AF729761

BENJAMIN FERREY

A Victorian Architect

TO THE GLORY OF GOD AND IN MEMORY OF BRAVE MEN WHO FOUGHT IN THE GREAT WAR 1914-1918 THEIR NAME LIVETH FOR EVERMORE

BENJAMIN FERREY

A Victorian Architect

HARRY SPAIN

UNICORN

To Matthew Ferrey,
whose steadfast generosity and dedication made this work possible

Published in 2026 by
Unicorn, an imprint of Unicorn Publishing Group
Charleston Studio
Meadow Business Centre
Lewes BN8 5RW
www.unicornpublishing.org

Text copyright © 2026 Harry Spain

All rights reserved. No part of the contents of this book may be reproduced, stored in or introduced into a retrieval system, or transmitted, in any form or by any means (electronic, mechanical, photocopying, recording or otherwise), without the prior written permission of the copyright holder and the above publisher of this book.

Every effort has been made to trace copyright holders and to obtain their permission for the use of copyrighted material. The publisher apologises for any errors or omissions and would be grateful to be notified of any corrections that should be incorporated in future reprints or editions of this book.

ISBN 978 1 911397 95 3
10 9 8 7 6 5 4 3 2 1

Design by newtonworks.uk
Printed in Serbia for Publikum

FRONTISPIECE Interior of All Saints, Blackheath.

Contents

Preface

Benjamin Ferrey was a Victorian architect through and through, in that he worked mostly and thoroughly in the Gothic Revival style. He was the youngest son of Benjamin Ferrey Senior, a draper who later rose to become the Mayor of Christchurch, which in those days was in Hampshire. The crucial moment in Ferrey's childhood was when he was sent to London to study under Augustus Charles Pugin, alongside Pugin's son Augustus Welby Northmore Pugin. Gothic seeds were to be sown in young Benjamin's mind which would later flourish.

In his early twenties he plunged enthusiastically into designing a new seaside town, Bournemouth. His later church-building practice would earn him high praise, with Charles Eastlake writing in his *History of the Gothic Revival* that Ferrey was 'one of the earliest, ablest and most zealous pioneers of the modern Gothic school', adding that his work 'possessed the rare charm of simplicity, without lacking interest'. Ferrey was twice elected vice-president of the Royal Institute of British Architects, and in 1870 was awarded the Royal Gold Medal – no mean achievement.

Nor was it only churches that were blessed by his hand: Ferrey built grand houses, cemetery chapels, mausoleums, and many, many schools. The output is that of an ambitious and enthusiastic architect who over the course of several decades built up a varied and healthy practice.

My excitement was considerable when I determined that as well as designing St Mark's parish church at Hedgerley in Buckinghamshire Ferrey might well have designed the very house in which I live: the Old Rectory next door – a house that I love and cherish. Such a possibility is intoxicating. Although the jury remains out, I am convinced that I know for certain that Ferrey was the man responsible. St Laurence's in Slough is just a stone's throw from Hedgerley. It is one of the many churches that Ferrey restored, and is one that has always particularly moved my heart. It stands on what can only be described as a most miserable spot on a ring road roundabout, but such is the huge charm of the church that all the horror of its situation vanishes.

Ferrey has suffered over time from a certain amount of bad press which this present biography happily contradicts. The image of Ferrey that now appears is of an affable and smiling man with a keen sense of humour. Those tempted to view his buildings as the work of a po-faced or staid Victorian might visit St Swithun's at Wickham in Berkshire. There they will encounter a church rich in carved foliage and flamboyant tracery. What's more, if they venture into the north aisle they will be faced with eight lushly attired, and if you please golden, Indian elephants holding up its roof. The papier maché pachyderms had been spotted by the church's then incumbent, William Nicholson, at the 1862 Paris Exhibition and he had thought how excellent they would look amidst Ferrey's work. So it is bravo to Benjamin Ferrey for designing a church which could so happily house such an original intervention – BRAVO !

Lucinda Lambton

Introduction

Benjamin Ferrey is an architect whose reputation has suffered. Where his contemporaries have been cast as pioneers of the Gothic Revival, he has more often been relegated to the margin of architectural history: competent rather than inspired, industrious rather than talented – in the words of Basil Clarke in *Church Builders of the Nineteenth Century* (1938), 'a close adherent of precedent' rather than a 'bold originator'. Such judgments, repeated often enough, have hardened into popular assumption. Yet they sit uneasily with the evidence.

This book sets out to challenge that judgment. Such a view is not merely reductive but actively misleading. When his work is traced in its totality, Ferrey emerges as a capable architect, draughtsman, and antiquary, often at the very forefront of the architectural debates that gripped Victorian Britain.

If Ferrey has suffered from neglect, he has also suffered from comparison. His early training under Augustus Charles Pugin placed him at the heart of one of the most fertile artistic environments in history, but it also ensured that his career would be read against that of Augustus's son, Augustus Welby Northmore Pugin, an undoubted genius and figure of volcanic intensity and polemical clarity. Ferrey's temperament was different. He was measured where others were dogmatic, accommodating where others were combative. When he settled down to write his 1861 biography of A. W. N. Pugin, he might have observed how life had dealt an uneven hand to them both. His childhood friend had died at the age of forty in the midst of his own success. Ferrey lived to old age and saw the Gothic Revival contort itself beyond all recognition. He refused to adapt to changing tastes; by his fiftieth birthday in 1860 the doggedly Puginian churches and houses that he continued to put up were beginning to look old-fashioned. It is alas the buildings of those years that have secured his unexceptional reputation, not the churches of the 1840s, full of confidence and brio.

One of the principal difficulties in writing about Ferrey is the paucity of surviving personal papers. Unlike some of his contemporaries, he left behind no substantial personal archive of correspondence, diaries, or working notebooks. Large parts of his professional and private life therefore resist close reconstruction. A year-by-year narrative, tracing his movements and thoughts with documentary precision, is simply not possible. What survives are fragments: published writings, drawings, occasional recollections, some project files, and the buildings themselves. This absence shapes the present study. Rather than attempting an artificial completeness, this biography seeks to present a representative cross-section of Ferrey's buildings and interactions, from the remarkable to the forgettable. A more sustained attempt at biographical reconstruction is reserved for the final chapter, where the available strands are drawn together to give a better sense of Ferrey 'the man'.

The preceding chapters trace Ferrey's formation from his provincial upbringing and early exposure to medieval architecture through his rigorous education in Pugin's drawing school to his emergence as an architect navigating the competing claims of nineteenth-century taste. Ferrey's was a career that began with the design of decidedly polite marine villas for a backwater baronet and ended with a muscular (if imperfect) mansion built for one of Queen Victoria's imperial governor sons: thus he witnessed first-hand the birth of an entirely new generation of 'great men'.

This book does not seek to elevate Ferrey artificially, or to cast him as a misunderstood genius. Rather, it aims to restore proportion. By attending closely to what survives – his buildings, drawings, publications, and the testimony of his contemporaries – it becomes clear that Ferrey was neither a footnote nor a failure. He was, instead, a thoughtful and capable architect whose reputation has dwelt for too long in the shadow of some of his more brilliant contemporaries.

Oxford, October 2025

CHAPTER 1

The Ferreys of Christchurch

Sunday 1 April 1810 marked the commencement of a period of feasting and pageantry in Paris. That afternoon at 2 o'clock, Napoleon Bonaparte processed through the Palace of St Cloud with Marie Louise, the nineteen-year-old daughter of the Holy Roman Emperor. A magnificent retinue of equerries, dignitaries, princes and princesses moved slowly through packed cabinets and chambers before reaching the Saloon of Mars. There, placed at one end of the hall was a canopied dais with two armchairs and a table underneath it. On that table stood an inkstand and the registers of the Civil State. This was the backdrop for the formalisation of one of history's most important marriage alliances, the moment when Napoleon's inexorable rise to international glory was consolidated. As the register was signed the marriage was formalised and gun salutes rang out across Paris, beginning celebrations that would last for days. There were church services, banquets, firework displays, and many processions. Napoleon's France seemed mightier than ever, and Britain watched on nervously.

As Paris was celebrating, so too were the residents of a set of rooms above a draper's shop in Christchurch, Hampshire (now Dorset), a few miles over the English Channel. As Napoleon's cortege made its steady progress through the Palace of St Cloud, Benjamin Ferrey was born above the family shop, the sixth and last child of Benjamin and Ann Ferrey – the newest product of that nation of shopkeepers.

That April, Christchurch would have been watching developments in France with particular anxiety. For three hundred years the town feared invasion from the sea. As well as occupying a vulnerable position on the south coast, Christchurch was in a relative state of poverty and underdevelopment. Even today the town seems remote and secluded from the rest of the world. Its main beauty, a vast medieval priory church, looms over expanses of marshland which lead out to the sea. The last prior of that church, John Draper, had written to King Henry VIII about Christchurch and its residents just as the King was beginning to dissolve monastic houses in 1538. Christchurch, he wrote, is 'set in a desolate place, in a very barren country out and far from all highways, in an angle or a corner, having no woods nor commodious country about it, nor right nor good town, but only the said poor town of Christchurch which is a very poor town and slenderly inhabited'.[1]

As John Draper was writing, invasion from European Catholic powers seemed imminent. When Benjamin was born in 1810, the threat of invasion was no less tangible. By then, though, the town was better equipped to repel an invading army.

OPPOSITE
Detail of Figure 147.

During what have been called the 'invasion years' of the French Revolutionary Wars, a preemptive campaign of defensive building took place throughout the region; almost a hundred regiments and battalions were stationed in the county from 1793. In 1795 a barracks was built in Christchurch to house a cavalry regiment; as well as military protection, this development brought parades, military balls, and newfound commercial opportunities to the town. In 1811 the necessity of having troops stationed in Christchurch had evidently not waned: as Benjamin was approaching his first year of age, construction was beginning on a large extension to the barracks to make provision for more guards.

While the construction and subsequent development of the barracks might have proved a worrying spectacle for the more anxious residents of Christchurch, it was good news for the Ferreys and their business.

George Ferrey the Draper

Benjamin's grandfather, George Ferrey, had set up shop in 1760 shortly after his twenty-third birthday. His life in many ways told the story of the developing shopkeeping middle classes of the mid-eighteenth century.

There had been at least four generations of Ferreys living in Hampshire before George was born in February 1737. His great-grandfather appeared in the parish records of Hordle, a village six miles east of Christchurch: Symon, the son of William, baptised on 14 March 1628. The old family story, which Benjamin often repeated, began with Huguenot ancestors who had fled France, probably during the sixteenth or early seventeenth centuries. It is a probable theory: there had certainly been an influx of Huguenots bearing the surname Ferré[2] across the south coast during the late sixteenth century. Different pre-1598 derivations of the surname do exist in England and Scotland, but the Ferreys were sure of their Huguenot origin, the details of which were probably known to them but lost to us.

Perhaps a further clue to the family's pedigree might be deduced from George's trade in textiles, a typically Huguenot enterprise if ever there was one, though there is no surviving evidence of the family having worked with textiles when his earliest traceable ancestor William was buried in October 1638. It is also worth noting that George's father had married a Jane Vesey in 1758 after the death of his first wife. Vesey is another surname with strong Huguenot connections, derived from the French town Wassy where there had been an infamous massacre in 1652.

George's upbringing was a respectable one. His father, also George, had been Parish Clerk of Milford and Old Hordle Church. A suitable match was soon found for his eldest son in Martha Sparks, the daughter of Benjamin Sparks, from whom the family's use of the name Benjamin originated. Sparks had inherited a small tenement in Puddletown and was able to endow his daughter with a suitable dowry. Once married in 1760, George Jr and his wife left Milford and established a draper's shop in Christchurch.

George bought a modest house with a shop window looking out over Castle Street, one of the main thoroughfares in the town [**1**]. Given the size of the shop,

1 Benjamin Ferrey's birthplace, in Castle Street, Christchurch, Hampshire.

he would have operated out of a small room stacked with bolts of fabric and occupied by two busy journeymen and an apprentice.[3] He specialised in making outerwear for Christchurch's gentlemen, labourers, and middle classes. As well as clothing, George and his apprentices would also often find themselves making carpets and curtains for the houses of some of their more fashionable customers.[4] When cavalry regiments came to Christchurch in 1795, poised to repel Napoleon's navy, and, as it happened, hordes of smugglers who terrorised the town, George Ferrey must have been delighted at the prospect of increased business. There was now a new market for the tailoring of all manner of uniforms for parades, drills, and balls. Military tailoring would fast become a mainstay of Ferrey's business.

By this point, George's son was on hand to assist the apprentices and learn the trade himself. Benjamin was George's ninth child, but only his third to survive into adulthood; many of his siblings were stillborn, and several survived for months rather than years. The eldest son, George, primed to take over the shop, died at the age of twenty-five long before his father, so it fell to the only remaining son, Benjamin, to apply himself to learning the trade as thoroughly as he could. This he did with considerable enthusiasm, and soon after his elder brother died in 1795 Benjamin found a wife and set about starting a family of his own.

Christchurch and Wimborne

By the time our Benjamin was born in 1810, business was booming for the Ferreys, and there must have been more comings and goings in the shop than ever before. In 1805 George Ferrey had died at the age of sixty-nine, working right up until his death. The ledger that he had kept so assiduously for almost half a century was quickly altered: where the title page of the 1804 accounts had read 'George Ferrey and Son, Taylor, Christ Church', that became 'Benj. Ferrey, Taylor, Christ Church', the father's name crossed out and the son's interposed.

Benjamin Jr's early childhood had been a happy one, filled with all the hustle and bustle that came with living above the family shop. There were three generations all housed under one roof, with four young children, and a modest team of household staff. One of Ferrey's earliest surviving sketches shows the drawing room of his house – a smart Georgian room with good panelling [**2**].

Benjamin's earliest memories were of this busy draper's shop and of his elderly grandfather working alongside his father. Ferrey & Son had a very full diary during the first few years of the century and an atmosphere of industry and productivity pervaded Benjamin's early childhood. The pleasures of doing good business and turning a profit were not lost on the family, who for generations seemed genetically predisposed to making a success of their careers. Certainly, for Benjamin this early exposure to the vigorous world of commercial enterprise instilled in him a keen sense of industry, one that he never lost.

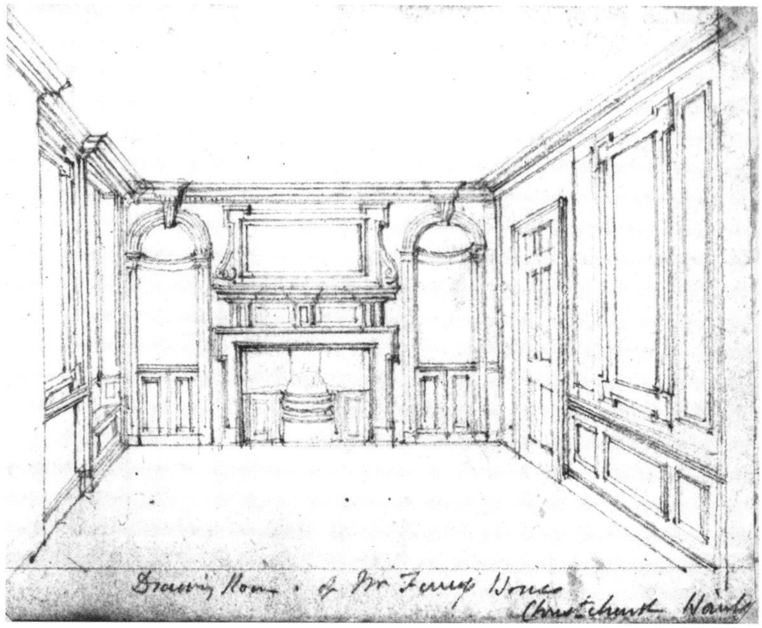

2 'Drawing Room of Mr Ferrey's House' – one of Ferrey's earliest drawings, showing his father's handsomely panelled room.

Just as important to Benjamin's formation were those glimpses of the medieval past that awakened his imagination [**3**]. Chief among them was the continual presence of the priory church, an ever-present sight out of the bedroom window [9]. Even today, the view from the house over to Christchurch Priory remains a perfect vision of untamed Gothic romance. The ruins of a Norman castle among which cattle used to graze lead the eye onwards to the priory, which despite both the Reformation and the Commonwealth avoided a fate similar to that of the castle and stands sentinel over marshland looking out to the sea beyond. During his 1811 tour of the West Country, J. M. W. Turner paused outside the window of Mr Ferrey's shop to make a sketch of the view over to the priory, such was its beauty [**4**].

3 'Ruins of Christchurch Castle & ancient Bridge' – a youthful sketch of the road leading up to Ferrey's childhood home. The overgrown ruins of Christchurch Castle are visible to the left.

4 The view from Ferrey's childhood home as sketched by J. M. W. Turner in 1811.

Those first few decades of the nineteenth century were a turning point in the history of English architectural appreciation. Some time around 1816 Thomas Rickman had visited Christchurch Priory to take notes for his seminal treatise, *An Attempt to Discriminate the Styles of English Architecture from the Conquest to the Reformation*, published in 1817. In it, Rickman attempted a system of classification by which hitherto misunderstood medieval buildings could be dated and understood. It was a system that stuck, and largely continues in use up to the present day. Rickman's stylistic eras – 'Early English', 'Decorated' and 'Perpendicular' – would form the vocabulary of the nascent Gothic Revival.

In those early days, when Benjamin was still a boy of seven, the new world which was being revealed through the antiquarian efforts of Rickman *et al.* seemed uncharted and thrilling. The ruins of the castle and the stately priory, the backdrop of Benjamin's early childhood, suddenly took on a new form. No longer were they the curious remnants of a distant and superstitious medieval past: they became representative of the artistic efforts of skilled craftsmen cognisant of style and form. The veil was slowly being lifted, and what had previously appeared in the gloomy light of mystery now appeared somewhat brighter, and, more importantly, worthy of both protection and replication.

While we can hardly imagine Benjamin reading Rickman's treatise at the age of seven, the effects of a changing tide in architectural appreciation would have been difficult to ignore, even for a boy. Having had the good fortune not to have been born the eldest son, Benjamin Jr was able to avoid inheriting the family business. He was allowed to turn his attention away from the draper's shop and, fortunately, towards architecture.

Christchurch, despite the commercial developments of the previous century, remained a town with more than ordinary levels of poverty and destitution. The Ferrey family with their established business occupied an enviable social position: Benjamin Sr would later become Mayor of Christchurch, and their surname peppered notices in local newspapers alongside the names of the great and the good. Therefore Benjamin, unlike most of his peers, was not enrolled at the school across the road from the family home but was instead sent to the ancient Grammar School in Wimborne, eleven miles north-west [**5**]. The headmaster, James Mayo – the first of a series of Mayos to serve in that role – advertised that 'at Free Grammar School, Wimborne, Dorset, young gentlemen are boarded and educated etc. for fees of 25 guineas per annum'. At the most basic level, the schooling on offer at Wimborne included 'classical instruction, writing and accompts, and washing'; for extra money the more ambitious boys could be taught French, dancing, music and drawing, all of which Benjamin studied and excelled at.

5 The original Grammar School building at Wimborne in Hampshire.

Had Benjamin instead been sent to the Free School in Christchurch, he would have been educated in a gloomy upper room at the priory, romantically named St Michael's Loft. Situated directly above the Lady Chapel, it was thought to have been a relic house before the Reformation turned it over to its educational use. Some decades later, Ferrey would make a pleasing antiquarian discovery in that same room (see p. 141).

Wimborne Grammar School was founded in 1497 by Lady Margaret Beaufort. By the time Benjamin arrived, it occupied an attractive old schoolhouse crammed with thirty students. Another James Mayo took over from his father as headmaster in 1822, and his brother Charles reported with some pride that the boys read Xenophon and Homer in Greek, and Cicero and Virgil in Latin. French was apparently so well taught by a Monsieur Le Prince that it was a common sight to see the young scholars reading French novels of their own volition in the dormitories.[5] Benjamin applied himself to his studies assiduously, but what caught his attention more than Cicero or Homer was the minster church next door to the schoolhouse.

6 Wimborne Minster.

Although modest in scale compared to Christchurch Priory, Wimborne Minster had more than enough historic substance to stimulate a young boy's imagination [**6**]. The tombs of King Æthelred and the Beauforts are there, and so too is the second largest chained library in the country. It was there, among the early printed books on history, gardening and architecture, that Benjamin could be found during his free time, or, just as frequently, he would be sat among the tombs of the minster's churchyard feverishly sketching the building and recording the most minute details of medieval stonework.

With carefree afternoons spent sketching the buildings of Wimborne and happy hours passed in the classroom of the schoolhouse, Benjamin's schooldays were contented, surprisingly devoid of the usual encounters with sadism that one expects in nineteenth-century schooling. He displayed a propensity to excel at almost everything he turned his hand to, and, just as crucially, possessed a friendly disposition. These dual qualities endeared him to the whole school. He was subsequently remembered as the favourite of both the headmaster and the boys, amongst whom he would distribute his drawings as gifts. Decades later, some of his contemporaries recalled how they were 'always glad to have a sketch by little Benjamin'.[6]

The poet Thomas Gray, when watching schoolboys playing blithely at Eton, asked 'Why should they know their fate? When sorrow never comes too late.' For Benjamin, his formative years had been carefree and untouched by sorrow or tragedy; however, on 7 January 1824, as he was approaching the final few terms at

Wimborne, his mother died quite suddenly at the age of thirty-seven. For the first time came a sadness that affected the sensitive thirteen-year-old considerably. Ann's death was to mark the point at which the halcyon days of Benjamin's early life came to a close. He was shortly going to leave the cheerful security of Wimborne and the south coast completely. London beckoned.

A copy of an anthology entitled *The Poetical Epitome or Elegant Extracts Abridged from the Larger Volume for the Improvement of Scholars at Classical and other Schools*, used at Wimborne Grammar School by Benjamin and his classmates, survives today in the archives at Christchurch. One extract from *Hamlet*, spoken by Polonius to his son Laertes, is marked enthusiastically in pencil by an asterisk. The title: 'A father's advice to his son, going to travel'. We might imagine Benjamin preparing to leave Wimborne to embark on the next stage of life and pausing to consult the page of his textbook so tellingly highlighted. As he did, he would hear his father's voice pronouncing:

Give every man thine ear, but few thy voice;
Take each man's censure, but reserve thy judgment.
Costly thy habit as thy purse can buy,
But not express'd in fancy; rich, not gaudy;
For the apparel oft proclaims the man.
This, above all, to thine own self be true;
And it must follow, as the night the day,
Thou canst not then be false to any man.

CHAPTER 2

Pugin's Drawing School

> 'You see', said Mr Pecksniff, passing the candle rapidly from roll to roll of paper, 'some traces of our doings here. Salisbury Cathedral from the north. From the south. From the east. From the west. From the south-east. From the nor'west. A bridge. An almshouse. A jail. A church. A powder-magazine. A wine-cellar. A portico. A summer-house. An ice-house. Plans, elevations, sections, every kind of thing. And this,' he added, having by this time reached another large chamber on the same storey, with four little beds in it, 'this is your room, of which Mr Pinch here is the quiet sharer. A southern aspect; a charming prospect.'

The scene that greeted Ferrey when he first entered Augustus Charles Pugin's drawing school might easily have been taken from Dickens's *Martin Chuzzlewit*. Ferrey, by now fifteen years old, stepped out of his coach at Great Russell Street to be greeted by a jolly and somewhat frantic Frenchman. Once inside the house, he would have been shown up to his shared bedroom, passing through rooms full of elevations and half-finished watercolours all worked on by a small brigade of pupils.

A few years earlier, A. C. Pugin had begun work on two volumes entitled *Specimens of Gothic Architecture*. This publication, intended to serve as a pattern book of Gothic architectural details, was the product of a collaboration with the Roman Catholic architect E. J. Willson, who had approached Pugin in Lincoln offering to write the text if Pugin would provide illustrations. The celebrated antiquary and topographer John Britton [15], notorious for his monumental publishing enterprises, also involved himself in the publication, reminiscing decades later with some frustration that 'I declined to place my name in the title-page but soon found that nearly the whole of the business department devolved on me.'[1] Despite the originality and quality of *Specimens* and its engravings, the venture was not a financial success; however, it probably led to the foundation of Pugin's drawing school. While preparing *Specimens*, Pugin seems to have realised that one way to offset his financial burdens and increase productivity would be to acquire a small workforce of pupils. In achieving the latter objective, the drawing school would serve him well for the remainder of his career.

Mr Pugin was a memorable figure, with untidy hair and penetrating eyes [**7**]. The portraits that survive show a man possessed of a wry half-grin. One can almost hear the favourite far-fetched anecdotes and jokes flowing forth from the sitter, all of them verbalised in broken Franco-English. When Ferrey came to set down his own recollections of the Pugins some thirty-five years later, he faithfully recounted the tall tale of A. C. Pugin's early life as he had no doubt heard it from the man himself.

7 Augustus Charles Pugin, by Joseph Nash, published in Ferrey's *Recollections of A .N. Welby Pugin, and his Father, Augustus Pugin* (1861).

> The elder Pugin was born in France, in the year 1762; his birthplace is unknown, but he was descended from a family of distinction, his ancestor being a nobleman who raised a hundred soldiers for the service of Fribourg, the Senators augmenting his arms '*d'un oiseau sable*', for his valour in having defeated a hundred cavalry at Morat, when besieged by Charles Duke of Burgundy in 1477. Pugin witnessed many of the fearful scenes in the French Revolution, and it is said that he fell fighting for the king, and was thrown with some hundred bodies into a pit near the Place de la Bastille, whence he managed to escape by swimming across the Seine, flying to Rouen, and embarking from that place to England.[2]

This account bears all the hallmarks of an exaggerated story designed to captivate his impressionable students; as A. W. N. Pugin's biographer Rosemary Hill has pointed out, 'the fact that the Bastille is on the north bank of the Seine is only the most obvious anomaly in this colourful tale'.[3] Nevertheless, when repeated often enough, stories like these take on their own sense of credibility. The peculiar thing about A. C. Pugin's account is that there appears to have been a small element of truth, contorted into something rather more extraordinary. Ferrey's repetition of the fabricated escape from France does not necessarily equate to a total naivety on his part: many of the elder Pugin's claims were also taken literally by his own family and his other pupils. (Charles Mathews, whom we shall meet, is one example.) The fanciful stories told by Augustus seem to have occasionally, and quite understandably, caused delusions of grandeur in his son, the high-flown architect A. W. N. Pugin.

In reality, Auguste Charles Pugin was born in Paris some six years later than Ferrey's estimation, in 1768 or 1769, the son of François Joseph Pugin (himself the son of a farm labourer) and his affluent middle-class wife Marguerite Duchêne. It was possibly the aspirational figure of his mother that helped form some of Augustus's *folies de grandeur*. Another obscure relation also fuelled Pugin's speculations. The 'nobleman' referred to by Ferrey was in fact a lawyer, Etienne Pugin, who in 1629 was received into the patriciate of Fribourg for good military service. This modest provincial honour conferred on a remarkably distant ancestor was seemingly enough to confirm the family's claims of a noble descent. Nevertheless, A. C. Pugin himself would have to eke out a living in pre-Revolutionary Paris as an illustrator for the magazine *Le Cabinet des modes*. Pugin existed on the margin of Paris's community of commercial artists, hardly a glamorous existence but one that helped to develop both his sense of humour and his industry. It was a world that he never quite managed fully to escape. Throughout his life, even in Britain, A. C. Pugin found himself eternally impecunious.

As with so much of the elder Pugin's biography, his flight to Britain is shrouded in mystery. It seems probable that he crossed the Channel around 1791, not having fled the Bastille in fear for his life but more likely having been driven on by the prospect of favourable professional opportunities in Britain. Despite finding his earliest days overseas difficult, Pugin eventually came across the employment that he had been in search of, as a draughtsman for John Nash (1752–1835). This job was to place Pugin at the forefront of the contemporary British architectural world. In Nash Pugin found an equal in both wit and imagination: in 1795 the two men notably put on a production of Sheridan's *The School for Scandal* in Carmarthen, where Nash appeared as Peter Teazle and Pugin fulfilled the role of scenery painter. Ferrey recorded in his *Recollections* how during those first years in England Pugin had 'according to the fashion of that day, [worn] a three-cornered hat, carried his muff and gold-headed cane, and made frequent applications at the post-office for letters'. Ferrey went on to emphasise Pugin's Gallic conspicuity, writing: 'his repeated inquiries … constantly received the same petulant answer, "I tell you there are no letters for Monsieur Augustus Pugin, but plenty for Monsieur Puggen."'[4]

Besides forays into theatre, Augustus's work for Nash saw him produce drawings for a wide range of commissions. Pugin's particular ability lay in producing perspective views. Nash and many of his contemporaries would come to depend on these views for their special power of evocation and expression. Pugin's representational method was straightforward and yet distinctive: buildings were set in their context, in many cases with much more artistic attention afforded to scenery than the buildings. Busy scenes generally packed with people and livestock took centre stage, all set under dramatic skies with flawless shadows and light cast forcefully onto the buildings themselves. This method had the obvious benefit of conjuring up the ideal effect of a building as one might encounter it in person. It was a method that Pugin would teach his pupils. Ferrey was especially quick to absorb the art of the perspective view and clung onto it for the rest of his career. The earliest drawings produced for the redevelopment of Bournemouth in 1834, discussed at greater length in the next chapter, show the strong influence of Pugin's style [36].

Ventures into architectural design were to prove few and far between for the elder Pugin. There appears to have been some disappointment when Nash failed to give him a promised commission to design a set of cottages in 1802. Rosemary Hill supposes that these cottages may have been part of Nash's works at Attingham.[5] Of Pugin's other designs we are afforded only occasional glimpses. His contribution of an elevation and plan of an imagined (and rather eccentric) dog kennel in an 1820 edition of Peter Beckford's *Thoughts on Hunting* provides one such insight [**8**]. The signature is of 'A. Pugin Archt'; the debt of inspiration the design owes to Nash is clear.

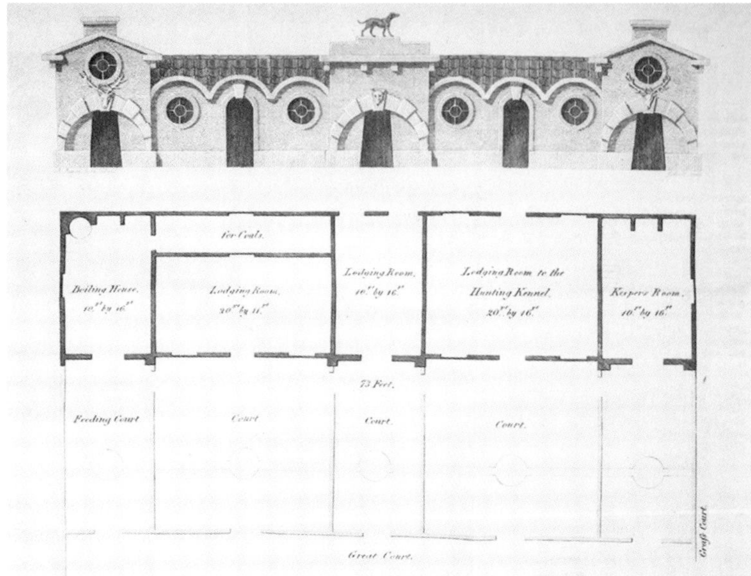

8 A rare architectural design by A. C. Pugin – a dog kennel.

It is tempting to see something of Mr Pecksniff in A. C. Pugin, the self-styled architect. Of Mr Pecksniff's professional engagements, Dickens wrote that they were 'almost, if not entirely, confined to the reception of pupils … of his architectural doings, nothing was clearly known, except that he had never designed or built anything; but it was generally understood that his knowledge of the science was almost awful in its profundity.'[6] It seems plausible that Augustus's school was among a number of sources of inspiration for Dickens in *Martin Chuzzlewit*, a novel dedicated to Angela Burdett-Coutts, who would become one of Ferrey's most significant patrons. Ferrey's view of A. C. Pugin as a great expert on Gothic architecture was totally sincere. While he was not an architect, nor seriously claimed to be one, he was a skilled draughtsman, and in many ways a discerning Gothicist. The image that emerges of Augustus is, like that of Pecksniff, of an eccentric. But unlike Pecksniff, Augustus Pugin seems to have been a genuinely likeable character.

Admission to the School

Exactly how Ferrey came to enrol at A. C. Pugin's drawing school is uncertain. Charles Mathews, later a renowned actor, was one of Pugin's first pupils and left a volume of memoirs in which he described his own admission to the drawing school. Mathews recalled:

> From the first I was passionately fond of drawing and mathematics … architectural subjects especially took my fancy, and … my ambition was to become an architect … Somewhere about the year 1797 when [my father] was a struggling actor on the Welsh circuit, he made the acquaintance of Mr. Nash, the builder, at Swansea who was a great patron of the theatre … John Nash, the humble builder of Swansea, was now the celebrated London architect in the zenith of his fame, and my father lost no time in calling upon him, to ask his advice as to the best mode of forwarding my architectural aspirations. The recognition was most cordial; and another acquaintance was brought to his recollection by Mr. Nash, in the person of the late Augustus Pugin, who had painted the scenes for the little Welsh theatre of bygone times. …
>
> By Mr Nash he was recommended as the man of all others required to undertake my instruction. The early friends fraternised, and all went up on

> wheels. A heavy premium was paid for my initiation, and on the 4th of May, 1819, I was installed in Pugin's office for a period of four years as an articled pupil.[7]

Mathews' account is revealing. Admission to Pugin's school, for him at least, was based on familial acquaintance and a recommendation – that and 'a heavy premium'. By the time Ferrey arrived in London some six years later, Pugin's drawing school was better known and therefore not quite so dependent on Nash's recommendations. Despite this, there still exist commonalities between Mathews' and Ferrey's cases. Both had shown an early aptitude as draughtsmen and had fixed their sights on careers as architects. Both seemingly had fathers keen to encourage their ambitions. Both also belonged to an emerging wealthy middle class. Ferrey failed to record the nature of his own admission to the school when he came to set down his recollections of the Pugins in 1861, but we are left with several intriguing clues.

In 1825 A. W. N. Pugin, then aged thirteen, became ill and was rushed out of London by his mother in order to recuperate. He was sent to Christchurch to take advantage of the sea air. Ferrey later reproduced a sketch of Christchurch Priory made by the young Pugin [**9**]; tantalisingly, the view is the same as that afforded from outside the Ferrey family's shop. In the absence of any more direct evidence, we are left to speculate. Ferrey, the promising young draughtsman, had just left Wimborne Grammar School and was in search of architectural training. Several of his sketches of the priory made around that time survive; when not in Wimborne, he seems to have spent much of his time sketching the priory. Could his first fateful meeting with A. W. N. Pugin have occurred when the two budding young architects were simultaneously sketching the priory in 1825? And might Mrs Pugin, having spotted Ferrey's talent and keeping an ever watchful eye on her husband's financial

9 A facsimile reproduced in Ferrey's *Recollections* of A. W. N. Pugin's sketch of Christchurch Priory, made in 1825, the year Ferrey entered Pugin's father's drawing school. Coincidentally, this was the view from outside the Ferrey family's shop.

condition, have recommended the drawing school to the recently widowed Mr Ferrey? It certainly seems possible.

In any case, Ferrey entered Pugin's drawing school that same year at the age of fifteen. By then, in Ferrey's own words, 'Pugin's office was in great repute and always filled with pupils.'[8] He went on to note how remarkable it was that 'of the many youths who were articled to him very few followed the profession of architects in after life'. Some died, others changed their pursuits or inherited property; but to use one of Pugin's quaint expressions, 'none sunk into filth or perished on the scaffold'!

Pugin was by then an established artist. His association with another immigrant, Rudolph Ackermann, whom he met in 1806, had proved crucial to his professional development and came to dictate the nature of much of the work that he produced for publication. Ackermann, a German Lutheran, had like Pugin married an Englishwoman and founded a drawing school, at 101 Strand. These premises principally operated as what Ackermann had rather grandly christened 'the Repository of Arts', out of which he ran a gallery, a shop, a publishing house, and a tearoom. It was the publishing house that engaged Pugin, initially jointly to produce *The Microcosm of London* (1808–10), the brainchild of Mrs Pugin. The result, a series of Pugin's watercolour views of London (on which he collaborated with Thomas Rowlandson), was presented alongside text by Ackermann. It was a masterpiece, and led to Pugin and Ackermann making many more joint ventures into publication, including the *History of Westminster Abbey* (1812), *History of the University of Oxford* (1814), *History of the University of Cambridge* (1815), and *History of the Colleges of Winchester, etc.* (1816). These publications are commonly thought of as some of the most splendid illustrated volumes of the early nineteenth century; they were certainly the basis of Pugin's reputation.

10 One of A. C. Pugin's watercolours of Nash's Brighton Pavilion, 1824.

11 The Pugin family house at 105 (since renumbered 106) Great Russell Street. It was here that Ferrey lived and worked under A. C. Pugin's tutelage.

Nevertheless, A. C. Pugin's architectural credentials and his association with illustrious luminaries appears to have caught Ferrey's biographical attention far more than his work with Ackermann. In his overview of Pugin's professional credentials in *Recollections*, Ferrey affords fewer than ten words to his master's work with Ackermann, and dedicates almost the entirety of the same page to relating a story which Pugin 'never failed to mention whenever he had opportunity' of how, when working on drawings for Nash at Brighton Pavilion in 1824 [**10**], he knocked over a colour box when scrambling to stand for the King. To Pugin's surprise, and Ferrey's boyish delight, the King stooped down to pick it up 'with an expression of apology'.[9] It was that sort of anecdote that obviously captivated Ferrey and the other pupils and from which Augustus derived a great deal of their youthful admiration.

When Ferrey arrived at 105 (now 106) Great Russell Street in 1825 he was set straight to work [**11**]. The Pugins had only moved there two years earlier from a smaller house in Keppel Street to accommodate the growing drawing school. Augustus had the boys practice their art on site by assisting with perspective views and using the camera obscura. Out of London, Pugin would encourage exploration, observation, and sketching. This was no doubt a source of excitement for Ferrey. In the space of a year he had swapped Wimborne Minster for Westminster Abbey, a building he would visit almost immediately upon his arrival in London. One sketch of figures on the tomb of John of Eltham there, made during his earliest days at Great Russell Street, shows signs of a developing eye and hand [**12**].

12 Figures from John of Eltham's tomb in Westminster Abbey, one of Ferrey's earliest sketches after his arrival at the drawing school in 1825.

At Home and Abroad

No sooner had Ferrey arrived in London than he was swept across the English Channel on one of Augustus Pugin's legendary drawing tours. These tours were a staple of the drawing school's curriculum and opened up a whole series of new architectural spectacles for the pupils to observe, study, and draw. More often than not, the tours were marked by chaos and coloured with outlandishness. The 1825 tour departed in August from Brighton and landed in Dieppe before proceeding to its first significant destination, Rouen. This was the first time Ferrey had been abroad. Having spent the vast majority of his childhood in his native Hampshire, in the space of a few months he had both moved to the Capital and crossed the Channel. The impression that Rouen made on the fifteen-year-old is difficult to overstate. His companions, among whom were A. W. N. Pugin, Thomas Talbot Bury and Joseph Nash, were more seasoned members of Pugin's school and had seen France before.

13 Eustache-Hyacinthe Langlois, one of several characters encountered by Ferrey in Rouen on his first tour abroad in 1825.

In Rouen A. C. Pugin went in search of local antiquaries and artists. The first port of call was E. H. Langlois [**13**], an impoverished artist who Pugin and his pupils found living with a wife and seven children in a deserted convent, poverty-stricken, yet surrounded by a vast collection of medieval antiquities and manuscripts. A year earlier, Langlois had begun teaching drawing to young students in Rouen. It says something of A. C. Pugin that he would be on equal terms with someone in Langlois' situation, and just as much of A. W. N. that he would remain friends with him for the rest of his life. Ferrey remained a little more cautious. Of Langlois he wrote:

> In M. Langlois, a member of the Society of Antiquaries of France, Pugin met with a remarkable artist. He was the type of a class of man who rank high in French estimation. Well versed in ancient literature, and able professor in science and art, this man of genius['] … apartments were meanly furnished, and all his arrangements characterised by economy; but still in everything about him there was an evidence of taste and a cultivated mind. In his person M. Langlois was extremely plain, and his manners were unpretending; but in social position, notwithstanding his humble mode of living, he visited and ranked with people moving in the highest circles.
>
> In this country things are rather different; it must be admitted that, in general, a man of talent unfortunately placed in M Langlois' circumstances could not mix in society on equal terms. In France a man is estimated by his mind and accomplishments, and treated accordingly, without reference to the size of his dwelling, or the style of his establishment.[10]

Ferrey, the son of a provincial tailor, let something show of his own English fixation on social class in recalling his brief association with Langlois. His reaction to the Frenchman falls somewhere between pity and awe.

Of course, the tour to Normandy was not without an ulterior motive on the part of the elder Pugin. As well as providing an important opportunity for his pupils to observe the wonders of French architecture, it gave him the chance to gather measurements and drawings for another joint enterprise with John Britton: *The Architectural Antiquities of Normandy*. This project had been underway since 1824, and Pugin's pupils had already made one tour to Normandy in the autumn of that

year in order to begin measuring and sketching those buildings that were of particular interest to their master. In Normandy in 1825, Ferrey recounted that the party took in the churches of St Ouen, St Maclou, the recently mutilated convent of St Amand, the Hôtel de Bourgtheroulde, and the Palais de Justice.[11] The party also travelled to other sites within easy reach of Rouen. When *The Architectural Antiquities of Normandy* finally went to print in 1827, it featured a single engraving based on a drawing by Ferrey, which thus constituted his first published work [**14**]. The drawing, an elevation of the church of Notre Dame in Caudebec alongside details of the church's stonework, was probably made during this 1825 tour of Normandy. The resulting engraving is signed with the customary Puginian formula: 'A. Pugin Arch[t]. Direx[t]. B. Ferrey del[t]'.

A great deal of hilarity occurred during this visit to France. Ferrey recalled one instance at Jumièges when A. C. Pugin's orders not to loot antiquities were disobeyed. It is worth reproducing his account in full:

14 Ferrey's only contribution to *The Architectural Antiquities of Normandy* (1827), an elevation of Notre Dame in Caudebec, where Ferrey and several other pupils were perilously lowered inside a vaulted ceiling to inspect its construction.

> Within a few miles of Rouen upon the banks of the Seine are situated the beautiful ruins of the once famous Abbey of Jumièges. These Pugin determined to visit, having been especially invited by the mayor of the commune. The passage from Rouen to Jumièges by the River Seine had been made in a market-boat, which leaving Rouen at an early hour in the morning returned again late at night. On the arrival of this boat with Mr. Pugin, accompanied by four of his pupils, he was warmly greeted by the mayor, who politely accompanied him to the abbey, anxious to hear his remarks upon the peculiarities of its architecture. In the course of their examination the pupils found a beautifully carved capital in a position which offered such facilities for removal, that they determined, in spite of previous warnings, to attempt the enterprise; but to accomplish the deed it was necessary to divert Mr Pugin's attention elsewhere. This was done by one of the pupils who, being in the secret, remained at Pugin's elbow, constantly suggesting fresh points for discussion between him and the mayor, and adroitly keeping them away from the spot where a mason was engaged in breaking away the useless and unnecessary stone from the capital to be removed. The noise of the chipping often roused the suspicions of the mayor, who was repeatedly on the point of rushing to the spot from whence the sound came in, but his attention was immediately drawn by some remark of their watchful pupil to an opposite portion of the ruins. At length the bulk of the stone being cut away, and the capital made

> portable, it was concealed under a camlet coat and stealthily hurried down the banks of the river just as the Amazonian boatwomen blew a tremendous blast from the cow-horn to summon the passengers on board this being the signal for departure. On Pugin's discovering the manoeuvre which had been practised in order to obtain this ornamental fragment, he was exceedingly indignant, and no future attempt of a similar kind was ever ventured upon by his pupils.[12]

The 1825 tour proceeded on towards Caen and Bayeux before ending in Paris in October of that year. It had proved an extensive and eventful expedition. Ferrey later listed a selection of luminaries who they had met along the way, including not least 'the hapless Beau Brummel, whose conversation enlivened the table d'hôte at Calais'.[13] Of Ferrey's labours during this tour little remains beyond the aforementioned drawing of Caudebec. One watercolour of the Banque de France in Paris emerged at Christie's in 2019, inscribed with the date 1825 [18]. The same image was used as the basis of an engraving which appeared in *Paris and its Environs*. The idea for that publication was formed two years later, in 1827, so it would seem likely that the Christie's sketch dates to a later French tour.

The Architectural Antiquities of Normandy was to prove something of a disastrous turning point for the Pugin family's fortunes, fortunes they previously had cause to be cautiously optimistic about. When the volume was published by John Britton [**15**] in 1827, payment to Pugin and the engravers John and Henry Le Keux was not forthcoming. Pugin pressed Britton for money, lost patience, and hastily took legal action – costly action which ultimately failed. The rights to his share of the *Antiquities of Normandy* and of another volume, *The Public Buildings of London*, were lost, and much of the family's hope for financial stability.

15 John Britton (1771–1857), the antiquary with whom both A. C. Pugin and Ferrey published.

Augustus, not one who was easily deterred, quickly started work on another project which he hoped might rival the work that he had previously undertaken for Britton. This was *Paris and its Environs*, published in 1829 by Robert Jennings and William Chaplin, specialists in topographical books. Ferrey, having returned from a second tour of France in 1826, was whisked off on two more expeditions across the Channel in 1827 and 1828, this time with the intention of executing watercolours of Paris. Of the engravings featured in the book, Nash produced 83, Bury 45, and Ferrey 36. A. W. N. Pugin, three years the junior of Nash and Bury, contributed 15. A handful of Ferrey's watercolours for *Paris and its Environs* survive. They are sketches in the true sense of the word, executed at speed and with a great deal of frenetic energy. It is easy to imagine Augustus standing over his pupil and hurrying him along to the next building as soon as one sketch was finished. Ferrey's watercolour of the church of St Roche

ABOVE
16 Ferrey's watercolour of the church of St Roche, made in preparation for *Paris and its Environs*.

ABOVE RIGHT
17 The engraving of St Roche as published in *Paris and its Environs* (1829).

demonstrates this: the figures and details are approximate, left to be worked out later by the engravers [**16**, **17**]. The watercolours produced on the tour to Paris were simply exercises in recording scale, perspective, and light. The watercolour of the Banque de France [**18**] is demonstrative of that same fact: Pugin encouraged his pupils to record light and shade above all else.

18 Ferrey's watercolour of the Banque de France in Paris, inscribed '1825' but probably drawn on a later tour.

Life at Great Russell Street was proving just as taxing for Ferrey. One of the primary bones of contention that many critics, both contemporary and modern, pick with Ferrey's 1861 *Recollections of Pugin* is his portrayal of Catherine, A. W. N.'s mother. Ferrey, a fair-minded and generous man, did however have some justification in depicting her as an authoritarian. Catherine was a relatively distant scion of the Welby family of Denton Hall in Lincolnshire. Her father, William, had been an attorney at the King's Bench but was never called to the Bar; despite this, Ferrey later promoted him to a 'distinguished barrister'.[14] As Rosemary Hill suspects, this exaggerated curriculum vitae was probably the invention of Catherine rather than Ferrey.[15] Catherine was reportedly a great beauty who had in her youth gained the moniker 'the Belle of Islington'.[16] Fundamentally, though, Mrs Pugin was class-conscious, assertive, and shrewd. Augustus had met her at the beginning of the century when he was working for Nash in Islington, and it was there that they married in February 1802. Ferrey, despite his other misgivings, did concur that Mrs Pugin was beautiful and intelligent. In introducing her in *Recollections*, he wrote:

> In proof of her good looks she was accustomed to relate the circumstance that once at a dinner party, a gentleman sitting next to her, with whom she had been in close conversation, availing himself of one of those mysterious pauses which sometimes occur at the table, and looking her earnestly in the face, suddenly exclaimed, with animated gesture, 'Madam, how exceedingly like you are to the devil.' This expression caused no small surprise amongst the company; but far from discomposing Mrs Pugin, she gracefully bowed her thanks and accepted the remark as a compliment to her personal appearance. Familiar with the works of Milton, and especially Paradise Lost, she recognized in the seemingly rude observation an allusion to the fascinating form of Satan as there described by the great poet.[17]

At times Ferrey was inclined to take a less generous view of Mrs Pugin's devilishness. The daily routine at 105 Great Russell Street seems to have taken Ferrey by surprise, and although he was diligent and hardworking in later life, the amount of time spent at work in the drawing school seemed excessive to the young boy. He later explained that Mrs Pugin woke at four o'clock and 'thought it salutary that the pupils should commence their studies at six o'clock in winter as well as in summer'.[18] One bell was rung for the maids, followed by another shortly after to rouse the pupils, and then a final bell summoned the boys to the office where they would begin work immediately. Ferrey recalled the 'pitiable sight' of seeing 'shivering youths reluctantly creeping down … to waste their time by a sleepy attempt to work before breakfast'. Breakfast was to prove another ordeal for Ferrey. After two and a half hours of early morning work, the pupils processed in, made a profound bow to Mrs Pugin at the head of the table, 'the neglect of which would quickly have been visited with reproof', and ate their breakfast in silence. Upon leaving the room, the same homage was duly paid. 'During dinner the like silent system was enforced, similar obsequious respect paid, and then retiring, the pupils continued to work incessantly at the desk till eight o'clock.'[19]

Ferrey had his own reasons for disliking Mrs Pugin. His own mother had died only a year before he entered Pugin's school, and any hopes he might have had of finding a sympathetic maternal influence in London were seemingly dashed by Catherine Pugin. Christchurch was also too far away for Ferrey to make regular trips home at the weekends, a luxury afforded to most of the other pupils; he might easily have grown to resent Mrs Pugin simply through overexposure. Her religious habits were certainly a source of irritation. On the regular occasions that Ferrey was resident in London at the weekend, he was forced to accompany Mrs Pugin to the Irvingite church on Cross Street in Hatton Green. There, Ferrey was exposed not just to a 'miserably ugly' building but to 'cold and tedious services' with 'long-spun' sermons after the Presbyterian manner.[20] Ferrey, who attended Westminster Abbey whenever he could escape Mrs Pugin's Irvingite excursions, later blamed A. W. N. Pugin's conversion to Roman Catholicism on this early exposure to churchgoing at Hatton Green. He remarked: 'It never could have been expected that such a youth would submit to be pent up for hours together without any relief, in a pew like a cattle-pen when so magnificent a building as Westminster Abbey, with its beautiful and solemn services, was within reach.'[21] But Mrs Pugin, despite Ferrey's reservations, was intelligent and fiercely practical: it was she who suggested the idea for *Paris and its Environs*, and managed, by enterprise and inheritance, to keep her husband's head just above water.

As at Wimborne Grammar School, Ferrey seems to have been a favourite of his master. He remembered Augustus Pugin with fondness even though, by Ferrey's own admission, he could be just as quick to show disapproval as he could favour towards his pupils. Unsurprisingly, given the fact that the pupils were there to work as well as learn, favour was shown to those who 'excelled in their artistic efforts' rather than those who 'were sluggish and unsuccessful'.[22] 'The former', Ferrey writes, 'were always naturally in favour, and [he] never failed to express approval or displeasure in a very decided and graphic manner to each youth according to his merits.'[23] The young A. W. N. Pugin went so far as to create a wheel of fortune charting who was in and out of favour with his parents! Ferrey remembered how 'every week the rotary machine was sketched with great spirit, each pupil being represented standing upon a projecting bracket attached to the wheel. The favourite was always at the top, capering and laughing with pencil in hand, while the one least fortunate was seen hurled to the ground by the revolution of the wheel.'[24] The young Pugin managed to win the affection of his peers by sharing in the trials of life under the watchful eye of his parents.

Ferrey and A. W. N. Pugin appear to have been close friends during this period [**19**]. Ferrey recalled, inaccurately, that the young Pugin had excelled academically during his short spell at Christ's Hospital School and had shunned the company of his classmates in favour of adults. There may be some truth in the latter statement, but Pugin certainly neglected his studies at school, probably distracted by higher thoughts. Ferrey, who spent all his free time at Wimborne sketching and was a favourite of both his masters and his peers, may have found in Pugin, two years younger, something of an equal in terms of precocity. The pair spent a good deal of time together on tours of England and the Continent, and seem to have got on very well; Pugin wrote in his diary in 1829 that he had explored Herstmonceux Castle and Hatfield House with 'my friend Ferrey'. Both boys were spurred on by Augustus's enthusiasm for publication and dreamt up schemes of their own. In July 1826 the two Pugins and Ferrey visited Rochester to inspect the castle there. A. W. N., enraptured by 'tales of chivalry and romance',[25] had determined that he would apply his attention to the production of a study of castles, which alas never made it to press. The party spent a number of days in Rochester, sketching, measuring, and producing drawings of the castle as if it were restored. Despite his prodigious talent, it is easy to forget that Pugin was still a fourteen-year-old boy, mesmerized by the imaginary worlds conjured up by Walter Scott.

19 Augustus Welby Northmore Pugin (1812–1852), Ferrey's childhood friend, at about the age of twenty-eight.

Ferrey later recalled how the young Pugin spent his time in Rochester in a great excitement characterised by intrepid bravery. He ordered excavations to inspect the foundations of the castle, and amazingly had himself lowered in a bucket to the bottom of a well inside the inner wall of the keep in search of treasure rumoured to have been thrown down there during a siege. Ferrey, less convinced by the existence of buried treasure, stayed above ground and remarked, possibly with some self-satisfaction, that Pugin's efforts were 'only rewarded by the acquisition of a few pieces of pottery and glass of Queen Elizabeth's period'.[26] Pugin's inspections of Rochester Castle's foundations almost ended in tragedy. On one occasion a trench collapsed moments after Pugin had climbed out of it, and on another a beam that he was leaning on while taking measurements slipped, throwing him backwards and narrowly missing his head as it fell.

The year 1827 was to prove equally important for the pupils of A. C. Pugin's drawing school. Jeffry Wyatville was coming to the end of his work at Windsor Castle, work which had been occupying much of King George IV's attention for several years. The King now appointed a French émigré, Nicholas Morel, to furnish the new apartments. Morel had worked at Brighton Pavilion with Nash, furnishing the rooms there, and had met his fellow countryman A. C. Pugin during that time. Now it was to Pugin that Morel looked in 1827 to help with his work at Windsor. Pugin, quick to accept the offer, sent a party of his pupils to Windsor, where they were engaged for several years. The younger Pugin famously came to design furniture for the King at the tender age of fifteen, but Ferrey's work was confined to helping

OPPOSITE

22 Ferrey's 1831 view of Windsor Castle, one of the finest of his early watercolours.

20, 21 An urn and a mantle clock in King George IV's collection, drawn by Ferrey at Carlton House in London.

create a pictorial inventory of furniture that could be moved from Carlton House to Windsor. Four watercolours made by Ferrey during this time survive in the Royal Collection – two urns, a candelabrum, and a mantle clock [**20**, **21**]. During a visit to Windsor in 1831 Ferrey made a watercolour of the castle from the end of the Long Walk [**22**], later engraved by John Shury.[27] Also in the Royal Collection, it shows just how far Ferrey had developed during his time at Pugin's school. The light, detail, and composition of the painting are the work of a proficient artist. Groups of soldiers, ladies, and herds of deer populate the foreground, and a dramatic sky

offers the perfect foil for the delicacy of the architectural detail. It is a perspective view that Augustus himself might have been proud of.

Indeed, it seems that Augustus was increasingly recognising Ferrey's talent. There was a flurry of publication in 1831, works which had all been in progress for several years. One of the most significant of Pugin's publications was *Gothic Ornaments*, which Augustus published himself 'at his office' on Great Russell Street. The ornaments were measured and drawn by Pugin and his pupils 'both in England and France during the years 1828, 1829, and 1830'.[28] Ferrey contributed several of the drawings, including details of buildings in Norfolk, in Rochester, Coventry, and Rouen, demonstrating the breadth of travel afforded by Pugin to his pupils. Ferrey also contributed to *Examples of Gothic Architecture*, the first volume of which appeared from 105 Great Russell Street in 1831; Pugin was working on this project shortly before his death, and the following volumes appeared posthumously. Intriguingly, Ferrey appears as a subscriber to this volume, afforded the dignity of 'architect'.[29]

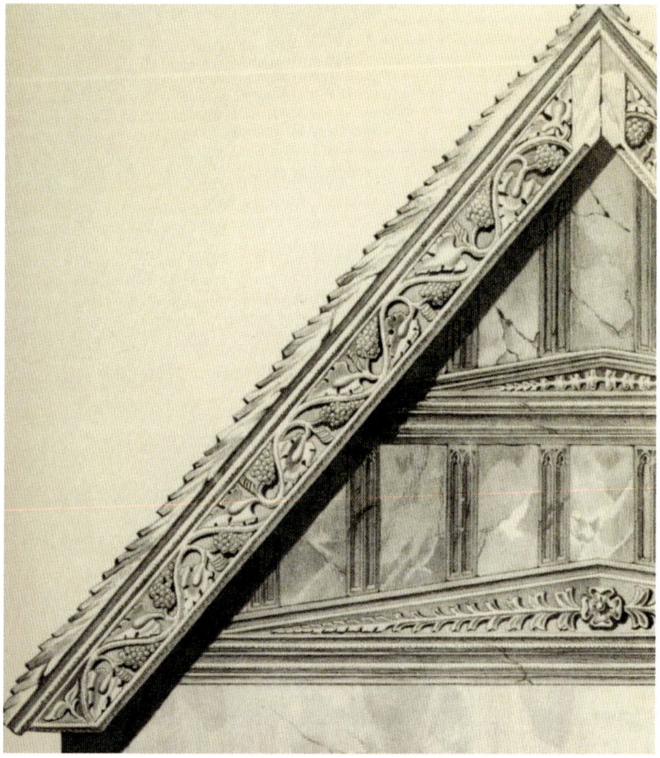

23 A Coventry gable, from *Ornamental Gables*, 'selected' by A. C. Pugin 'and drawn on stone by his pupil B. Ferrey', 1831.

Another product of Pugin's 1831 venture into publication was a collection of drawings of timber gables, with the title *Ornamental Gables selected from ancient examples in England by Aug^s Pugin, Architect and drawn on stone by his pupil B. Ferrey* [**23**]. On this occasion Ferrey had been entrusted with working on a volume of his own, a unique accolade bestowed by A. C. Pugin. Most of the drawings in *Ornamental Gables* were made during the trips that Ferrey had undertaken with Pugin and the other pupils to prepare drawings for *Examples of Gothic Architecture* and *Gothic Ornaments*. The majority are from Coventry; despite the title of the book, several gables from Abbeville are also included. The quality of the drawings is far beyond anything that Ferrey had achieved before: the publication of *Ornamental Gables* proved an important turning point for the twenty-one-year-old and marked the point at which he made the first steps towards fledging his nest at 105 Great Russell Street. To have produced a volume in which he was named on the titlepage was a valuable achievement for Ferrey just as he was preparing to launch his own career. As A. W. N. Pugin had done some years earlier, Ferrey had escaped the strict regimen of the drawing school and was evidently somewhere between being a 'pupil' and an 'architect'.

On 30 May 1831 a report from Christchurch appeared in the *Hampshire Chronicle* noting how 'a most magnificent Communion Table was presented to this parish by Augustus Welby Pugin … through his friend Mr. B Ferrey, jun.' [**24**]. According to

24 A. W. N. Pugin's altar at Christchurch Priory in Dorset, presented 'through his friend Mr. B Ferrey, jun.' in 1831.

Ferrey's recollection, Pugin had become enraptured by Christchurch following the period of recuperation he spent there in 1825, and, no doubt, as a result of subsequent visits with Benjamin. Ferrey wrote that Pugin 'was truly delighted with the magnificent priory Church, the ruins of the Castle and Castellan's House, as well as the beautiful marine scenery of the town and neighbourhood'; Christchurch 'struck [Pugin] as being particularly well calculated for his retreat when desiring to study apart from the turmoil of business in London'.[30] Pugin had by now formed the desire to build himself a house away from London, ultimately realised in 1843 by his residence in Ramsgate (and before that at St Mary's Grange, Salisbury), but in 1831 his focus was set on acquiring a spot for a house near Christchurch. Ferrey recalled how 'upon hearing that the site for a house in a retired situation near the town of Christchurch, called Holfleet … was to be obtained, a negotiation for its purchase was at once set on foot'.[31]

By 1832 A. C. Pugin's health had taken a turn for the worse. Now in his mid-sixties, he was still working and teaching, out of necessity more than anything. On 19 December he died at 105 Great Russell Street, the drafts for the next volumes of *Examples* still on his desk, almost complete. It was to prove the end of an era for Ferrey and his classmates. Pugin had been cut down during one of his most productive periods, and any hopes that Ferrey might have entertained for further collaboration died with his master. In a double blow for the young Pugin, his mother, Catherine, died just four months later, on 28 April 1833.

As Ferrey watched A. C. Pugin's coffin enter St Mary's Church in Islington, he must have reflected how death had once more closed a chapter of his life and opened a new one. Fortunately, he was now of an age to make his own way in the world. The seven years he had spent at 105 Great Russell Street, although not always easy, had provided him with the strongest of foundations on which to begin building a career.

CHAPTER 3

Early Career

Serving his Articles

Even before A. C. Pugin's death, Ferrey would begin his search for gainful employment. In the summer of 1832 he entered the office of William Wilkins, who was then at the height of his career and was engaged on what would be his final major commission: the design of the National Gallery [**25**]. Wilkins, an imposing and exacting figure, was among the most influential Classical architects of his generation, and his office offered Ferrey an invaluable introduction to the formal practice of architecture. It was probably through Pugin's *Examples of Gothic Architecture*, to which Wilkins had subscribed, that he had become acquainted with Ferrey's name. Wilkins recognised in him both technical precision and a draughtsman's sensitivity to form that made him ideally suited to the exacting work of preparing elevations and perspectives for the National Gallery.

Ferrey's time in Wilkins's office proved an early education in the realities of architectural practice. The National Gallery project was beset by revisions, public scrutiny, and bitter controversy, an atmosphere that must have tested the patience of the young draughtsman. But amid this turbulence, Ferrey acquired a practical and moral understanding of the profession. From Wilkins he learned both the discipline

OPPOSITE
Detail of Figure 33.

25 William Wilkins' National Gallery in London shortly after its completion in 1838. Ferrey's work on plans for the Gallery introduced him to the tumultuous cut and thrust of national architectural debate.

of large-scale design and the hazards of public dispute. Where Wilkins met criticism with outbursts of public anger, Ferrey would cultivate a more measured temperament. His two years in Wilkins's office also broadened his architectural sympathies beyond the Gothic, exposing him to Grecian Classicism and also to the administrative and political complexities of taking on major commissions. When he left in 1834, Ferrey was finally ready to navigate the aesthetic and ideological crosscurrents that would come to define his later career.

Rebuilding Parliament

A turbulent and long-drawn-out public debate was born on 16 October 1834. For much of the day a chimney fire had been smouldering unnoticed in the Palace of Westminster, having been sparked by the careless and unauthorised burning of tally sticks in the heating furnace below. By 6 p.m. the fire had spread, and a few minutes later a doorkeeper's wife spotted the House of Lords in flames. Within half an hour the sky of London was illuminated by the conflagration, and a crowd of onlookers gathered outside [**26**].

One spectator was Charles Barry [30], who, watching the flames consume the building, exclaimed the immortal line 'What a chance for an architect'. The tale of what happened next has been told,[1] but it goes without saying that Barry's casual remark would prove prophetic when he was eventually appointed to the task of rebuilding.

We do not know whether Ferrey was in the crowd that gathered that evening. He had recently set up a practice just over a mile away, and it is almost inevitable that he would have rushed to the scene if he was in town. Either way, by the next morning there was very little else being spoken of, especially among those who had a vested interest in the rebuilding that would follow.

In 1835 a Commons select committee produced its report on how Parliament should be rebuilt. Valiant firefighting efforts and a change in the wind had saved several parts of the old building, including Westminster Hall and St Stephen's Chapel. The committee set out how the two houses should be arranged, laying out practical considerations to do with scale and organisation, crucially also making a proclamation on how an architect would be appointed and in what style the new buildings should be executed. The committee stated: 'it is expedient that the designs for the rebuilding of the Houses of Parliament be left open to general competition' and 'that the style of the buildings be either Gothic or Elizabethan'.[2]

The stipulation about style was surprising, and would provoke a great deal of controversy and debate. Gothic

26 A contemporary illustration of the Houses of Parliament engulfed by fire on 16 October 1834.

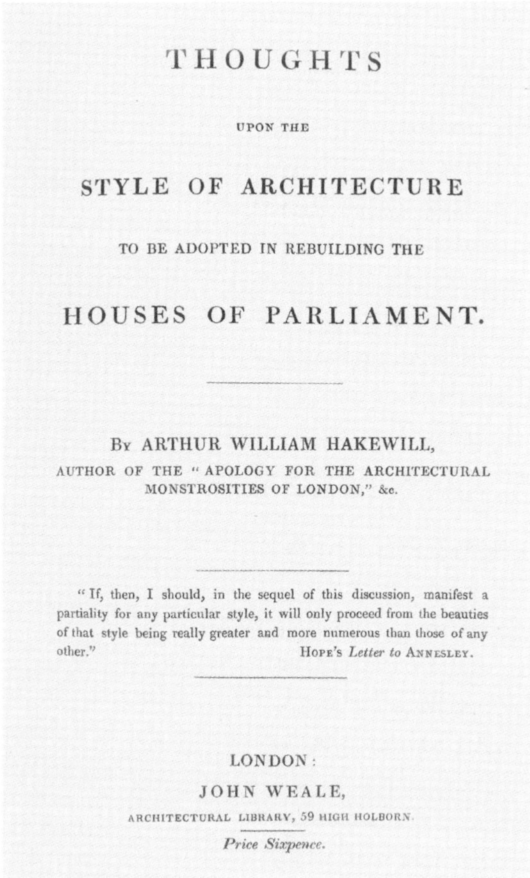

THOUGHTS

UPON THE

STYLE OF ARCHITECTURE

TO BE ADOPTED IN REBUILDING THE

HOUSES OF PARLIAMENT.

BY ARTHUR WILLIAM HAKEWILL,

AUTHOR OF THE "APOLOGY FOR THE ARCHITECTURAL MONSTROSITIES OF LONDON," &c.

"If, then, I should, in the sequel of this discussion, manifest a partiality for any particular style, it will only proceed from the beauties of that style being really greater and more numerous than those of any other."
HOPE'S *Letter to* ANNESLEY.

LONDON:
JOHN WEALE,
ARCHITECTURAL LIBRARY, 59 HIGH HOLBORN.
Price Sixpence.

27 The titlepage of A. W. Hakewill's controversial pamphlet which provoked both Pugin and Ferrey to enter into a public debate against him in favour of the Gothic.

was far from being established as a dominant national style in 1835; indeed, apart from A. W. N. Pugin there were hardly any unbendingly dogmatic Goths to be found. A number of agitators in the Commons would do their best to frustrate the competition that was to follow.

Outside Parliament, a bitter dispute was brewing. Debates raged over the question of style, with a majority of published opinion suggesting that Classical styles had been unfairly prohibited. While some voiced their opinions discreetly, others turned to pamphleting. In the summer of 1835 a little-known architectural theorist, Arthur Hakewill, published his *Thoughts upon the Style of Architecture to be Adopted in Rebuilding the Houses of Parliament* [**27**]. It was a vigorous and highly provocative denouncement of the Gothic style in favour of the Classical. Hakewill's language was intended to provoke a reaction: the Gothic was denounced as obsolete, and those portions of the medieval Palace of Westminster that had survived the fire were called a 'clump of thistles'.[3] The pamphlet attracted several responses, including one from Pugin and another from Ferrey.

Pugin's subsequent involvement in rebuilding Parliament is well known; so too is his response to Hakewill, which represents his earliest published writing. In his *Letter to A. W. Hakewill, Architect* Pugin issued a spirited defence of Gothic architecture as a distinctly moral, Christian style:

> these buildings you term weeds, impeding the planting of the Greek Flower, which you wish to establish. Yes, Sir, they do impede it, for while such wondrous proof of the consummate skill of the builders of the ages (termed by you barbarous) remain, you will have some difficulty in persuading the country that their vicinity should be disgraced by another of those half-English, half-Pagan erections which have so woefully disfigured the architecture of the last century.[4]

Pugin continued with an impassioned conclusion:

> No, Sir, believe me, the day is passed when such enormities can be perpetrated: a feeling of admiration and respect for the noble works of our forefathers has arisen, which I trust and believe will never be suppressed … I trust fully that Anglo-Greek will shortly cease to exist, except in the buildings erected during the last few years, whose slight constructions give great hopes of their speedy decay, a result most fervently wished for.[5]

By 1835 his friendship with Ferrey had begun to cool. Just a month before publishing his pamphlet, Pugin had been received into the Roman Catholic Church, thereby rendering himself something of a social pariah in many circles. Ferrey, a committed Low Church Anglican, found Roman Catholicism an impossible pill to swallow. In his pamphlet he even suggested that the Gothic might be somehow associated with 'the superstition and pageantry which attended the Popish rites'.[6] He continued though by asking whether the 'hecatombs and human immolations' or the 'sanguinary and cruel exhibitions which stained the arena of the Coliseum' with which the Classical style was associated were somehow 'more congenial to our sympathies' than 'the splendid Archæological Architecture included under the term and period of the middle ages'.

This line of reasoning marks the principal distinction between the architectural theories of Ferrey and Pugin. For Pugin, the Gothic was inherently moral and Christian; for Ferrey, architecture and art were to be judged primarily on their beauty. Unlike Hakewill, Ferrey was able to recognise this beauty as readily in the medieval sculpture of Rouen as in the Elgin Marbles. His pamphlet, measured in tone, was considered by several commentators to be the best produced during the pamphlet war.

Of course, Ferrey had a horse in the race. When the Office of Woods released their specifications to competitors, he set to work immediately on his own design. No drawings, alas, survive for his proposal, though his own description does. His design was submitted to the judges under the pseudonymous motto *Quod potui perfeci* ('I have done my best'). He had projected a building in the Tudor style, desiring 'to avoid the ecclesiastical appearance so inseparable from Gothic architecture of an earlier period'.[7] The 700-foot-long river frontage was to prove a challenge even for Barry; Ferrey writes adroitly of this obstacle and the difficulty of adapting Tudor or Gothic architecture to so extended a façade:

> In the composition of this front I considered that, however advantageous the length of ground might be for buildings of Greek or Roman design, where horizontal members are predominant, its latitude, under prescribed styles, presented some difficulties; as the architecture to be employed, depending chiefly upon perpendicular masses, compelled in some degree, such a distribution of parts as should ensure its legitimate character, at the same time that it should combine breath and effect of grandeur.[8]

Quite how Ferrey tackled this elevation is not clear. The northern end, near Westminster Bridge, was worked into a quadrangle arranged symmetrically with New Palace Yard behind. Ferrey noted that he had resisted the temptation to introduce 'a degree of richness' into his design, having instead 'rigidly adhered to a presumed necessity of economy'.[9] There is perhaps a hint of bitterness in that remark, since Pugin's competition drawings for Barry were resplendent with rich architectural detail.

In the aftermath of the fire, Ferrey had spent a good deal of time sketching ancient houses in England, perhaps in readiness for the competition. Athelhampton received much attention from his pencil, as did Milton Abbey, where he drew the great hall [**28**, **29**]. These sketches were no doubt put to use when he designed

28, **29** Sketches by Ferrey of the great halls of Athelhampton House and Milton Abbey in Dorset, made in preparation for his proposed Houses of Parliament design in 1834.

the Parliamentary chambers. Ferrey wrote that he had endeavoured to present the two Houses of Parliament as distinct halls, the focal point of the entire design, themselves based 'upon the model of … ancient Halls … in the palatial and baronial mansions now remaining'.[10] The entrances for the Lords and Commons were placed at the southern end of the site towards Old Palace Yard and were bounded by a gatehouse 'on the plan of such appendages to ancient noblemen's residences'.[11] There the King would be received on state occasions and conducted up a short *scala regia*. This description provides the only fleeting glimpse of Ferrey's competition entry.

30 Charles Barry (1795–1860), who triumphed in the competition.

When the deadline for submissions finally arrived in December 1835, the Office of Woods had received no fewer than 97 entries. It had been a fraught process. The instructions were initially issued incorrectly, and there was widespread confusion about the terms of the official directives. One competitor, Francis Goodwin, even died from the stress caused by the whole affair. On 29 February 1836 the result was finally announced: Charles Barry [**30**], who had been assisted by Pugin, was awarded the commission to rebuild the Houses of Parliament. The rest, as is well known, is history.

The debate, however, was far from over. A bitter dispute quickly erupted between the judging committee and a group of unsuccessful architects. Ferrey was among this latter number. Two particularly aggrieved competitors, Lewis Cottingham and Thomas Hopper, would make public accusations of cheating, bribery, and plagiarism against Barry. It was an unfortunate development.

31 Charles Robert Cockerell (1788–1863), chairman of the committee of disgruntled architects.

Rumours of Barry's success had circulated for some time before the official announcement, prompting a committee of competitors to meet on 4 February 1836 in an attempt to pre-empt the judgment. Confident that the Commissioners tasked with adjudicating between the 97 entries 'must have [by now] made their selections with ability, judgement, and impartiality',[12] the committee sought to organise a public exhibition of all the designs. Their aim was explicit: to challenge the Commissioners' expertise and elicit a contrary opinion from the public. At the first meeting, Ferrey was elected Honorary Secretary.

In retrospect, it was perhaps an unfortunate cause for Ferrey to have aligned himself with. At heart he was an agreeable, even-tempered man, but as Honorary Secretary his signature appeared beneath every one of the committee's challenging proclamations. When Barry's victory was announced, it was hardly surprising that many unsuccessful architects, embittered by rejection and the contest's confused administration, reacted forcefully. Letters soon appeared in the press, protests were lodged with MPs, and demands were made for the whole matter to be reconsidered. The committee, chaired by Charles Robert Cockerell [**31**], sought to lend the protestations of disappointed competitors a degree of dignity and articulation. In this Ferrey's innate good humour proved an asset.

In March 1836 the committee met again at the Thatched House Tavern and passed several stern resolutions unanimously, including a denunciation of the Commissioners, chaired by Charles Hanbury-Tracy, as 'avowedly deficient in practical and professional knowledge'.[13] The main point of contention, however, arose with the public exhibition. Parliament had endorsed it, and the Chancellor of the Exchequer, Thomas Spring Rice, declared that it would display 'all the plans for the new Houses of Parliament, the unsuccessful as well as the successful'.[14] However, when the exhibition opened in Wilkins's National Gallery, the first, second, third and fourth prize drawings were withheld by the Office of Woods. Many unsuccessful competitors interpreted this as confirmation that the winning design was substandard. The committee accused the Commissioners of avoiding public scrutiny, while Cottingham and Hopper attempted, in vain, to gain access to the drawings.

Finally, on 28 April the four successful drawings were added to the exhibition. The embittered competitors predictably dismissed them: Barry was accused of plagiarising Hopper's proposal [**32**], while Wilkins ensured that his pamphlet, *An Apology for the Designs of the Houses of Parliament Marked Phil-Archimedes*, was handed to every visitor. Cockerell, the committee chair and a committed Classicist, took aim at the 'barbaric carvings and disgusting monstrosities of Gothic architecture'.[15] These were, of course, strange bedfellows for Ferrey, who had already defended the official endorsement of the Gothic style. His objection was not to Barry's proposal *per se* but to the evident mismanagement of the competition. Popular opinion in the press largely favoured Barry, but the committee persisted, claiming the exhibition demonstrated that 'the selection of the Commissioners [had]

32 Thomas Hopper's proposal for the Houses of Parliament. The disappointed competitor had this, and several other, views published as lithographs in 1842.

not received that approbation and confirmation from the public which a Commission appointed by His Majesty for this object was expected to have elicited'.[16]

The matter culminated in a parliamentary debate on 21 July 1836. A group of thirty-six competitors petitioned Parliament, through Joseph Hume MP, to reconsider the results of the competition. The petition objected to the validity of the results for a variety of reasons. Among them were technicalities like the facts that only four of the five Commissioners had signed the report and that the question of expense had been ignored; attacks however on the judges themselves and the prize-winning designs were also forthcoming. Barry's proposal, they noted, was in 'direct contravention of the instructions' regarding the arrangement of the Houses of Lords and Commons.[17]

The day before the crucial debate, Ferrey travelled to Downing Street for an interview with the Chancellor, accompanied by Cottingham, Hopper, John Taylor, and James Savage. Whatever objections they may have raised, their complaints were ultimately in vain. After a lengthy and impassioned debate in the Commons, Barry was formally authorised to proceed.

The controversy did not immediately subside, but Ferrey wisely withdrew. Though he had conducted himself with greater dignity than many co-petitioners, he had become embroiled in a bitter dispute. Relations with Pugin, who had collaborated on the winning design, were unlikely to have been helped. Nevertheless, Ferrey might have felt a sliver of optimism: several visitors to the National Gallery exhibition praised his designs, and one reviewer suggested that his entry might well have made a worthy fifth, which, out of ninety-seven, is no mean feat.

What might a victory have meant for Ferrey's career? The 'what if' question remains irresistible. Would he have become a household name? Might he have been dubbed Sir Benjamin Ferrey? How would his practice have evolved? We shall never know.

Whatever the case, other grand projects soon called him onwards to Bournemouth.

Bournemouth

By 1836 Ferrey had begun to establish a reputation as a capable architectural mind. He had made a fine proposal to rebuild Parliament and had published accomplished drawings of Christchurch Priory – but he still had no buildings to his name.

It was thanks to A. C. Pugin that Ferrey had published *Antiquities of the Priory of Christ-Church* in 1834. The book followed the model that Pugin had perfected: a series of illustrations accompanied by explanatory text. Pugin's former collaborator, John Britton, acted as Ferrey's publisher, while Edward Wedlake Brayley, who had also worked with Pugin, contributed the text. Ferrey had been preparing the watercolours as early as 1831 [**33**], and the drawing of a medieval statue of Christ that decorates the front cover was executed when he was only sixteen [**34**, **35**].

The first advertisement for *Antiquities* appeared in September 1831, announcing that the work would correspond 'in size and general execution'[18] with Britton's *Cathedral Antiquities*, an ambitious series begun in 1814 with Brayley and others. Subscriptions were to be 'received by B. Ferrey, 41 King Street. Soho'.[19] When the volume finally appeared three years later, it was warmly received. Among its subscribers were many of the most notable figures in the architectural world. Alongside his old associates, A. W. N. Pugin and Wilkins, were Robert Smirke, James William Wild, Anthony Salvin, and numerous others; Ferrey also ensured that a copy reached Sir John Soane. Equally revealing are some of the other subscribers, including the Duke of Wellington. Several of these aristocratic patrons would, in time, commission work from Ferrey. The publication of *Antiquities* thus afforded him a degree of professional exposure that proved invaluable at the outset of his career.

33 A watercolour of the north choir aisle of Christchurch Priory in Dorset, made in 1831 by Ferrey in preparation for his *Antiquities of the Priory of Christ-Church.*

Two surnames on the subscribers' list – Tapps and Tregonwell – point to the story of Bournemouth in Dorset. Captain Lewis Tregonwell, whose son John subscribed to Ferrey's book, has been hailed as the founder of Bournemouth. In 1810 he purchased eight and a half acres of heathland and built himself a house there, having visited the nearby beach with his wife and been captivated by its scenery. Over the following twelve years, Tregonwell gradually acquired additional land and ultimately established an estate of 36 acres with several properties for visitors and household staff. By the time of his death in 1832, he had effectively created a small seaside village.

Three years later, in 1835, Sir George Ivison Tapps, the local landowner who had sold Tregonwell his initial eight and a half acres,

34, 35 Ferrey's youthful sketch of the statue of Christ at Christchurch Priory, made in 1826, later used as a vignette in his *Antiquities of the Priory of Christ-Church, Hants*. (1834).

died. The baronetcy passed to his son, George, who appended the ancestral name Gervis to his surname. Tapps-Gervis, having observed Tregonwell's development, recognised the potential to create a fashionable resort along similar lines to Brighton. Having subscribed to Ferrey's *Antiquities* and noted his skill as a draughtsman, he engaged Ferrey in 1836 to develop the Westover estate at the mouth of the River Bourne.

Tapps-Gervis understood that the success of the scheme required careful planning. Ferrey's familial roots in nearby Christchurch may have contributed to his selection, but the commission also reflects Tapps-Gervis's confidence in Ferrey's ability. Ferrey approached the project with enthusiasm, designing a series of houses and public buildings. By October 1836 his designs were complete, and he began translating them into large perspective views. One of these watercolours, now held by the Russell-Cotes Gallery, displays some of Ferrey's finest draughtsmanship [**36**]. It is a bird's-eye view of the development, looking inland from the sea, and demonstrates a dramatic use of light and perspective reminiscent of Joseph Gandy. Even in comparison to A. C. Pugin's work it is striking in its clarity and ambition.

These perspectives were soon engraved and published. They depict the development as envisioned rather than as it was ultimately realised, but they give a clear sense of Tapps-Gervis's overall plan. Sixteen of the villas shown on the left

36 Ferrey's magisterial perspective watercolour of 1834 showing a projected plan for Bournemouth in Dorset, Puginian in its conception and execution.

were eventually built, collectively known as the Westover Villas [**37**]. Each villa was unique – some in picturesque, non-committal Gothic, others in the Italianate style [**38**]. The designs drew heavily on the pattern books of the early nineteenth century. John Claudius Loudon's *Encyclopaedia of Cottage, Farm, and Villa Architecture* (1833) clearly influenced Ferrey's planning, particularly in the arrangement of gardens and the orientation of principal rooms to take advantage of sea views. Italianate towers, several of which he designed for Westover, fulfilled this purpose by providing elevated vantage points for observation and light. Construction had begun by July 1836, and by June 1838 twelve villas were complete. Rather than being built by the estate, Ferrey's designs were selected and constructed by individual speculators, with Tapps-Gervis serving as ground landlord. Early owners included a bricklayer turned estate contractor and Samuel Bayly, a retired draper from Christchurch and former competitor of Ferrey's father.[20] The houses that Ferrey designed in a series of interconnected crescents were never built.

37 Detail of an engraving of another of Ferrey's perspective views of Bournemouth, showing his proposed Westover Villas.

The Westover development was conceived primarily as a health resort rather than a pleasure destination. On the far left of Ferrey's watercolour perspective [36] is the bathhouse, also in an Italianate style, featuring a central tower to accommodate the furnace. The main elevation is framed by verandas opening onto a library and newsroom; beyond these lay eight warm baths and associated dressing rooms. The scale of the building is evident in another of Ferrey's perspectives, taken from a hilltop looking toward the sea. The bathhouse as designed was never built. Instead, a modest boarding house, the Belle Vue, occupied the site.

The focal point of Ferrey's watercolour perspective is a church, perched 'like a diadem'[21] atop the hill and illuminated by sunlight. It was his first church design, and it stands alone in his ecclesiastical output. It is octagonal in plan and resembles the Gothick of a generation earlier, with echoes of James Wyatt's Fonthill and Lee Priory. It has four gabled elevations (the east and west ends and transepts) and lancet windows grouped in threes. Crowning the structure is another octagon, inspired

38 A contemporary engraving of 1 and 2 Westover Villas in Bournemouth.

39 The chapel of ease at Wisbech in Cambridgeshire, built in 1827, perhaps an important source of inspiration for Ferrey's unexecuted church at Bournemouth.

by Ely Cathedral's lantern, surmounted by a stone spire. Octagonal churches were rare; a few however had been built around the same time – these include St Dunstan-in-the-West, Fleet Street, and a chapel of ease in Wisbech [**39**] – but Ferrey's design is unique in its inclusion of a spire. Here, ambition collided with inexperience: in striving for innovation, Ferrey produced a design he would later have acknowledged as unattractive. The church was never built, and local residents continued to travel to Poole or Christchurch on Sundays. One contemporary reviewer critiqued not Ferrey's design, but rather the placement of the building:

> it will not do for invalids with delicate chests and damaged lungs to climb up the Capitol, either to return home after a walk on the sea-shore, or to attend at church on a Sunday, to be blown away in endeavouring to reach the House of God, or blown upon on coming out of it by the boisterous south-wester, – and so, chilled into a pleurisy or an additional vomica, thereby destroying the benefit which Bournemouth is calculated to yield to the sick. Has the architect, has the landowner ever reflected upon such a consideration as this?[22]

Time has dealt an unfortunate hand to Ferrey's Bournemouth. Of all that he built for Sir George Tapps-Gervis only the Bath Hotel survives, and it has been so altered as to be almost unrecognisable. Classical in style, it opened on Queen Victoria's coronation day in 1838. It formed the centrepiece of the new resort and from there many of Ferrey's Westover Villas were auctioned. Tapps-Gervis died of a stroke in August 1842, and Ferrey was soon replaced in his role as the estate's supervising architect by Decimus Burton.

Although his vision for Tapps-Gervis's resort remained largely incomplete, Ferrey played a crucial, and now largely forgotten, role in creating modern Bournemouth. By 1842, this once-obscure headland had been transformed into a flourishing coastal resort. Thomas Hardy, in *Tess of the d'Urbervilles* (1891), described 'the lofty roofs, chimneys, gazebos, and towers of the numerous fanciful residences of which the place was composed'.

Ferrey's 'city of detached mansions; a Mediterranean lounging-place on the English Channel' was his first and last attempt at civic architecture on such a scale. As the century progressed, he was drawn away from domestic projects and increasingly devoted himself to church-building.

CHAPTER 4

Ferrey the Church-Builder

OPPOSITE
Detail of Figure 86.

It was clear, even from an early age, that Ferrey was destined to become a church architect. His youthful fascination with Christchurch Priory and Wimborne Minster was nurtured by his time at A. C. Pugin's drawing school, which offered him a valuable education not only in domestic architecture but also in an extensive range of English and French ecclesiastical buildings. Throughout his life, Ferrey remained a follower of the younger Pugin; yet, unlike his childhood friend, it was primarily the archaeological principle of the Gothic Revival rather than its religious connotations that guided his practice.

Ferrey's brief partnership with a former classmate, Thomas Larkins Walker, ended when both men chose to pursue careers as ecclesiastical architects. Very little survives from their collaboration, most of it having been concerned with publication and secular commissions. In 1838 their partnership dissolved, and the two architects immediately embarked on separate projects: Walker began work on All Saints, Spicer Street, in east London,[1] while Ferrey designed his first church, St Thomas of Canterbury at Compton Valence in Dorset. The respective ambition and energy demonstrated in these commissions may help explain why their partnership did not endure.

Despite it being Ferrey's first church, St Thomas of Canterbury is a confident and assured building [**40**, **41**]. The commission came from one of his earliest and

40, **41** St Thomas of Canterbury, Compton Valence, Dorset (1838–39), Ferrey's first church, designed and built with considerable input from Arthur Acland.

most important patrons, Robert Williams (1767–1847), a banker and sometime Member of Parliament [**42**]. Williams had purchased an estate at Bridehead in Dorset at the end of the eighteenth century, and in 1838 he commissioned Ferrey to build a stable block there [165]. Impressed by the result, Williams engaged Ferrey to rebuild the parish church at Compton Valence, five miles away, where he held the living. Ferrey was to be assisted in this task by Arthur Acland, an in-law of the Williamses [200]. The medieval church was in a state of disrepair [43]. Following a pattern he would repeat throughout his career, Ferrey retained the old tower while rebuilding the remainder of the structure. For a first restoration, the work was remarkably sensitive: he preserved the character of a Dorset village church, carefully matching stonework and retaining as much of the original fabric as possible. The result, despite it being Ferrey's earliest, ranks among his most striking interiors, with an exceptional vaulted apse.

42 Robert Williams of Bridehead (1767–1847), one of Ferrey's earliest and most important patrons.

The exterior, while straightforward, demonstrates Ferrey's skill. The nave and north aisle, both funded by Williams, are well proportioned and constructed of heavy ashlar, left bare to match the tower. By contrast, inside, the north arcade and chancel arch feature tall, elegant piers of warmer local limestone, creating subtle visual distinction. The whole character is that of a fifteenth-century village church realised in an archaeological, rather than merely revived, style. Ferrey's handling of the chancel is where his youthful talent is most apparent. The medieval church, which he sketched in 1839, had a low chancel of two bays and a flat east end [**43**]. Quite in contrast, Ferrey built a vaulted polygonal apse with tall Decorated windows in each wall, admitting light from three sides. It is an arrangement that owes as much to Continental churches as to English medieval examples such as Tidmarsh in Berkshire. The whole rebuild puzzled Pevsner, who wrote:

> Now the point is that Dec as a choice, a polygonal apse as a choice, and the more general tendency to let a village church appear 'real', i.e. a real medieval village church, is usually connected with Pugin and Scott. But neither did this sort of thing before 1840 (although the short apsed sanctuary is exactly what one would expect for the date). So here is an advanced guard of proto-Ecclesiological church architecture, carried out by a group highly influenced by the Oxford Movement. Compton Valence is therefore of more than local significance.[2]

Ferrey's work at Compton Valence prefigures the approach later adopted by the most celebrated Gothic Revival church-builders. Thanks largely to the influence of Williams and the input of Acland, it anticipates the movement toward creating churches that appear genuinely medieval. For a thirty-year-old architect designing his first church, the outcome is extraordinary.[3]

43 Ferrey's sketch of the medieval church at Compton Valence in 1839.

Yet Ferrey's career as a church-builder has often been underappreciated. Only occasionally did he produce work of groundbreaking brilliance, and much of his output was considered competent but conventional. While he rarely designed a poor church, his reputation has suffered from the comparative extraordinary excellence of contemporaries such as Pugin and Scott. In churches like Compton Valence, Morpeth, and Buckland St Mary, however, Ferrey demonstrated that he was capable of excellence.

Basil Clarke's 1938 summary of Ferrey's work, quoting his obituary in *The Builder*, typifies the traditional assessment: 'His churches are numerous. They are all timid, orthodox, and harmless, for Ferrey was "rather a close adherent of precedent than a bold originator."'[4] The following survey of Ferrey's ecclesiastical output focuses on his new churches rather than restorations. By the time of his death at seventy, he had designed almost sixty new churches – an average of roughly one and a half per year between 1840 and 1880.

As will be seen, the promise of his early work was not always sustained. During the 1840s, as he experimented with the Romanesque style, he produced a series of less remarkable buildings before achieving immense success. This trajectory, the tension between early innovation and later conventionality, defines the arc of Ferrey's career as a church architect.

The Romanesque Churches

On a wet Thursday afternoon in December 1842 the failure of a vault at St Nicholas, East Grafton in Wiltshire foretold a greater collapse – that of the Romanesque Revival. This fleeting revival, a curious spark of creativity during the Gothic Revival's infancy, never fully recovered from the early blow it was dealt at East

Grafton; by the end of that decade, the style had almost entirely disappeared back into the obscurity from which it had emerged.

In the early 1840s architects still practiced free from the rigid doctrines which were soon to be imposed by the likes of the Cambridge Camden Society. The Society, founded in 1839, had not quite found its popular voice by this point. Not then the arbiter of taste it would later become, the Society's journal, *The Ecclesiologist*, featured a review of Ferrey's church at East Grafton in the pages of its very first edition of 1843. The design, it reported, is 'externally of pleasing effect and correct detail, and one which is highly creditable to the architect'.[5]

By the latter half of the 1830s the smoke from the Battle of the Styles might have been beginning to clear, but victory had not yet been declared. The competition to rebuild the Palace of Westminster had proved this somewhat starkly. George Vivian, an artist turned architectural critic who had published in favour of adopting the Greek style for Parliament, described the stylistic tensions of the first decade of Queen Victoria's reign by writing that 'at present all is unsettled – each professor has his idol'.[6] For some, Vivian recorded, it was the Hindoo, for others the Jacobean, and indeed for a growing number of architects it was 'Norman ugliness'.[7] Antiquarian texts, especially A. C. Pugin's *Specimens of the Architecture of Normandy* on which Ferrey of course had worked, were an important factor in disseminating measured sources from which this supposed 'Norman ugliness' could be copied. While some measure of public consensus had basically been reached – that Grecian was the correct style for large public buildings, as Tudor was for houses, and Gothic for churches – the lack of consistency in the tastes of individual architects, and therefore the sub-categories of Gothic they favoured, was proving to be a major weakness for the Revivalists. If the Revival was to flourish, one consistent expression of Gothicism was thought vital. It was a uniformity that Ruskin would later call for in *The Seven Lamps of Architecture* (1849): the seventh lamp, 'Obedience', expounded universal conformity to one rule of architecture, which, in Ruskin's estimation, was the Middle-Pointed. The Ecclesiologists would offer much stylistic policing, but at the beginning of the 1840s no such substantive move towards stylistic standardisation had taken place, and a disarray of styles emerged out of the confusion. What was unfairly called 'Norman ugliness' had become one of the more fashionable of the various modes of church building by the 1840s, and was briefly in favour with both the Ecclesiologists and commissioning patrons.

44 Pugin's St James, Reading, Berkshire (1837–40). An unusual Romanesque experiment for Pugin, which he disavowed even before the church had been consecrated.

In 1837 Pugin began work on St James's Church in Reading [**44**]. It was to be among the very first of his churches and was designed in an unapologetically

Romanesque style cribbed from St Laurence, Castle Rising. This was a curious decision, given that Pugin had already declared the unique correctness of those 'noble edifices of the fourteenth and fifteenth centuries'.[8] But the choice was not wholly his own. At just twenty-five, the young architect had deferred, understandably enough, to the vision of his patron, James Wheble, who insisted that his new Roman Catholic church should evoke the style of the neighbouring ruins of Reading Abbey. Even before its consecration, Pugin had disavowed his work at St James's. He would return to the Norman style only three more times, and only once for the construction of a new church: St Michael the Archangel, Gorey, in Ireland, where enthusiasm for the Romanesque proved more enduring and widespread.

Pugin's brief flirtation with the Romanesque style was not without the wider context of an emerging revival. This revival, though still relatively tentative, had already found expression in isolated but determined efforts – Samuel Pepys Cockerell's fantastical encasement of the Norman church at Tickencote in Rutland in 1792 stands out as one ambitious and early example. By the 1820s, churches like St Clement in Oxford began to spring up with more regularity, but it was only in the 1830s and 40s, through the efforts of architects like Thomas Penson and Ferrey, that the style began to achieve a firmer and more respectable architectural footing.

Even so, those early ventures, like Pugin's at Reading, typically rested on some plausible historic pretext. The invocation of the Norman style was seldom arbitrary: it was, at least in part, often an appeal to some local historical memory.

An Unbuilt Chapel for Cardiff and Holy Trinity, East Hyde, Bedfordshire

On first glance, it appears that Ferrey was not as early to the Revival as Pugin, since it was not until 1840 that his first Romanesque church appeared. However, in 1837, the same year that Pugin had begun work on his Romanesque church in Reading, Ferrey was engaged by John Crichton-Stuart, the 2nd Marquess of Bute, to construct a chapel near Cardiff. Lord Bute, later hailed as the founder of modern Cardiff, had only been seriously considering the commercial expansion of that city for a short time when he engaged Ferrey in 1837.

Lord Bute was one of the major landowners of that period, owning some 100,000 acres spread across Scotland, England and Wales. The family also owned a house at Highcliffe near Christchurch. In 1831, Lord Bute's cousin, the 1st Baron Stuart de Rothesay, had commissioned William Donthorne to design a Gothic castle to match his new Gothicised title. The Ferreys knew of the Stuarts, and it is plausible that the Stuarts would have known of the Ferreys: despite being members of a commercial middle class, George Ferrey's family were on the up. George would become Mayor of Christchurch in 1840, and his eldest son would also later serve in that role. Intriguingly, in his biography of Pugin Ferrey related a story of how Pugin had almost been engaged to rework Donthorne's newly erected work at Highcliffe. Sketches that Pugin had drawn up on site and presented to Lord Stuart de Rothesay at dinner were not greeted with the immediate approval that he had hoped for, so much so that when his host expected to continue discussions over breakfast the next

45 The chapel designed at the behest of Lord Bute for Cardiff, illustrated in *The Civil Engineer and Architect's Journal* in 1837. It remained unbuilt.

morning, it was found that Pugin had risen early and left by coach. Whatever the truth of that story (and it is quite possible that Ferrey heard it directly from the family), in consulting Ferrey Lord Bute made a safer decision than his cousin had done.

Bute would go on to build several docks which would transform Cardiff's fortunes, but he first commissioned a chapel. He requested from Ferrey a building in an ancient style, hinting more specifically at the Romanesque, a style with which Ferrey was yet to experiment. In October 1837 an article appeared in the first edition of *The Civil Engineer and Architect's Journal* revealing what Ferrey intended to build [**45**]. It reported: 'this chapel … although upon a small scale … and sufficiently economical in regard to decoration, is marked by considerable piquancy of character and architectural effect'.[9] The engraving that accompanied the article shows precisely that: a small box of a chapel greatly enlivened by the addition of an unusual double staircase at its west end. Ferrey had copied this directly from the twelfth-century Norman staircase that once led to the Poor Pilgrims' Hall in Canterbury. He took this and mirrored it, making provision for steps leading up both sides of the chapel's west front. Among Ferrey's earliest sketches is one of the Canterbury staircase, executed in some detail in 1835 [**46**]. His proposed reinterpretation of it for Cardiff is one of

46 Ferrey's sketch of the Norman staircase of the Poor Pilgrims' Hall at Canterbury, made while he was courting his first wife in 1835.

the most oblique references to an existing building he would ever make in his own work.

The double staircase projected for Cardiff had a practical function. The round-headed central portal leads to the west door, the stairs to its left lead into the small tower that abuts the northernmost corner of the wall, and the other stairs lead inside to a gallery. One must not forget that the Revival was still in its early stages; galleries were still *de rigueur*, though they would become anathema to committed Goths a few years later. This was still the era of the 'Commissioners' Churches' erected after the Church Building Act of 1818. A growing disdain for those churches was becoming apparent. Elsewhere an 'infuriated ox' had been driven through the ceremonial laying of a foundation stone,[10] and the reviewer of Ferrey's designs for Lord Bute did not miss the opportunity to make a dig at the Commissioners when discussing the arrangement of the staircase: 'Perhaps, indeed, the Church Commissioners might object to such arrangement; it is therefore fortunate that on this occasion Mr. Ferrey has had nothing to do with them, nor been obliged to accommodate his design to the Procrustes bed of their regulations.'[11]

Procrustes was the bandit in Greek mythology who habitually attacked victims by stretching them or severing their legs in order to fit them into an iron bed. Despite the favourable coverage in *The Civil Engineer and Architect's Journal* and its suggestion that Ferrey's chapel was 'about to be erected',[12] the plans were shelved at the eleventh hour: even with its galleries, it was thought to be too small for the purpose.

Ferrey seemingly thought no more of the Romanesque Revival for another three years, during which time he was primarily engaged on his grand plans for Bournemouth and Dorchester. He built just one church between 1837 and 1840, St Thomas of Canterbury in Compton Valence [40, 41], that church being as far removed from the Romanesque as one could imagine. It was not until Ferrey received further correspondence from Lord Bute at the end of 1839 that he would once again return to the style. The church which had been projected for Cardiff was to be built after all, but at a different location – not in Wales but in Bedfordshire.

In 1837 the Diocese of Ely subsumed the counties of Bedfordshire and Huntingdonshire from the Diocese of Lincoln, and thus gained Luton. The estate of Luton Hoo had been in the possession of the Crichton-Stuarts since 1763; the Robert Adam house there had been remodelled at the 2nd Marquess's behest a few years earlier by Robert Smirke. Luton and many of its surrounding villages relied on the medieval church of St Mary, and Joseph Allen, Bishop of Ely, instigated a campaign to provide churches for these far-flung hamlets. East Hyde was one such hamlet. Lord Bute, in collaboration with the Bishop, gave land from his estate, £600 (about £50,000 today), towards the cost of the new church, and an architect in the form of Ferrey. What Ferrey built was the church that had been projected for Cardiff in 1837.

Holy Trinity, East Hyde (now St Charalambos, Greek Orthodox), is a puzzling church, quite unlike anything that Ferrey would produce again [**47**]. It must be

OPPOSITE
47 Holy Trinity, East Hyde, Bedfordshire, 1841 – now in the care of the Greek Orthodox Church and rededicated to St Charalambos.

remembered that it was only his second church, and that it was built very much according to the broadly unacademic principles of the period. Timothy Mowl described it thus: 'East Hyde, Bedfordshire, is a Commissioners' box lit by slim round-arched lancets … The church is the work of a young man following an old-fashioned plan but attempting to enliven it by an irrelevant display of historical detail.'[13] While that is a strong assessment, it would be difficult to characterise it as unfair. Ferrey was still finding his feet, and unlike at Compton Valence was working to a tight budget of just £1,000 (about £155,000 today). Despite Pevsner's assessment of the west front as 'a distressing display',[14] it actually represents an undeniable degree of architectural imagination and provides an elegant (if slightly unusual) solution to the need for access to the galleries. This was an element of the design that a reviewer of Ferrey's Cardiff church project in 1837 had noted, writing: 'We trust … that although it is the first, it will not be the last modern instance, of staircases leading to the galleries of churches, being so placed, and thus made to conduce very strikingly to exterior design.'[15] And indeed, when Ferrey's Romanesque design was eventually realised at East Hyde in 1841, the Canterbury staircase was noted by other architects. Robert Wallace included a strikingly similar set of staircases in his design for the National Scotch Church in Covent Garden a year later [**48**], and Samuel Sanders Teulon's sketchbook contains a design for a double-staircased church copied directly from Ferrey.[16] Beyond this brief flurry of interest, the idea hardly caught on.

Where Ferrey's church at East Hyde fails most noticeably is in its choice of building material [**49**]. The Cardiff chapel was projected to be constructed entirely of stone, with details executed in moulded brick or terracotta. But given the limited budget at East Hyde, this church was to be built entirely of brick – Luton Greys,

48 Robert Wallace's National Scotch Church in Covent Garden, London, designed in 1842, the year after Holy Trinity, East Hyde, was built.

sourced from a brickyard owned by Lord Bute. The broad appearance of a 'Commissioners' box' is only further accentuated by the meanness of the brick, which has, alas, recently been cleaned; the accumulation of a century and a half's dirt had at least lent it the vague appearance of ancient granite.

49 The brick in Ferrey's church at East Hyde appears somewhat jarring.

In the same year that East Hyde was consecrated, John Mason Neale was anonymously declaring the unsuitability of brick in a pamphlet for the Cambridge Camden Society. He wrote: 'Brick ought on no account to be used [for churches]: white certainly is worse than red, and red than black: but to settle the precedency in such miserable materials is worse than useless.'[17] It is highly improbable, but not entirely impossible, that Neale's words were a reaction to the church that had just been completed at East Hyde.

Pevsner's assessment of the church places it in the context of Ferrey's developing ability: 'Ferrey was one of the first to take archaeological accuracy seriously. He began to do this just about 1841. Yet here he is still entirely in the Commissioners' vein.'[18] This is almost true. The skeleton of a Commissioners' church is undoubtedly noticeable at East Hyde, but what Ferrey did was to dress that skeleton in an archaeological skin and thereby vivify it. In incorporating a practical double staircase based on the Canterbury precedent from his sketchbooks, he lent his brick box a momentary glimmer of intrigue and energy. On account of that alone, it must never be accused of being a church entirely driven by formula: it is simply the work of an enthusiastic and promising young architect who was yet to find his feet. That was soon to change.

St Nicholas, Corfe, Dorset, and St Nicholas, East Grafton, Wiltshire

In 1841 Ferrey was appointed as the Diocesan Architect for Bath and Wells, an appointment that would have a significant impact on his practice. One of the first churches he built in the Diocese was St Nicholas at Corfe in Dorset in 1842 [**50**]. This was his second foray into the Romanesque style and proved a more archaeological affair with no whiff of the influence of the Church Commissioners about it. Unlike at East Hyde, Ferrey carried the Romanesque into the church's interior, making it more than simply an encasement. As Timothy Mowl noted, 'for the pulpit design he cleverly re-used the interlaced arcading of Corfe's genuine Norman font'.[19] The rest of the church's detail is executed in a style entirely in harmony with itself. The

50 St Nicholas, Corfe, Dorset, 1842.

justification for using the Norman style at Corfe was clear, given the twelfth-century work that survived in the church that Ferrey's replaced. But it still represents, albeit to a lesser degree than East Hyde, the work of an architect getting to grips with the style: the plate tracery of the west window, for instance, is unsatisfyingly simplistic. Charles Edmund Giles would make significant additions to the church in 1858, including the addition of the south aisle and the north-west tower, the scale of which clashes uncomfortably with Ferrey's work. Giles, with good intentions, probably looked to Ferrey's work at East Grafton for inspiration when he came to design the tower.

With the Norman Revival gathering steam and Ferrey's reputation growing for work in the style, his patrons soon started to expect Romanesque work from him. In Wiltshire the energetic incumbent of Great Bedwyn, John Ward [**51**], received a visit on 27 December 1841 from the Marchioness of Ailesbury, whose husband owned the Great Bedwyn estate. She reported that her husband, having been frequently urged by Ward to consider the necessity of additional church accommodation, was determined 'to take active measures for carrying such a work into execution'.[20] The population of Ward's parish had outgrown its church in Great Bedwyn, with some thousand people living three miles away in East Grafton. At the beginning of 1842 the Dean of Salisbury was presented with a petition to provide a parish church for East Grafton. Permission was granted, and land was carved out in the Marquess of Ailesbury's estate.

51 The Rev. John Ward (1795–1861), instigator of work at East Grafton.

Ferrey was appointed as architect later that year, and was specifically requested to design a church in the Norman style. He set to work with celerity and produced designs which demonstrated an accomplished and careful handling of the style that he had been working for several years to master. The church drew almost all its inspiration from the church at Thaon in Normandy. As a boy Ferrey had visited that with A. C. Pugin, who included an illustration of the church in *Specimens of the Architecture of Normandy* [**52**]. Moreover, in the early 1840s there was a brief flurry of interest in Thaon as a model to copy. As John Sell Cotman had observed twenty years earlier, the church was a specimen of 'the true Norman style, unaltered, and also uninjured'.[21] In 1841 the Cambridge Camden Society reported in *The Ecclesiologist* that George Selwyn, Bishop of New Zealand and a patron of the society, had requested plans of a model church from which he could base designs for new churches in his diocese, and the Camdenians sent a design 'modified from that of Than [*sic*] church, near Caen, in Normandy'.[22] That design was true to the basic form of the Norman church in that it consisted of 'Chancel, Nave, two Aisles to each, Transepts, and central Tower'.[23] In practice, Selwyn would only refer to this exemplar very loosely, if at all.

52 The Romanesque church at Thaon in Normandy, illustrated in A. C. Pugin's *Specimens of the Architecture of Normandy* (1827).

Incidentally, as *The Ecclesiologist* was publishing its first volume in which the reference to Thaon was printed, work was beginning on a new church at Albury in Surrey, based on that same Norman church [53]. The story of the three churches in that small parish must be one of the most bizarre footnotes in the architectural and religious history of the period, but one which is, alas, largely beyond the scope of this study. In short, Albury's squire, Henry Drummond, was a founder of the Catholic Apostolic Church, to whose services

53 St Peter and Paul, Albury, Surrey, designed by William McIntosh Brookes for Henry Drummond, 1839–42.

Ferrey had been reluctantly dragged as a boy by Mrs Pugin. Drummond disliked his villagers, especially the fact that they lived so close to his parkland, so he simply moved them a mile to the west of Albury Park, promising them a new parish church to replace the old parish church that he had closed. It is worth noting that he would commission his friend Pugin to design a mortuary chapel in the disused Saxon church – one of Pugin's finest reorderings.

Drummond had himself reportedly visited Thaon and was impressed by the church he saw there. In 1839 he commissioned William McIntosh Brookes to design both a Catholic Apostolic church and a new parish church for the resettled villagers. The latter was to be based on what he had seen at Thaon. The result, St Peter and St Paul [**53**], executed to Drummond's annoyance in brick rather than stone, is a relatively unacademic single-cell Romanesque church with a tower copied from Thaon, but unlike the original positioned at the north-west corner. The church was completed in 1842, just as Ferrey was beginning work at East Hyde.

Whether there is any relationship between East Grafton and Albury is a question that deserves further investigation. It is however worth noting that work was taking place at the same time in Thaon to demolish parts of the church, which became redundant in 1840. Whether this was known to those involved in the construction of the churches is unclear. While it is difficult to discern the original outline of Brookes's church, owing to later interventions by Arthur Blomfield, it bears key similarities to Ferrey's church at East Grafton [56], especially in the placement of its tower at the north-west corner. This may well be coincidental, but that Ferrey knew of the work taking place at Albury is possible given Pugin's involvement there.

Whatever the case might be, on 17 March 1842 work began on digging the foundations for Ferrey's new church at East Grafton [**54**]. The survival of architectural

54 St Nicholas, East Grafton, Wiltshire, engraved by Thomas Talbot Bury after one of Ferrey's drawings.

drawings, together with the diaries of both the incumbent and the builder, make this one of Ferrey's most thoroughly documented projects. Those diaries would, in time, acquire a further significance. The church Ferrey designed was by some margin his most accomplished in the Norman style to date [**55**]. It was to be constructed entirely of limestone and rubble, with a nave and aisles of five bays and an apsidal chancel. The narrow clerestory windows lend the exterior an oddly uncomfortable appearance, and yet they also confer a certain solidity and authenticity where another architect might have yielded to the temptation of a more flamboyant treatment. In arranging the west front [**56**], Ferrey looked to precedent from the Norman church at Castle Rising in Norfolk. The tower, which provided the most oblique allusion to the church at Thaon [52], is placed at the north-west corner, a position prefigured by the turret at Holy Trinity, East Hyde, and Brookes's tower at Albury. Ferrey's tower, with its prominent gargoyles and pyramid roof, lends the church an exotic aspect amidst the rural Wiltshire vernacular. It is undeniably incongruous.

The earliest drawings show a barrel vault spanning the entire length of the nave [**57**]. By that point in the nineteenth century few new churches had been given stone vaulting, Ferrey's was an ambitious scheme, intended to lend the church an unprecedented degree of stylistic legitimacy. At a meeting of the Oxford Society for Promoting the Study of Gothic Architecture (otherwise known as the Oxford Architectural Society) in June 1841 a paper written by Ferrey was read. The subject was 'The principles of the construction of a particular class of vaulted stone roofs, in which the outer roof and the inner roof or ceiling are united into a solid mass

OPPOSITE TOP
55 St Nicholas, East Grafton, from the north.

OPPOSITE BOTTOM
56 St Nicholas, East Grafton.

possessing great strength and exhibiting much scientific skill and ingenuity'.[24] Ferrey used as his case study the fourteenth-century St Catherine's Chapel in Abbotsbury. Drawing on several other examples as well, it was Ferrey's aim to demonstrate the strength of such a vault, which, 'though constructed of many pieces, would hold firmly together without cement'.[25]

One member of the society who was seemingly present at that meeting was Thomas Mozley, a Tractarian fellow of Oriel College in Oxford and the brother-in-law of John Henry Newman. Mozley, a keen amateur architect, was a friend of John Ward, who he later recalled as 'a great archæologist … [with] a fine collection of models'.[26] Ward had conducted several excavations on the site of a Roman villa in his parish. In July 1842 Mozley happened to be visiting a relative of one of his pupils in Great Bedwyn and decided to go and inspect the works at East Grafton. Two months earlier the foundation stone had been laid by the Marquess of Ailesbury, and work had continued apace. By the time Mozley visited, the aisles and chancel were mostly complete, the tower was under construction, and work was about to begin on the nave.

57 A detail from Talbot Bury's engraving showing East Grafton's interior as originally projected, with a barrel-vaulted nave.

The Ecclesiologist published a description of the new church in its first edition and made mention of Ferrey's intention to build a stone barrel vault. The Society's preference for a quadripartite vault was duly noted. Mozley, having read this description and seen the work in progress, quickly formed his own opinion that the proposed vault was not only aesthetically flawed but also liable to collapse. It is difficult to say how much of Mozley's account benefitted from hindsight: he recounted the whole affair at East Grafton some forty years later, in 1882, two years after Ferrey had died, but he was keen to portray himself as one who offered unheeded warnings. He had evidently done so in writing after his visit in July 1842, as Ward had written to invite him to inspect the works in the company of John Henry Parker, an archaeologist and architectural writer. Mozley's *Reminiscences* give the strong impression that it was Ward himself who particularly wanted the stone barrel vault. A date for the visit could not be set until the end of August, by which point 'the whole of the vaulting lay on the ground, beautifully shaped, ready to be put up'.[27] Any objections that Mozley and Parker might then have raised were very likely to be useless.

Ferrey and Ward had made applications for funding to the Incorporated Society for Church Building which were quickly approved, only for their surveyor to refuse to allow a stone vault to be built. Ferrey was undeterred, and wrote to Robert Willis concerning the security of the vault. Pevsner called Willis 'the greatest English architectural historian of the 19th century',[28] who alongside his architectural writing was one of the earliest professors of mechanical engineering at Cambridge. Willis wrote back to Ferrey confirming that his projected vault was indeed sound, and the ICBS quickly dispensed with the advice offered by their surveyor. We are told that

Mozley persisted in his objections, and Ward, probably exhausted by his repeated interventions, wrote to Ferrey to express what he had been told.

The crown of a barrel vault exerts a strong downward pressure which must be properly supported by the curved sections of the vault, the haunches, the natural tendency of which is to bulge outwards. The haunches must therefore either be supported by some external means, like buttresses, or loaded from behind with a sufficient quantity of material to counteract the outward pressure. It was Mozley's contention that the loading was insufficient. In October Ferrey referred Mozley to an Oriel contemporary, Robert Williams (son of one of his most important patrons), who in turn pointed to the example of the aforementioned chapel at Abbotsbury, with its barrel vault which 'had no abutment, only rising from a good thick wall, and no loading'.[29] That had, Mozley noted, 'stood all the storms of the Atlantic' in a solitary position on the Dorset coast.[30] However, Ferrey's projected vault at East Grafton had a much greater curvature.

58 The first page of the diary of John Lloyd, the builder.

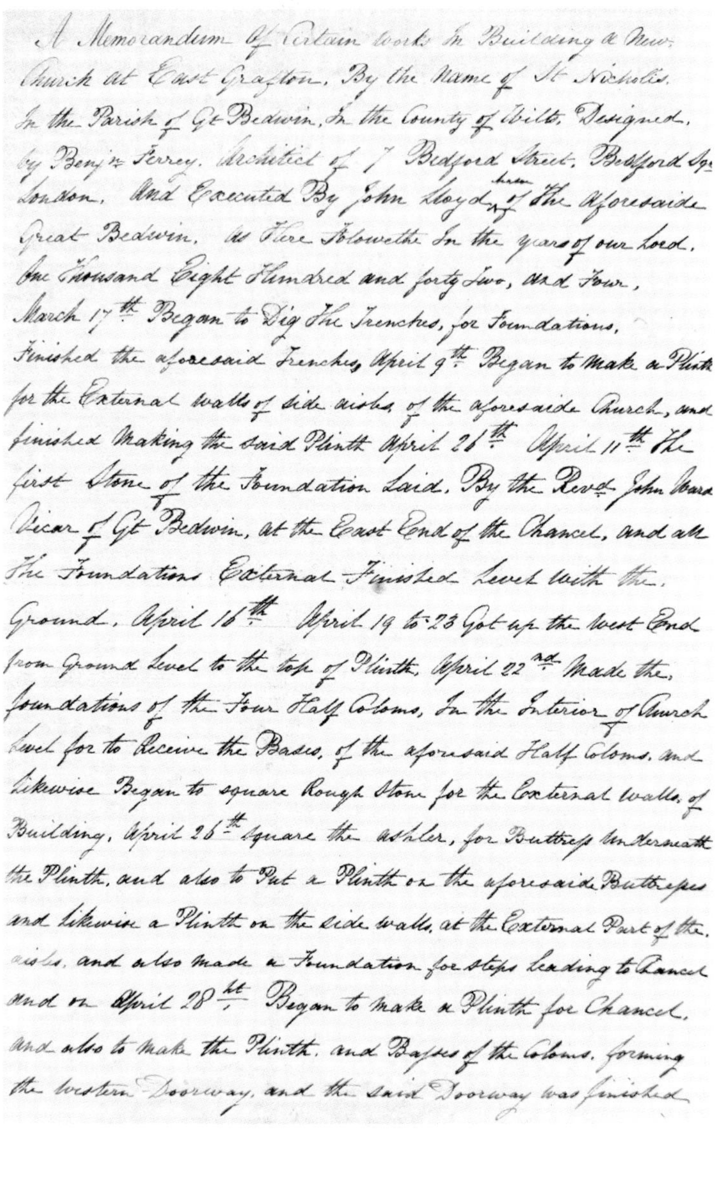
A Memorandum Of Certain works In Building a New Church at East Grafton, By the Name of St Nicholas. In the Parish of Gt Bedwin, In the County of Wilts. Designed, by Benjn Ferrey. Architect of 7 Bedford Street, Bedford Sqr London. And Executed By John Lloyd, Mason of The Aforesaide Great Bedwin. As Here Followethe In the years of our Lord, One Thousand Eight Hundred and forty two, and Four, March 17th Began to Dig The Trenches, for Foundations, Finished the aforesaid Trenches, April 9th Began to make a Plinth for the External walls of side aisles, of the aforesaide Church, and finished Making the said Plinth April 21st April 11th The first Stone of the Foundation Laid, By the Revd John Ward Vicar of Gt Bedwin, at the East End of the Chancel, and all The Foundations External Finished Level with the Ground, April 16th April 19 to 23 Got up the West End from Ground Level to the top of Plinth, April 22nd Made the foundations of the Four Half Coloms, In the Interior of Church Level for to Receive the Bases, of the aforesaid Half Coloms, and Likewise Began to square Rough Stone for the External walls, of Building, April 26th Square the ashler, for Buttress Underneath the Plinth, and also to Put a Plinth on the aforesaide Buttresses and likewise a Plinth on the side walls, at the External Part of the aisles, and also made a Foundation for steps leading to Chancel and on April 28th Began to make a Plinth for Chancel, and also to make the Plinth, and Bases of the Coloms, forming the western Doorway, and the said Doorway was finished

On his first visit to East Grafton in July, Mozley would have noticed buttresses which were about to be built, flying from the aisles up to the clerestory walls. These internal buttresses were intended to support the walls, about a yard thick, from which the vault would spring; it was a solution suggested by the church at Great Bedwyn, which 'at some remote period'[31] had similar internal buttresses fitted after its wooden roof had pushed the arcades of the nave outwards. For Ward they were the chief architectural excitement of his church there, and he was very keen to introduce similar buttresses to his new church at East Grafton.

Ferrey's builder at East Grafton was John Lloyd of Great Bedwyn. Lloyd's family had been practicing as stonemasons since 1790, and the family company still operates today. Lloyd and Ward, independently of each other, made diaries outlining the building work as it progressed. Ward's diary is concise and matter-of-fact: a list of dates is given with a few accompanying words recording relevant milestones. Lloyd's is written as a continuous narrative in a flowing hand which belies some of his more provincial grammar [**58**]. His entry for 8 November 1842 reads: 'began to prepare stone and vault the nave of church'.[32] Ward's diary records the rest of the progress that month. The chancel vaulting (which remains intact today) was brought to completion [**59**]; then 'the first bay of the nave vaulting being the easternmost' was finished on the 26th;[33] and work on the second bay commenced the next day.

Mozley, much troubled by the work at East Grafton, depicted the next episode with a somewhat overzealous sense of drama which one cannot help but take with a pinch of salt. He wrote:

> On one of the first days of December I saw a hearse pass my parsonage towards Salisbury. There were few people to die between me and Marlborough, and I had not heard of anyone likely to die. I immediately thought of East Grafton Church. As they would be sure to stop in the village, I sent my servant to make inquiries.[34]

Whether or not Mozley's mind immediately turned to East Grafton when he saw that hearse passing his parsonage, someone had indeed met their end there.

59 The chancel of St Nicholas, East Grafton – the first part of the church to be finished, and the only part to retain its original vaulting.

On 1 December 1842 Lloyd's men were busy preparing slates for the chancel roof when a party of visitors arrived at the church. At the head of the group was Earl Bruce [**60**], the son of the Marquess of Ailesbury, accompanied by the Rev. George Augustus Montgomery [**61**], James Galbraith (the clerk of works), Ferrey, Ward, and a few other individuals involved in the construction. George Montgomery, rector of Bishopstone in Wiltshire, was the illegitimate grandson of the 10th Earl of Pembroke. According to Mozley he was 'an amiable and excellent man, of great taste, and fond of church architecture'.[35] Mozley records that Sidney Herbert, younger son of the Earl of Pembroke, was also present, but this is not corroborated by any of the other contemporary accounts. It is worth noting that T. H. Wyatt and David Brandon were building their famous Italianate church in Wilton at the time, funded by none other than Sidney Herbert. It is not entirely dissimilar from East Grafton in its imported flamboyance and basic profile. The Herberts might therefore have taken a particular interest in East Grafton.

LEFT
60 Charles Brudenell-Bruce (1773–1856), 1st Marquess of Ailesbury, on whose land St Nicholas's was built.

RIGHT
61 The Rev. George Augustus Montgomery (1793–1842), a grandson of the 10th Earl of Pembroke.

It had been a wet November; rain had continued to pour until the morning of 1 December, but it had abated by the time the visitors arrived. Lord Bruce and the Rev. Montgomery appeared at about half-past one in the afternoon and were met by Ward and Ferrey. Ward went ahead with Montgomery, and Ferrey followed, accompanying Lord Bruce towards the church. For an account of what happened next, we must turn to Ward's report, given at the coroner's inquest on 2 December and published in a local paper not long afterwards:

> [We] walked straight through the nave of the church into the chancel, where conversation not more than a minute's duration passed generally between us. Mr. Montgomery and I then separated to the easternmost part of the chancel, noticed some rib mouldings which were lying on the floor. I then said to Mr. Montgomery, 'You can see the effect of these mouldings in the nave, where some of the ribs are already erected.' I advanced into the nave, followed by Mr. Montgomery, and, passing towards a spot where I intended to show Mr. Montgomery the rib in question, I heard over me a cracking of some wood-work, and immediately sprang into the south aisle, and heard the crash of the stone vaulting follow. On recovering myself from the alarm, I turned round and approached the spot where the stones lay, and heard that somebody was buried underneath. I saw the clerk of the works approach, and lift a stone from the head of the deceased. Lord Bruce immediately sent me for medical assistance. From the time that the deceased left Lord Bruce's carriage to the moment that the vault fell could not have been more than four or five minutes.[36]

Montgomery died instantaneously, at the age of forty-seven, having suffered a fracture to the back of his skull. Accounts vary as to precisely how he was struck. Mozley suggested that he had been hit by a stone that rebounded off a scaffold pole, but Ward's explanation seems the most reliable. Galbraith, the clerk of works, gave a rather more graphic account of the scene, reported in the *Salisbury and Wiltshire*

Herald on 2 December: 'I ran to him and took several stones from his body; a great deal of blood flowed from his mouth, his head was much injured, and his left thigh was broken; I assisted to carry him out of the church to a neighbouring house.'[37] That issue of the paper also featured an obituary for Montgomery:

> The loss of so good, so truly pious, so exemplary a man, even under the ordinary circumstances incidental to our common nature must have been deeply and severely felt by all around him; but there is something inscrutable to mortal comprehension in that awful – nay, appalling – dispensation of Providence, by which a life so thoroughly devoted to the service of God, and to the good of his fellow-creatures, was in an instant terminated, – even whilst he was engaged in the pious duty of inspecting the progress made in the erection of a new Church.[38]

It was a tragedy of some magnitude, not only regarding Montgomery's death but also Ferrey's reputation. By 3 December garbled reports of the incident had reached most local and national newspapers, giving the strong impression that the vault had been of unsound design. Ferrey found himself frantically writing to editors to set the record straight. One such letter of clarification appeared in the *London Evening Standard* on 7 December and is worth quoting in full:

> TO THE EDITOR OF THE STANDARD.
>
> 7, Bedford-street, Bedford-square.
>
> Sir, – I must beg the favour of your immediate insertion of this letter, to correct a most erroneous statement (copied from the Salisbury Herald), of a lamentable accident that took place at East Grafton Church (not Bishopstone Church), on Thursday last.
>
> It was a part of the unfinished compartment of the vaulting in the nave that fell, owing to the negligence of the mason in not wedging up the centering when ordered to do so. Had this duty been attended to, no calamity could have happened. The chancel of the church, which is of similar construction to the nave, has been finished for some weeks, and is perfectly sound. It was owing to no failure whatever in the principle of the vaulting, the walls, or any other part, or the want of strength in either, but entirely to the above cause, as the evidence produced at the inquest will abundantly prove. Deeply lamenting so sad an accident, I feel it my duty at once to contradict an account so incorrect as to the causes, and one calculated to do such unmerited injury to others.
>
> I am, Sir, your very obedient servant,
>
> BENJAMIN FERREY[39]

In writing these clarificatory letters Ferrey was setting out his defence – namely, that there was no fault in the design of his vault. Rather, according to Ferrey, the cause of Montgomery's death was the disobedience of his builder, Lloyd. The whole case had already been rehearsed by Lloyd, Galbraith, Ward, and Ferrey at a coroner's inquest, held the day after the accident. Ferrey's and Lloyd's testimonies are revealing.

The basic evaluation of the accident was that the vault collapsed because its wooden centering (the frame upon which it was constructed, and which temporarily held it in place) had been removed prematurely. The vault was incomplete, covering just one bay, and the rain had further weakened its structure. The question was whether Ferrey had ordered the removal of the centering or Lloyd had done so without his approval.

Ward, whose account was quoted above, took the side of his architect during the inquest. He produced a letter which was crucial to clearing Ferrey of the blame. It had been written on 28 November and read to Lloyd by Ward the next morning. In it, Ferrey wrote: 'on no account let Lloyd neglect instructions that I have given about the vaulting: he must build on the haunches, as I have directed; he does not see the importance of it, but I do.'[40] This was a difficult piece of evidence for Lloyd to be faced with, and he made no attempt to contradict or deny Ward's account in this respect. He admitted that he had not loaded the haunches as Ferrey had instructed, because 'the stones were so wet from the rain, that they would not lie one upon the other'. His defence was that Ferrey had given the instruction to lower the centering on 1 December, only to insist at one o'clock that it be re-engaged. Lord Bruce's arrival at half past one was, according to Lloyd, half an hour earlier than had been expected, so he was engaged in replacing the centering when the visitors arrived. He recalled: 'on his arrival I was in the act of going down the ladder from outside of the building to get planks, hurdles, and poles, when the greater portion of the vaulting fell in'.

Ferrey's account was clear in its accusations against Lloyd. He testified that after the chancel vault had been completed, with sufficient care paid to loading the haunches and keeping the stone dry, he was confident to proceed with constructing the nave vault. 'In a matter of such vital importance as this work', Ferrey said, 'I took special pains to give the most urgent orders to load the haunches.' Lloyd neglected to do this – so much so that the purpose of Ferrey's visit to East Grafton on 1 December was not just to greet Lord Bruce but to remonstrate with Lloyd in person and make him follow the instructions that had been communicated to him in writing. On arriving at the church Ferrey was irritated but unsurprised to find the haunches unloaded; he however noted that the vault seemed to stand well enough, and he ordered the centering to be lowered by two inches. Lloyd evidently obliged, but as another downpour of rain came on, Ferrey instructed that the centering be replaced into position. Ferrey's account of events diverges at this point from Lloyd's. He claimed that he had been forced to repeat his order fifteen minutes before the arrival of Lord Bruce, and he presumed that it had finally been followed. He went on to testify that he had gone out to greet the party of visitors, and they then

> went straight through the body of the building into the chancel, when some remarks expressive of approbation were made by his Lordship and the deceased upon the chancel vaulting, and they then turned round to look at the nave. At this juncture, I looked at the centering of the compartment, and exclaimed loudly to the clerk of the works, 'That centering is wedged up, is it not?' I had scarcely

> received his answer in the negative when I saw the arch open just above the haunches, exactly at the point where the loading would have resisted the strain, and I believe the first stone that came down fell upon the back of the deceased.

Ferrey then delivered the damning line: 'This catastrophe would have been averted had the centering been wedged up when I gave the order.' It was clear that the cause of the collapse had been the removal of the centering, and, added to that, the lack of any loading. Lloyd was surely at fault for the latter, given that he had been ordered to load the haunches in November, but Ferrey was aware of this when he ordered the removal of the centering. Had the haunches been loaded, it is likely that the collapse would never have happened. The jury returned a unanimous verdict of accidental death. Both Lloyd and Ferrey were cleared of directly causing Montgomery's death. This was probably the fairest conclusion. Lloyd had undeniably been negligent in not loading the haunches, and, seemingly, in not replacing the centering in time. Equally, Ferrey had ordered the centering to be removed in the first place, and had in Lloyd's estimation left it rather late, but crucially not too late, for it to be reengaged. To hold one man or the other entirely responsible would seem unfair.

Equally, there have been suggestions that had the vault been carried through to completion, it would still not have been structurally sound. The lack of any external buttressing points might confirm this suspicion. There were internal buttresses in the aisles, but Mozley suggested that they abutted the clerestory wall below the point at which they would have been most useful. However, even if this had been the case, the consequences were unlikely to have been fatal. A similar case, noted by Timothy Mowl, was at Roecliffe Church in East Yorkshire, where Richard Hey Sharp built a stone barrel vault the year after the collapse at East Grafton: there the roof had to be shored up by large external buttresses, but only after several years of standing without their support. The security, or lack thereof, of Ferrey's projected vault at East Grafton will probably never be fully established. The engineer William Froude remarked of it, 'if the masonry was good [it] would stand; not otherwise'.[41]

Unsurprisingly, Ferrey and Ward both wisely decided not to attempt to re-erect the stone vault. The whole episode had been a thoroughly unpleasant experience, and, as Mozley pointed out, Ward would never have been able to get his congregation to sit under a replica of the unfortunate vault. Ferrey therefore designed a timber roof [**62**], literally pasting the new design over the old in his drawings. Remarkably, despite the very public row between Ferrey and his builder, Lloyd was kept in post at East Grafton, and by April 1844 had carried the work through to completion [**63**]. The church was consecrated on 11 April 1844 by the Bishop of Salisbury, who at the same service dedicated the altar to the eternal memory of the Rev. George Montgomery.

Ferrey's church at East Grafton suffered as a result of the 'lamentable accident' at the end of 1842. The interior, satisfying as it is with its archaeologically correct decoration and good proportions, was alas robbed of a good deal of the intended grandeur by the replacement of its stone vault with a timber roof. That collapse overshadowed an otherwise admirable church building [56] and, it has been argued,

OPPOSITE
62 Ferrey's redesign for the interior of St Nicholas, East Grafton, with a timber roof rather than a stone vault.

63 The interior of St Nicholas, East Grafton, as built.

led to the stylistic collapse of the Romanesque Revival. Still, it did little to harm Ferrey's professional reputation in the long run. His practice continued steadily to grow, and he even received a commission to build a near replica of East Grafton at Sandymount in Dublin just as work was finishing in 1844. His patron there was none other than Sidney Herbert, the uncle of the unfortunate George Montgomery. If this was not a symbol of absolution from blame, it is difficult to imagine what might be.

In an ironic postlude to the episode at East Grafton, Montgomery was buried in his parish church at Bishopstone under an extremely elaborate Gothic monument; its architect: Pugin.

St James the Great, Morpeth, Northumberland

As work was progressing at East Grafton, Ferrey received another commission for a Romanesque church, this time for Morpeth [**64**]. Whereas his other churches in

64 St James the Great, Morpeth, Northumberland (1844–46).

the style had been for villages, this one was to serve a large town. As Morpeth had grown and covered a larger geographical range, it became clear that the medieval parish church, situated on the other side of a river from what had become the main town, was too far for many congregants to travel, not least during inclement Northumbrian winters. As was so often the case, it took the initiative of a new and energetic incumbent to remedy this longstanding problem. Francis Grey was the incumbent in question. Grey was a younger son of the Prime Minister, the 2nd Earl Grey, and an early follower of the Oxford Movement, albeit in a fairly cautious way. At his institution as rector of Morpeth in 1842, the Bishop of Durham reputedly offered him two pieces of advice: always wear worsted stockings, and never keep a cow!

Grey's ministry in the parish stretched beyond what the Bishop evidently expected. Not only did Grey want a new church for Morpeth, but he had a clear vision of how it should look. He had encountered the twelfth-century cathedral at Monreale during his honeymoon in 1840 and decided that he would like a similar church for his new parish. Ferrey would use this source of inspiration only very loosely, but the interior with its lofty proportions and shallow apse possesses a vaguely Sicilian appearance.

The justification for Ferrey's use of the Romanesque however went beyond any relationship with Monreale to something altogether more substantial. In Morpeth he was finally building a Norman church where it seemed to belong. Whereas his experimentations to date had seemed somewhat incongruous in their respective settings, St James's is a church that sits comfortably and eloquently within its landscape. The site was given by the Earl of Carlisle, Grey's father-in-law, along with £400 (roughly £70,000 today), and after a series of similar benefactions building work on the church was able to commence at the beginning of 1844. In its scale it is Ferrey's most ambitious church, with seating for over one thousand congregants. St Stephen, Rochester Row, is the only other church by Ferrey that approaches St James's in size. The Norman style suited this monumental approach to church-building well. Ferrey could finally explore the true character of the style as expressed in mass and proportion rather than merely recalling it through decoration. It is thoroughly convincing.

The church sits comfortably at the east end of its site, set some distance back from the main road that runs past the western boundary of the churchyard. The approach from this direction is dramatic. An avenue of trees leads from a later stone wall on the street front[42] towards the west end of the church, which is striking in its solidity and vertical pull. Its three stages are satisfyingly arranged in a one-two-three scheme, with the door below two large round-headed lancets, and three smaller ones above set into interlaced arcading. The heavy buttresses that frame the west front give a functional solidity not previously seen in Ferrey's work. The structural strength of the building is again expressed in the façades of the transepts, where a central buttress forms the focal point of the composition. Those buttresses are chamfered, with slender round pilasters at the corners that rise to full height, emphasising both verticality and strength. That sense of 'functional solidity' may be what makes this one of the most pleasing Romanesque Revival churches: it is not merely an essay in archaeological decoration but a substantial building with a strong sense of form and construction.

This focus on structural integrity may not be surprising, given what had happened at East Grafton hardly a year earlier. St James's power is attenuated only by its lack of a stone vault. Ferrey can hardly be blamed for exercising caution at Morpeth, not least since the nave was a great deal wider than at East Grafton. Still, one cannot help but imagine what might have been had he not proceeded nervously. The angularity of the timber roof is the main weakness of the interior [**65**, **66**] – it is at odds with the elegant roundness of the nave arcades and the vast crossing-tower arches. Morpeth is a church that cries out for a barrel vault to tie its interior together, much more so than East Grafton.

65 One of Ferrey's perspective views for St James's showing the church before happy introductions like the rood screen and the apse's Clayton & Bell murals.

66 St James the Great, Morpeth – an interior that longs for a stone vault.

Still, in sheer scale Morpeth's interior is extremely striking. Its apsidal chancel, paved by a sea of Minton tiles, is especially satisfying [**67**]. Here interlaced arches appear once more, wrapping themselves round the east wall and emerging cleverly into stone screens that separate the chancel from a side chapel and the vestry. Above a plain wall (much beautified with later frescoes by Clayton & Bell) a tier of round-headed windows admit light – an arrangement that would have

67 The tall apsidal chancel of St James the Great, Morpeth, with a Minton tile pavement and frescoes by Clayton & Bell.

been instantly recognisable to Grey's parishioners as having been borrowed from Durham Cathedral's chapter house. The view from the nave towards the chancel is punctuated by a tall crossing tower. A bell chamber had been projected for it, but a lack of funds demanded that it be left open to its full height. This was a happy curtailment: the open tower affords an augmented sense of scale to the interior, and, more importantly, a valuable source of light. Outside, it rises nobly over the church.

St James the Great, Morpeth, was finally consecrated in October 1846 after almost three years of work. Ferrey's ambition had paid off. He had shown himself to be one of the most able practitioners of the Norman style in that time. It is striking, for example, to compare the quality of St James's with Pugin's similarly formed Romanesque church at Gorey. Timothy Mowl's assessment of Ferrey's work at Morpeth sums up its success: 'it not only looks convincingly of its region, Northumberland, but also convincingly Norman. … [Ferrey's] response to the essential weight of Norman design is very rare at this period and in itself marks [him] as a foremost practitioner of the revived style.'[43]

A Romanesque Postscript

Ferrey's other Romanesque churches are few and far between. Having mastered the style, he soon abandoned it at the end of the 1840s as fashions in church-building continued apace and the style began to diminish in popularity. The commission for his last two Romanesque churches came just a year after he had been engaged at Morpeth in 1845. The best of the two, Christ Church, Melplash, would develop the form of Romanesque church to which he had arrived in Morpeth – here rephrased for the context of a small Dorset village.

Ferrey would build another Romanesque church during this period, St John the Evangelist at Hale in Surrey, in 1844 [**68**]. This is a curious composition. The nave recalls East Grafton rather strongly, with its small round-headed clerestory windows and equally small windows in the aisles. There is no apse, just a small, flat east end with three more round-headed windows below a circular window which lights the chancel nicely. The rather clumsy transept was a later addition and interferes with the main curiosity of the church, its slender round tower, capped with a tall conical roof. This tower is an allusion to the 12th-century round towers found in Ireland and forms a rather unusual addition to the Surrey countryside. It might be appreciated better without the transept, but at present seems rather uncomfortably hemmed in; it has no space to breathe or reveal itself naturally from the east.

68 An early watercolour of St John the Evangelist, Hale, Surrey, 1844, showing the church before later additions.

Christ Church, Melplash, in Dorset, presents a much less frivolous effort, although its interior today is difficult to analyse since its nave was turned over to use as a badminton court in the 1970s [**69**]. Parishioners now meet in the north transept, the chancel having been refashioned into a baptistery. The effect is bemusing, and, needless to say, injurious to the interior – still, this creative response to dwindling numbers may well have saved the building from a worse fate.

The silhouette of the church from the road is striking [**70**]. Unlike Ferrey's other Romanesque churches, the main road passes its east end and the apse is the first thing that a passerby notices, its elegant roundness contrasting wonderfully with the solidity of the crossing tower which rises above it. As at Morpeth [64], the Romanesque that Ferrey employs here is solid and serious. A raw strength and purity of line are expressed, albeit on a more modest scale. That is indeed one of the most pleasing aspects of the church at Melplash: Ferrey has successfully translated the success he had building a large town church in Northumbria to a village church in Dorset. Here we find the proof that Ferrey had mastered a convincing and practical Romanesque style.

That is, however, where Ferrey's Romanesque churches end – at the point when he had seemingly perfected the style that he had spent the best part of a decade studying. The reality is that by the middle of the 1840s the Romanesque was already becoming unfashionable. What is more, the collapse of the roof at East Grafton had

BELOW
69 Christ Church, Melplash, Dorset (1845–46), its nave now a badminton court.

BELOW RIGHT
70 Christ Church, Melplash, seen from the road.

played some part in this decline. The incident there had attracted the attention not only of connoisseurs and pedants but of the national press and ordinary people. The Romanesque had become inseparably linked with structural uncertainty. Had the vault at East Grafton not collapsed, would the Romanesque Revival have gone from strength to strength? It is difficult to say with certainty. It is however easy to say that Ferrey would have thrown a stone vault over St James the Great in Morpeth and thus created an interior of considerable beauty. What effect might that have had on his career?

Ferrey would only return to the Romanesque a handful of times later in his career, almost always when restoring Norman churches. In Oxfordshire there was the satisfying restoration of a Norman apse at Swyncombe in Oxfordshire in 1850, and he would rather convincingly rebuild the tower at nearby Kirtlington in 1853 [**71**]. Ferrey's restoration of Romsey Abbey in 1855 provides an ironic footnote: there he constructed a barrel vault over the nave – not in stone but in timber.

71 Ferrey's Romanesque tower of St Mary the Virgin, Kirtlington, Oxfordshire, put up in 1853.

72 St Swithun, Wickham, Berkshire (1845–49), from the west. Next to the large north aisle is the Saxon tower, with a Romanesque upper stage by Ferrey.

The Middle-Pointed and Beyond

St Swithun, Wickham, Berkshire

Ferrey's church at Wickham might reasonably claim to be one of his most unusual [**72**]. The commission to rebuild the parish church there came in 1845, in the same month as the commission to build a new church at Melplash. His patron at Wickham was the Rev. William Nicholson, who seven years later would engage Thomas Talbot Bury, a former classmate of Ferrey's from Pugin's drawing school, to rebuild the neighbouring church of St Gregory at Welford. The rich interior of that church owes some debt of inspiration to Ferrey's at Wickham. It is an interesting coincidence that Ferrey had sketched the original church at Welford in 1842 [**73**].

It is curious that Ferrey, at the height of his powers as a practitioner of the Romanesque, should choose to build in an unapologetically Decorated style at

73 Ferrey's sketch of St Gregory, Welford, Berkshire, 1842.

Wickham, not least since the Anglo-Saxon tower might have naturally suggested another treatment. Ferrey reworked this tower, adding a new upper stage with some inoffensive Norman bell openings. He also revelled in the antiquarian aspect of work on the tower, noting Roman stonework which had been incorporated into the Saxon work and discovering soot marks inside which he took to indicate a former secondary function as a warning beacon.

At Wickham Ferrey had to deal with an unconventional floorplan: the north aisle dominates the exterior when the church is approached from the road at the west. It is extremely tall, gabled, and tacked boldly onto the tower, extending almost to its western extremity, quite in contrast to the modest lean-to south aisle which with the nave hides modestly behind the tower. The interior is indeed 'very sumptuous', as Pevsner found it [**74**].[44] Ferrey decorated the church with discernible enthusiasm. The capitals are composed of a wonderful variety of naturalistic foliage inspired by the leaves of Southwell Minster's chapter house [**75**]. At its west end, abutting the tower, a Saxon archway was blocked up and replaced with a small doorway set into a complete riot of blind curvilinear tracery, rich in the extreme. Only briefly does Ferrey's Gothic richness verge on clumsiness, as it does in the font. Like Pugin he had toured East Anglia in the 1840s, so it is unsurprising that he introduced an angel roof to the nave, a treatment he carried through to the north aisle.

74 The interior of St Swithun, Wickham, looking west.

However, angels no longer support the aisle's timber roof [**76**]. The church was complete in 1849, and within thirteen years its incumbent, William Nicholson, evidently felt moved to make alterations. On a visit to the 1862 Paris Exhibition he found three large papier maché elephants, dressed in tasselled blankets and headdresses. The effect these elephants had upon him was so great that he ordered another five to be made, and replaced Ferrey's East Anglian angels with these incongruous Indian elephants. The effect is

ABOVE
75 Naturalistic carved capitals at St Swithun, Wickham.

ABOVE RIGHT
76 The north aisle of St Swithun, Wickham, with papier maché elephants in place of angels.

outrageous in the most glorious of ways. Ferrey's reaction to this most peculiar of interventions is not, alas, recorded.

St Peter, West Lydford, Somerset

By 1846 Ferrey had developed a flourishing church building practice – he was at that point one of the most prolific ecclesiastical architects of the day. So prolific was he that when news broke of his appointment to rebuild the parish church of West Lydford, an acerbic note appeared in *The Ecclesiologist*:

> A small Perpendicular church has lately been taken down, and built again upon the old foundations and after the original design. Such a plan, if not ingenious, is at least safe. The architect employed was Mr Ferrey. How many cathedrals, churches, chapels, we wonder, would satiate a first-rate London architect? Or is his willingness to undertake jobs absolutely illimitable? There is need here of reform.[45]

Ferrey was quick to remonstrate with the Ecclesiologists over this attack. In the next issue of *The Ecclesiologist* there appeared a rather reluctant clarification: 'With respect to the connexion of a remark on the overwork of modern architects with Mr Ferrey's name, we can only say that our observation was meant to apply generally … the amount of church-work undertaken by an individual, must be left to his own conscience.'[46]

It was an accusation that would haunt Ferrey's reputation up to the present day. His prolificacy has all too often been equated to mediocrity. In the case of some of the later churches it is difficult for even the most sympathetic biographer to exonerate Ferrey from the charge levelled by the anonymous Ecclesiologist: his willingness to accept work, especially on low budgets, did result in an uninspiring church here and there, and there was also undoubtedly an amount of delegation to less talented pupils during the final few decades of his practice.

West Lydford however presents no such problem. The Rev. William Hungerford Colston, the rector, had been appointed to the living by its patron, his brother, Edward Francis Colston. It was at the joint expense of these two men that Ferrey rebuilt the parish church in 1846. The old church had been 'in a state of partial decay',[47] and was soon demolished to make way for its replacement. Ferrey retained the fifteenth-century tower, but encased it and carried it up higher. In designing the nave and chancel, he referred to the original church and built in a rich Perpendicular style; crucially, as Ferrey was keen to remind *The Ecclesiologist*, his work was not a mere copy of the church that he demolished. The result is pleasing, not least as an archaeologically correct essay in the Somerset Perpendicular, a style with which Ferrey had become well acquainted during his time as Diocesan Architect for Bath and Wells. In designing this straightforward village church Ferrey endowed its exterior with sustained touches of visual interest [**77**]. The nave and chancel are treated with careful delineation. The embattled nave gives way to a lower chancel

77 St Peter, West Lydford, by the River Brue in Somerset, 1846.

featuring a particularly elegant parapet pierced by quatrefoils within lozenges; for this motif Ferrey looked to the work of fifteenth-century masons in North Somerset churches like Brent Knoll and Wrington.

St Peter's at West Lydford must be one of the most picturesque of Ferrey's churches, reclining in a verdant churchyard on the bank of the River Brue. In no small part thanks to this setting, and in its unpretentious correctness, West Lydford is one of Ferrey's most pleasing smaller rebuilds. It was received with great enthusiasm when it was consecrated in August 1846, especially by its parishioners, who erected a triumphal arch of laurel and flowers over the approach to the church.

Twenty years later, another church by Ferrey was consecrated within a stone's throw of St Peter's: the church of the Blessed Virgin Mary in East Lydford (now deconsecrated) [**78**]. Intriguingly, Ferrey referred back to his sketchbooks when designing this church. Its curious octagonal tower is a clear nod to the medieval church at Welford which he had sketched in 1842 [73].

78 The former church of the Blessed Virgin Mary, East Lydford, Somerset (1864–66).

St Stephen, Rochester Row, London

79 The Devil's Acre in Westminster, awash, according to Charles Dickens, with 'the blackest tide of moral turpitude'. Gustave Doré recorded it in 1872.

The Devil's Acre, as it came to be known, was London's worst slum – indeed, it was the first place ever have that term applied to it [**79**]. The Acre comprised about six streets immediately to the west of Westminster Abbey and the Houses of Parliament. Despite its proximity to the heart of the British state, it remained 'the most deplorable manifestation of human wretchedness and depravity', where poverty, overcrowding, and crime existed on an unparalleled scale – a condition that had persisted for almost a century. By the 1840s disease had been added to the area's catalogue of miseries: the 'ever-present hazards of typhus, smallpox and other contagious diseases' were decimating huge swathes of its population each year.

In 1845 Parliament passed the Westminster Improvement Act, resulting in the construction of Victoria Street, which cut directly through the worst slums of Westminster and displaced some five thousand of the Devil's Acre's residents. The area, already grossly overcrowded, now became unsustainably so. By 1855 one six-room terrace house reportedly housed seventy-two people. Dickens wrote:

> The district, which is small in area, is one of the most populous in London, almost every house being crowded with numerous families and multitudes of lodgers. There are other parts of the town as filthy, dingy, and forbidding in appearance as this, but these are generally the haunts more of poverty than crime. But there are none in which guilt of all kinds and degrees converges in such volume as on this, the moral plague-spot, not only of the metropolis, but also of the kingdom. And yet from almost every point of it you can observe the towers of the Abbey peering down upon you, as if they were curious to observe that to which they seem to be indifferent.[48]

It was here that one of Dickens's correspondents would fund the construction of a new church, and in so doing would transform the face of the area more completely than anyone before or since. Angela, later Baroness, Burdett-Coutts (1814–1906) [**80**] was the daughter of Sir Francis Burdett and Sophia Coutts, the daughter of the banker Thomas Coutts. From her father Angela inherited a strong humanitarian instinct; from her mother, the largest fortune in England. It was to prove a powerful combination.

80 Angela Burdett-Coutts, later 1st Baroness Burdett-Coutts, *c.* 1840.

Angela's father, Sir Francis Burdett, 5th Baronet (1770–1844), was a radical parliamentarian. After Oxford he entered the Commons and soon established himself as a champion of popular liberties, denouncing the suspension of *habeas corpus* for radical campaigners, and the corruption of borough politics. His outspoken sympathy for the victims of Peterloo and his repeated calls for parliamentary reform earned him both wide popularity in the country and deep hostility from the establishment. Burdett was imprisoned several times for his outspokenness – once in the Tower of London – and became a symbol of resistance to arbitrary authority. The radical philanthropy of Angela Burdett-Coutts owed much to the character of her father. Upon his death in 1844 she sought an appropriate means of memorialising him.

In the autumn of 1846 Charles Blomfield, Bishop of London [**81**], wrote to Ferrey on behalf of Burdett-Coutts, asking whether he might submit plans for a new church in the diocese. Ferrey replied favourably and set to work. He had already collaborated with the Bishop through the Metropolis Churches Fund, which Blomfield had established a decade earlier with the aim of building two hundred new churches in London. Blomfield would found the Church Building Society in 1854, a body that became an invaluable source of funding for many of Ferrey's later commissions. Blomfield's role in shaping the architectural landscape of his diocese, and indeed of the nation, cannot be underestimated.

81 The Rt Rev. Charles Blomfield (1786–1857), Bishop of London.

Burdett-Coutts's plans for endowing a new church had evidently been under consideration for some time when Blomfield wrote to Ferrey. The earliest surviving letter on the subject, dated 12 January 1846, records Blomfield's satisfaction that 'I have found a site in a poor and populous part of Westminster where a Church would be of great benefit … near the Tothill Fields Prison.'[49] Blomfield went on to estimate that a church, with a tower and spire 'which I think desirable', would cost just over £6,000 (about £980,000 today).[50] Eight months later, having set Ferrey to work on the plans, Blomfield informed Burdett-Coutts that the architect was ready to present his proposals, though

82 Ferrey's sketch of Pugin's house, The Grange, next to the church at Ramsgate in Kent.

they were rather more expensive than had been anticipated. Still, he hastened to reassure her that Ferrey could 'reduce the cost by making the building somewhat less ornamental'.[51] Blomfield need not have worried – Angela Burdett-Coutts, the wealthiest woman in England, had in fact set aside £30,000 (almost £5 million today) for the purpose.

Ferrey first presented his plans to Burdett-Coutts in November 1846 at Ramsgate, where she was then staying. It was an interesting and timely visit, since his estranged friend Pugin had just completed The Grange, the imposing house in which he would die in 1852. On a later visit to Ramsgate Ferrey sketched Pugin's house from beyond its garden wall – a poignant little drawing [**82**]. The two childhood friends must have been within yards of each other, separated only by an impenetrable wall over which Ferrey peered, still full of admiration for his old companion's work. One might easily read this as a metaphor for the relationship between the two architects.

Whatever Ferrey's reaction to The Grange might have been in November 1846, his visit to Ramsgate was largely fruitful. Burdett-Coutts reported to Bishop Blomfield that she approved of the plans for the new church in Rochester Row, though she found them 'not quite so handsome in architectural ornament' as she had hoped.[52] New plans were therefore drawn up and presented, this time showing none of the restraint previously exercised.

Around the same time, Ferrey was also working on a new church at Penn Street in Buckinghamshire [**83**]. His patron there was the 1st Earl Howe, a Tory opponent of the Reform Act and a stalwart of the Royal Household, who commissioned Ferrey to build a school and a rectory as well as a church.[53] Howe was related by marriage to Ferrey's patron at East Grafton, Lord Bruce. By now Ferrey had amassed a large network of wealthy patrons, many connected by familial and political links, who were increasingly affording him the opportunity to build in style. Holy Trinity, Penn Street, was one such opportunity, and it must rank among the most striking of his churches. It has variously been described as 'chaste' and' 'simple',[54] curious terms to assign to a building of such dramatic power. Pevsner's assessment, 'very competent and dignified',[55] is more apposite. In reality it is at heart a simple church, a straightforward cruciform affair, its ornamentation largely executed in a restrained Decorated idiom. The chief point of architectural interest is

83 Holy Trinity, Penn Street, Buckinghamshire.

the handsome octagonal crossing tower, out of which issues a beautifully proportioned shingled spire. In 1848 Ferrey had been studying the fourteenth-century church at Shottesbrooke [**84**], for a commission to replicate the whole building at Kingswood (as we shall see). This model, with its elegant spire rising over a crossing tower, also inspired Penn Street's arrangement. The octagonal tower with a spire on top had been prefigured by Ferrey's church at Baughurst in Hampshire, built in 1845, where the tower stands detached at the south-west corner. Instead of a richness of decoration, Penn Street relies entirely on a sense of scale and proportion to achieve its effect, an effect greatly enhanced by its picturesque setting in the glade of a pine forest. This was a site supposedly pointed out by the Queen Dowager Adelaide while she rested under a tree on Lord Howe's estate.

84 St John the Baptist, Shottesbrooke, Berkshire, the medieval inspiration for several of Ferrey's churches, including those at Penn Street [83] and Kingswood.

The Queen Dowager had, through Howe, endowed several churches, and Howe himself had been an energetic patron of church building and restoration in several counties. The Queen Dowager – who would die seven months after Penn Street was consecrated – presented the stained glass for the east window there, a rather lifeless Resurrection by Thomas Willement. It was during one of her visits to the site in 1847 that she requested from Ferrey drawings of the proposed new church about which she had heard so much: St Stephen, Rochester Row [**85**]. Ferrey wrote to Angela Burdett-Coutts with tangible excitement:

> I attended the Queen Dowager yesterday in her inspection of the Church which I am building for Lord Howe at Penn St, and during Her Majesty's stay she alluded to your Church with great pleasure and expressed a desire to see the Drawings. I have therefore taken the liberty of sending the plans to Her Majesty at Bushy House, and they will be returned before Wednesday next. I felt that I should not be doing wrong in these steps.[56]

In May 1849 Holy Trinity at Penn was consecrated, and work at Rochester Row continued apace. Two years earlier, on 20 July 1847, the foundation stone had been laid in grand style. Special platforms were erected on the site for spectators, and a long procession with no fewer than four bishops entered the enclosure at two o'clock. The foundation stone, suspended from a truck on an elevated tramway,

85 Ferrey's proposal for St Stephen, Rochester Row, in London, published with an account of the laying of its foundation stone in 1847.

was lifted into place at the base of the tower and 'slightly struck thrice' by Angela Burdett-Coutts using a silver trowel.[57] Children from the local Green Coat, Grey Coat, and Blue Coat schools all sung a hymn, the Bishop preached and pronounced a blessing, and the congregation burst into 'God Save the Queen', giving three cheers as the procession retired from the site. Blomfield had announced in his sermon the hope that Ferrey's church would be 'one of those bright examples which would redound to the strength of the Church and the ultimate security of the country'.[58] It was a high ambition. The model for building a new parish church was well rehearsed. The Victorian preoccupation with social improvement necessitated the construction not only of a concomitant parsonage but of a church school as well. Ferrey had built along these lines several times before, and the school at Rochester Row was the first element of the project to be completed. By the middle of 1848 these ancillary buildings were almost ready to be occupied.

The letters that followed were jovial and familiar. Ferrey wrote regularly to Angela Burdett-Coutts, and it was clear that they had formed a friendly relationship. In July 1848 he wrote to his patroness to thank her for opera tickets; these were for a performance of Meyerbeer's *Les Huguenots* at Covent Garden at which the Queen was present, a performance which demanded the construction of a royal box for the first time in living memory. One might deduce Ferrey's churchmanship from the choice of opera, as well as that of Burdett-Coutts, and indeed the Queen. *Les Huguenots*, with its overture based on Martin Luther's *Ein Feste Burg*, was a shameless example of Low Church political marketing, and its message was not lost on Ferrey. Not only was he himself a fine musician and tenor, but his descent from persecuted Huguenots served to reinforce his own Protestantism.

In 1848 most of the structural work at Rochester Row was underway, and by December of that year the rough structure was almost complete. Ferrey had already been able to turn his mind to the smaller details of internal decoration, and the letters in the summer of 1848 are full of references to altar linens, carpets, and designs for furniture. Burdett-Coutts had been paying Ferrey and his builder, Mr Rigby, in regular instalments of about £300 (about £42,000 today) and £3,000 (about £420,000) respectively. Ferrey was able to report in September that 'the works are proceeding very rapidly and well, and I think there will only be one further instalment at all likely to be required about Christmas'.[59]

By the end of 1848 Ferrey had turned his mind to a ventilation system for the church. As well as being a place of worship, St Stephen's was seen as an instrument of social improvement, and a key part of that was a concern for the health and wellbeing of its impoverished parishioners. The Great Stink of 1858 was yet to come, but the Victorian preoccupation with 'bad air' had created a market for ventilating 'good air'. Being able to heat and cool a large building was also very appealing. Ferrey corresponded with John Sylvester, son of the chemist Charles Sylvester who had invented a system of warming and ventilating buildings. The younger Sylvester inherited his father's company and hoped to install one of his ventilation systems in both the church and the school at Rochester Row. Meanwhile, Angela Burdett-Coutts, from whom the concern for air quality stemmed, had engaged the leading chemist William Brande to inspect the site with Ferrey and make practical suggestions to him. By the summer of 1849 these consultations had evidently concluded, and Sylvester was invited to build two ventilation systems, one for the church and another for the school. The introduction of this system, with flues for both hot and cold air, was remarkably innovative for a church of its date.

After facing some obstacles in finding a location for the ventilation shafts for the school, attention once more turned to the execution of furnishings and decorations. Ferrey had successfully convinced Burdett-Coutts to allow a 'polygonal shaped' chancel roof as opposed to one of a 'far [less] correct waggon headed' shape.[60] Ferrey, well acquainted with many historic star-painted ceilings, had suggested that the chancel ceiling might be coloured a rich blue with gold stars painted on it (a few years later he would copy Giotto's starry ceiling of the Scrovegni Chapel in his sketchbook). Burdett-Coutts had in turn requested that the wooden bosses in the chancel be picked out in gold. Meanwhile, work on the chancel stalls progressed well, along with the seats for the church, so that by the beginning of 1850 all the necessary woodwork sat happily complete in Rigby's workshop.

Alas, things would soon begin to unravel. On 17 March Ferrey found himself writing to Burdett-Coutts to inform her that Rigby's premises had caught fire and burnt down the night before; all the woodwork for St Stephen's had been destroyed. Still, Ferrey was surprisingly undisturbed by the incident: 'there will be no difficulty', he wrote, 'in replacing the work which is required for the Church by the middle of June … we … need not apprehend any delay in the consecration of the Church.'[61]

Indeed, by the beginning of May Ferrey seems to have once more been contentedly dealing with the finishing touches for the church, concerning himself with details of inscriptions. It even appears that his wife, Ann, had been making drawings of heraldry for the carpets. However, as the day appointed for the church's consecration fast approached, this sense of blissful readiness was shattered by the arrival of an irate letter from Burdett-Coutts. The letter is no longer extant, but judging from Ferrey's reply it is evident that she had inspected the building at some point around 10 May and was deeply unsatisfied by what she saw. Ferrey had recently requested, on behalf of his builders, some unexpected extra payments which Burdett-Coutts had gladly made, but upon visiting and seeing the unfinished state of the church she had found herself suspicious of both architect and builders. Ferrey, quite rightly, was quick to defend himself and to assure her that the church was much nearer to completion than it might have appeared: 'I can assure you that I do not neglect the due over looking of the works at St Stephen's. I can quite understand that it appears to you as though the work went on slowly; and certainly the character of the work is of a kind which does not make a conspicuous appearance but I do not think the work could possibly go on faster.'[62]

As for the unfinished state of the decoration of the chancel roof, Ferrey explained that the successive layers of coloured paint required time to dry – it should, he thought, be ready by the end of the week. Equally, the woodwork had to wait to be installed until the glass (which was outside Ferrey's purview) had been put in the windows. For delays on carving and fixing the crocketed finials of the tower, Ferrey wrote that he had 'never hesitated to blame Messrs Rigby'[63] for the delays that had occurred in that respect. Still, he did not doubt that they would be finished in good time for the consecration.

Nevertheless, Ferrey was evidently shaken by Burdett-Coutts's sudden change of tone. Ferrey, who had recently became a father, hastily made plans to move his young family from Henley to London so that he might 'be <u>daily</u> at the church'[64] and was quick to communicate this development to his patroness, hoping to restore some of her confidence in him. Nevertheless, the succeeding letters from Ferrey to Burdett-Coutts continue in a penitent and occasionally panicked tone, quite in contrast to the relaxed friendliness of earlier correspondence.

As the date set for the consecration – 24 June 1850 – drew nearer, Ferrey's letters became more and more frantic. He soon found himself writing once again to 'express [his] penitence'[65] for an oversight which resulted in the replacement chancel stalls being made to an old specification which Burdett-Coutts had previously rejected. On 6 June Ferrey was desperately trying to find a new artist to execute the decalogue boards, having realised that the woman he had initially engaged, 'though very willing', was unlikely to finish them in time for the 24th.[66] One gets the strong impression that Ferrey might have underestimated both his workmen and his patroness. Working for Angela Burdett-Coutts was unlike anything

Ferrey had experienced before. He was much more accustomed to dealing with rural clergymen, and while it is true that he had often worked for much grander aristocratic patrons, none was quite so strong-willed or indeed wealthy as his patroness here. The stakes were much higher than they had ever been for Ferrey. He was not only designing one of his largest and most ambitious churches to date, but also the centrepiece of a grand programme of social reform. As such, attention from the press and public, even before the buildings had begun to rise, had been intense.

86 St Stephen, Rochester Row, 1846–50, from the north-east.

The Ecclesiologist eagerly awaited progress on the church, noting in 1849 that its completion would 'mark an epoch' in London church building.[67] Much interest had also been garnered by the appearance of one of Ferrey's watercolours of St Stephen's in the Architectural Room of the Royal Academy exhibition. This scrutiny finally reached a climax on 24 June 1850, the day appointed for the consecration of St Stephen's. Within the district many shops closed for the day and residents decorated their houses with flags and foliage. There were over fifteen hundred people inside the church, among whom were the great and the good of the clergy and aristocracy; several relations of Ferrey's old patrons, like the Greys and Carlisles, looked on keenly. At eleven o'clock the Bishop of London, Blomfield, who had of course helped instigate the project, entered the church in procession. When he reached the east end of the church Burdett-Coutts presented him with the deeds of conveyance, and the ceremonial proceeded 'in a very impressive manner',[68] with music provided by the combined choirs of the Chapel Royal, Westminster Abbey and the Temple Church. A grand lunch followed in the school rooms for selected guests, while the workmen and poor inhabitants of the parish enjoyed their own lunch in a marquee outside the church. Ferrey addressed this meeting with some sense of relief and proposed a toast to the health of Angela Burdett-Coutts. The building had, after all, been completed on time.

What Ferrey had erected was an ambitious attempt at a large Middle-Pointed city church in Bargate rag and Northumberland sandstone. The exterior, weighty and brooding, is dominated by the tower that stands away from the main axis of the church [**86**]. It adjoins the north-east wall of the nave, above which it rises confidently, culminating in a spire confected from medieval sources including Lichfield Cathedral. In placing the tower where he did, Ferrey formed a pleasing visual link between the church and the street, much enlivening the architectural rhythm of the exterior.

The nave is tall, with small clerestory windows, and aisles abutting it. On the north side is a handsome stone porch, with verses recording St Stephen's martyrdom from the seventh chapter of the Book of Acts carved in its interior cornice. The chancel, a good degree lower than the nave, is noticeably long for a church of the period. Ferrey employed an open parapet here pierced with quatrefoils, almost identical to that at West Lydford [77].

Inside, St Stephen's is light and spacious [**87**]. Much of Ferrey's decorative scheme is now lost, but a good impression of its original appearance can be gained from contemporary descriptions and illustrations. The chancel, the most richly decorated part of the church, has been altered the most. The star-painted ceiling, originally a rich deep blue, was painted an insipid light blue in more recent times, and Minton's terracotta diapering behind the altar, based on a medieval fragment from Canterbury Cathedral and originally picked out 'with gold and colours',[69] was whitewashed in the 1940s. So too were the walls, which had originally been painted with verses from Scripture and the Prayer Book order for Holy Communion. The textiles that once decorated the chancel have naturally long since perished. They originally formed a rather interesting collection. The sanctuary carpet – decorated with the Burdett arms alongside several others including the Sees of Canterbury, London, Adelaide, and Cape Town – had been executed by an army of Burdett-Coutts's friends and other 'ladies of distinction'.[70] Among them were Ann Ferrey, the Duchess of Northumberland, and the infant granddaughter of the Duke of Wellington. It had been rumoured that the Duke of Wellington himself had grown romantically attached to Angela Burdett-Coutts, though forty-five years her senior. Whatever the truth in that might be, Wellington did indeed endow St Stephen's with an altar cloth and a 'rich hanging' for the chancel – an Indian carpet that he had captured from the tent of Tipu Sultan, 'the Tiger of Mysore', in 1799.

For *The Ecclesiologist*, the church was a 'triumph of colour',[71] but it also had architectural substance. Looking down the length of the nave, the compound piers are at once both elegant and solid, crowned with foliate capitals. The pulpit is perhaps the most eye-catching feature in the nave, and it received a good deal of praise at the time [**88**]. It is handsomely carved with foliage and rich ogee-arched niches; what is unusual is the way in which it is approached. Ferrey was compelled by the diocesan surveyors to build a buttress which would project westwards into the north aisle. It was a tricky modification, not least since this buttress would cut across the steps up to the proposed pulpit. He therefore made a decorative element

OPPOSITE
87 St Stephen, Rochester Row, looking east.

of the buttress, panelling it with blind tracery and cutting an arch through it to provide an entrance to the pulpit. Even the most discriminating contemporary critic thought that Ferrey had handled the buttress 'with great taste'.[72] Such an assessment might more readily divide opinion today.

When he had started designing St Stephen's, Ferrey's ears were still ringing with *A Few Words to Church Builders*, a pamphlet reissued by the Cambridge

88 The pulpit at St Stephen, Rochester Row. On the left is the buttress imposed on Ferrey by the diocesan surveyors.

Camden Society in 1844. In it, the Decorated or Middle-Pointed style was declared as uniquely suitable for church building. This was part of the sustained attempt to create some sense of uniformity among Revivalists in that stylistically diverse decade. Ferrey duly subscribed to this developing philosophy, which had ultimately been prefigured and inspired by the writings of his childhood friend Pugin. At St Stephen's Ferrey made one of the earliest and most determined attempts at designing an ecclesiologically correct city church. As an archaeologically true building St Stephen's was highly successful.

In the review of the church that appeared in *The Ecclesiologist* soon after the consecration, however, the clerestory was criticised for being impotent, the spire for being too attenuated, and the inscriptions for being haphazardly executed.[73] The lowness of the chancel had been criticised in an earlier edition of the journal when construction had only just begun; there the critic recommended that Ferrey either heighten the chancel or remedy the visual discrepancy by the introduction of an elaborate ridge crest. The latter course of action was duly followed by Ferrey, but in the later review the height of the chancel was once more criticised:

> The great fault of S. Stephen's, both internally and externally, is the disproportionate lowness of the chancel compared with the nave, which gives it, particularly inside, too much of a country-church look. Outside, a lofty metal crest helps to palliate the mistake. This is more annoying, since it is of such satisfactory length; and it causes another collateral evil, that of bringing the windows, particularly the east window, too low.

The reviewer nevertheless maintained a strong enthusiasm for Ferrey's work at Rochester Row. The church had many 'points of great excellence' for which they 'most sincerely and warmly congratulate' Ferrey and Burdett- Coutts.[74] Two other London churches consecrated that year were also considered – St Barnabas, Pimlico, and St Mary, Crown Street – and of the three St Stephen's was judged to be the best architecturally. *The Ecclesiologist* ended the review: 'It is now time for us to conclude. May the poor of London long have cause to bless the three Saints' days of June, 1850; and may these three temples, then rendered to the service of our dear English mother, long remain to verify the saying of the wisest of men, "a threefold cord is not quickly broken."'

Ferrey might rightly have been both pleased and relieved to see what he had built in the heart of the 'Devil's Acre'.

St Paul, Island of St Helena, South Atlantic

When Angela Burdett-Coutts had been forming plans to build St Stephen, Rochester Row, she had also become involved in funding new dioceses in the colonies. In 1847 she had endowed both the bishoprics of Adelaide and Cape Town and would go on to establish the diocese of British Columbia ten years later. The sense of Christian duty that motivated her church-building work in the slums of London moved her to consider the religious condition of British subjects abroad. It would be an important

89 The Rt Rev. Robert Gray (1809–1872), Bishop of Cape Town, and husband of the amateur architect Sophy.

method employed by the civilising arm of the British Empire in the decades of its pre-eminence. The first Bishop of Cape Town, Robert Gray [**89**] (who later seceded from the Anglican Communion, much to the chagrin of his patroness), undertook the arduous duty of visiting the far-flung corners of his diocese in the first years of his episcopate.

In 1849 he finally made it to St Helena, a journey that took him some fourteen days by steam frigate. There he met Richard Kempthorne, who had arrived on the island ten years earlier and had been acting as the colonial chaplain. Kempthorne was the son of an evangelical clergyman. His brother was Sampson Kempthorne, the workhouse architect by whom George Gilbert Scott had briefly been assisted. By 1848 Richard had formed a desire to build a new church on the island, and with the assistance of Bishop Gray he established a building committee to oversee the task. His architect brother had designed several colonial churches in New Zealand, so it is curious that he was not approached. Bishop Gray's wife, Sophy, had designed some forty out of the fifty new churches in her husband's diocese; the Bishop, in one of his first communications to Kempthorne's building committee, enclosed two designs for the island's new church, subtly intimating in his letter that should one of those designs be selected, 'the working plans could be immediately prepared in His Lordship's own family'.[75] Diplomatically, Gray also sent Kempthorne an introduction to Ferrey, who we must conclude had been endorsed by Burdett-Coutts. By the end of 1848 Ferrey was making occasional references to work in South Africa in the course of his correspondence with her.

The building committee had politely and sensitively rejected Mrs Gray's proposals on the basis of economy, and on 3 July 1848 wrote to Ferrey to invite his designs for a new church. They requested a building capable of holding 450 people, with a chancel, tower, vestry and registry office, all within a budget of £3,200 (about £450,000 today). The committee were at pains to point out that this expense was a major burden on the island's rate-payers, so 'any such ornamental part of structure as may not be absolutely necessary … must be delayed until a future period'.[76] They thought that a Romanesque church would prove the most affordable. Ferrey had other ideas.

Ferrey's drawings had evidently been received promptly, as a few months later Kempthorne found himself writing to his bishop in October to record his qualified enthusiasm for Ferrey's proposal: 'The west end runs up into rather a high bell turret, containing three bells. This rather disappoints me, as I had set my heart upon a LARGE bell. It will however, if correctly carried out, be doubtless the prettiest building in the Island. The foundation is now being dug out.'[77]

The foundation stone was laid by the Governor of St Helena, Sir Patrick Ross, almost a year and a half later on 6 February 1850. The foundations had been dug in 1848, but a period of almost two years elapsed before any serious building work could commence. Ferrey, at the suggestion of the committee, had all the building materials prepared and cut by Messrs Winsland & Holland of Duke Street in Bloomsbury.[78] In January 1850 what was effectively the entire church was loaded aboard the *Glentanner* at Gravesend and sent on its way to St Helena – 'a novelty in exportation' as the *St Helena Gazette* observed.[79]

The church that arrived aboard the *Glentanner* was a modest Early English building, another style that had been associated with economy [**90**]. The result divided opinion. St Paul's is, unsurprisingly, a very simple church, single-celled, its walls pierced with small lancet windows. At the west end there is a tall double-tiered bellcote, but beyond that architectural interest hardly goes. It was a building dictated entirely by function and economy. As a ready-made church for a distant colony, it is perfectly admirable.

While some contemporary reviewers criticised the meanness of Ferrey's ornament, the main point of contention was the imposition of a very English vernacular on an exotic backdrop. A reviewer in *The Ecclesiologist*, not mincing his words, wrote:

90 St Paul's, Island of St Helena, shipped from England in 1850 and later promoted in 1859 to become the island's Anglican cathedral.

> we would ask such of our readers as have seen bananas and plantains grow, or who know what the colour and shape, and size of the basaltic cliffs of the Atlantic islands, all extinguished volcanoes, are, how they think a smart white smug 'Early English' church, all natty and nice, with its trim, neat windows, and a cocky little spire would look under such associations? Because this is exactly the principle of what Mr. Ferrey has done in sending out a ready made stone church.[80]

It was a view not unilaterally held. Lady Ross, Sir Patrick's wife, wrote in response to that review: 'The truth is that the scenery amidst which the church is placed is, with its hills, fields and hedgerows, exactly of an English character; so similar, that it might well be taken for a rural scene in one or other of the English counties.'

Owing to a dispute about the church being assigned to Gray's diocese, he was unable to consecrate it on his visit to the island in 1852. St Paul's had to wait another five years before he returned to St Helena in 1857, at which point he was finally able to say the rite of consecration inside it. Two years later, the diocese of St Helena was formed and Ferrey's little Early English church became a cathedral.

91 St Michael and All Angels, Littlebredy, Dorset, with Ferrey's thatched schoolhouse in the foreground.

St Michael and All Angels, Littlebredy, Dorset

Littlebredy today must surely have a claim to be the most perfect estate village in England. It remains almost untouched by time. There is a striking absence of tarmacked roads and cars, and hardly anything has been built there for two centuries. One can therefore gain a remarkably accurate impression of how the village appeared when Ferrey completed his work on the church and the village school in 1850 [**91**]. Littlebredy is idyllic in the extreme.

At one end of the village, a short walk from the church, is Bridehead [185, 186]. Until 2024 Bridehead was the seat of the Williams family, who had provided Ferrey with a consistent stream of work over several decades. Ferrey had worked on remodelling the house, assisted in this task by Arthur Acland [200], who had worked with him at Compton Valence. Acland remained in regular contact with Ferrey thereafter, consulting him on ecclesiological matters as he undertook minor church restorations of his own.

92 The younger Robert Williams of Bridehead (1803–1878), who inherited his father's estate in 1847 and set about rebuilding the church at Littlebredy.

The notion of rebuilding the church at Littlebredy had been under consideration for several years. Ferrey's first church, at Compton Valence, had been erected under the patronage of Robert Williams [42], who was succeeded in 1847 by his son, also Robert [**92**]. With the arrival of the new squire at Bridehead, plans to rebuild the village church at last began to take shape. In 1850 Ferrey began work on reconstructing the medieval church. Acland, Williams' brother-in-law, was appointed to assist and advise Ferrey.

Williams was an intriguing patron. When Ferrey had worked for his father in the 1830s, the younger Williams had been in the process of falling under the spell of the Oxford Movement. He had gone up to Oxford in Michaelmas 1833, only months after the Movement had sprung vigorously into life that July following John Keble's Assize Sermon at the University Church. It was a momentous time to begin an Oxford education, as the University entered the throes of a religious controversy that would shape the character of the century that followed. Moreover, Williams entered Oriel College, the very centre of Tractarian sympathies, and there formed a close friendship with John Henry Newman. On Newman's secession to Rome in 1845, however, Williams abruptly severed all contact. He not only burned his correspondence with Newman but reacted vehemently against the Oxford Movement itself. Within months he had gone from being a staunch Anglo-Catholic to a convinced Low Churchman.

Had Newman not converted, the parish church at Littlebredy might well have looked rather different. As it stands, St Michael and All Angels is a church designed to meet the needs of ordinary parish religion.

Ferrey's work at Littlebredy occupies an ambiguous position between restoration and rebuilding. It is included in this section since the amount of medieval fabric he retained is comparable to that preserved in other rebuilds such as Compton Valence and Wickham. At Littlebredy Ferrey lengthened the nave, added a north aisle, and entirely reworked the interior in Caen stone from Normandy. Yet he preserved many of the medieval windows, including the Early English lancets in the chancel, to which he added striking detached colonettes [**93**]. The nave arcade is notably solid and refined: its short, stout piers impart a certain muscularity to the interior. Externally, Ferrey appended to the tower an elegant spire, fastened

RIGHT
93 The chancel of St Michael and All Angels, Littlebredy, Dorset, 1850.

BELOW
94 The font at Littlebredy, carved by Arthur Acland himself. Acland set up a wooden hut in the churchyard and oversaw much of the work he had helped Ferrey design.

not with iron but with dowels of flint – perhaps an attempt to imitate the building of Solomon's Temple, in which 'neither hammer nor axe nor any tool of iron' was heard during its construction. Acland had in fact set up a shed in the churchyard from which he oversaw the church's progress and ensured that the workmen behaved reverently, so the pious work on which they were engaged was dignified. [**94**]. Encouraged by the partnership at Littlebredy, Acland would later rebuild the church at Huntsham with Ferrey after inheriting the estate there in 1852 (see p. 185).

The Church of St Michael and All Angels was completed within a year and has remained almost entirely unaltered [**95**]. It is a work of the highest quality, marked by great care in the choice of materials.

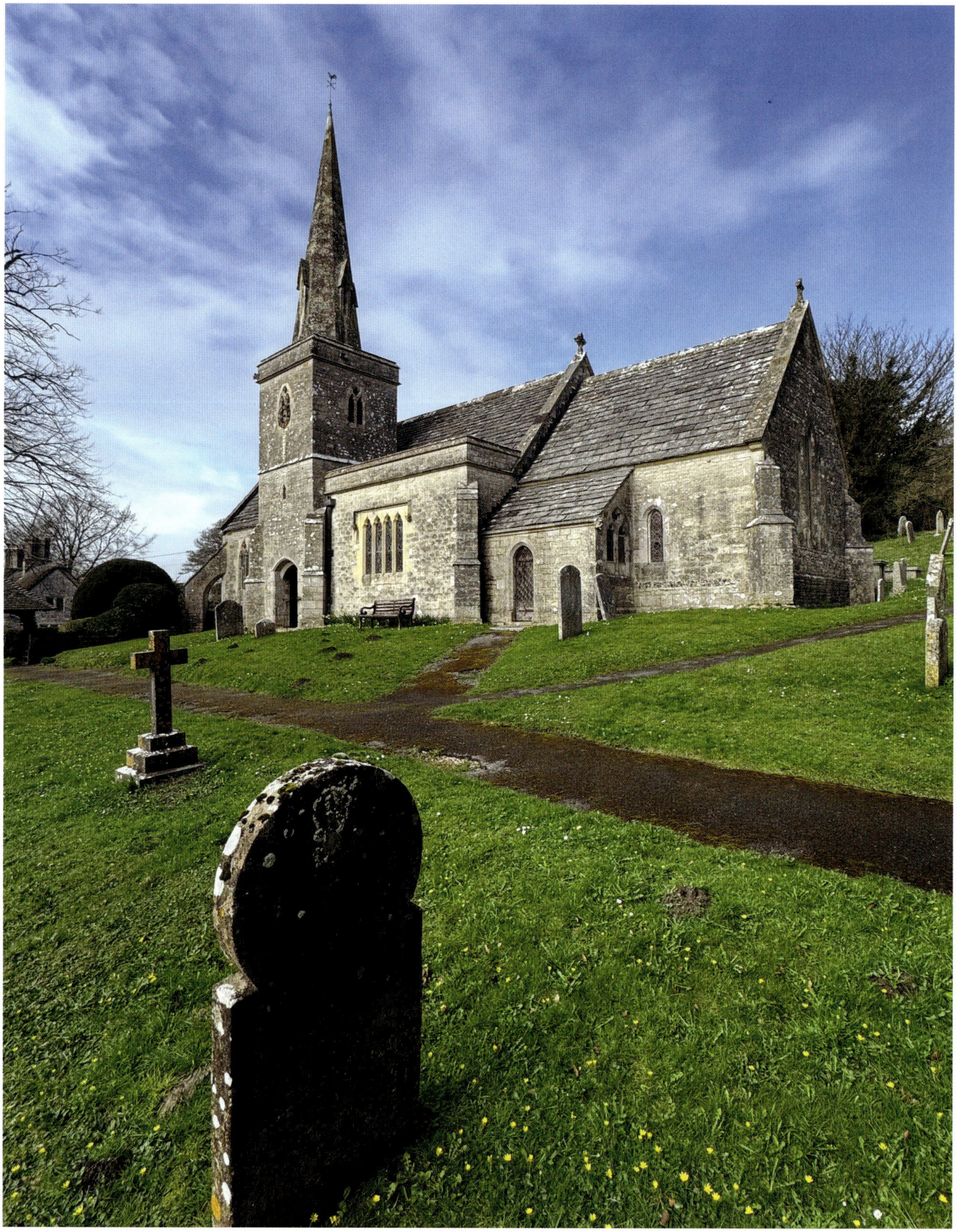

OPPOSITE
95 St Michael and All Angels, Littlebredy, seen from the north-east. The schoolhouse can just be glimpsed at the far left.

An estate bailiff was dispatched from Bridehead to Normandy to inspect and purchase Caen stone, and Williams even offered his newly laid oak library floor should better timber not be available for the roof. Ferrey's work at Littlebredy – not only the church but also the delightful thatched village school [91] – demonstrates an unusually sympathetic and restrained approach to the design of authentic rural buildings. To work so deftly within the Dorset vernacular was no small achievement.

St Mary, Buckland St Mary, Somerset

In 1853 came the commission for a new church at Buckland St Mary [**96**]. It would prove to be Ferrey's finest work in Somerset during his tenure as Diocesan Architect, and remains one of the county's finest Victorian church interiors.

When the Rev. John Edwin Lance was appointed to the living in 1830 the parish was a shadow of what it was to become under his patronage. Lance had inherited a stagnant situation. Buckland St Mary lacked the anchor of a dominant local landowner; its church was therefore deprived of the oversight and financial stability so often provided by the Victorian gentry. Consequently, the living had been vacant for over half a century. In the absence of a rector, the parish was served – if such a term can be generously applied – by Dr Palmer of Ilminster, who would travel between rural parishes on Sundays, conducting services in no fewer than five different parishes each week.

96 St Mary, Buckland St Mary, consecrated in 1863.

Into this somewhat hopeless situation stepped Lance, taking on a mission of reform in the fullest sense. He was to use architecture as a chief weapon in his mission for social renewal. During the decades that followed, Lance built, both figuratively and literally, upon the barest of foundations with remarkable vigour. The year of his arrival in the parish was said to be 'the year [that] was to change Buckland for ever'.[81]

It was not a glamorous calling. One of Lance's earliest duties at Buckland St Mary was the burial of a twelve-year-old boy who had been murdered by his own father. The man, it was reported, had 'been in the practice of treating the boy, who was a diminutive child, with extraordinary brutality … flogging him with a rope, at other times with a thick stick, and occasionally by kicking him'.[82] For Lance it was an eye-opening initiation into the grim realities of his new cure. Undeterred, he set about steadily reforming his parish over the course of the next two decades. He baptised and catechised his flock, and when necessary did not hesitate to offer firm political counsel to the more Liberal among them. A staunch Tory, he once rode uninvited to the scene of an impromptu Liberal rally in the village; no sooner had he appeared than the entire gathering dispersed.[83]

By 1853 the medieval parish church in Buckland had fallen into such a state of disrepair that it was impossible to use; its condition had reportedly 'become a subject of serious anxiety to the rector' [**97**].[84] Ferrey, in his role as Diocesan Architect, was commissioned to draw up plans for its replacement. The building of a new church represented the final stage in a broader scheme of local regeneration initiated by Lance. In 1840 he had funded the construction of a new church at Tatworth, just over five miles from Buckland, and in 1851 he engaged Ferrey to

97 A drawing of the old church at Buckland St Mary, demolished in 1853.

build a village school for his own parish. The school is a modest Tudor composition with a somewhat idiosyncratic elliptical window at its east end. There has been some debate over its authorship, but the building's inclusion in Ferrey's own list of works serves to settle the matter in his favour.

The church was to prove a more assured and ambitious work. By 1853 Ferrey had demonstrated his capabilities through a number of significant churches, not least St Stephen, Rochester Row, and had entered what might fairly be called the zenith of his career. The commission for Buckland St Mary arrived at an especially propitious moment, offering Ferrey the extraordinarily rare chance to build free from the usual constraints of economy and deadline. As it happened, the church took a decade to be completed. The result is arguably the most accomplished expression of Ferrey's ecclesiastical practice: in the richness of its interior and in the beauty of its scale and proportion, Buckland St Mary is one of the most refined – and least appreciated – rural churches of the Gothic Revival.

For so small a village, the scale on which Ferrey built at Lance's instigation is striking. The church is designed in what one contemporary reviewer with characteristic Victorian verbosity identified as the 'Second Pointed style of the later Floriated character'.[85] The nave is broad and lofty; a series of stained-glass windows by Clayton & Bell fill the aisle windows. Most of the stained glass was presented by benefactors connected with the church's construction. One particularly charming window was given by the church's builder, Henry Davis [**98**]: in it Solomon holds his temple and King David unfurls an architectural plan – appropriately enough, a plan of St Mary's. At the west end, the tower (which abuts the south wall) is afforded a soaring sexpartite vault of quite extraordinary scale, wholly unexpected in a village church such as this.

It is the chancel that draws the eye [**99**]. Here Ferrey created something unprecedently lavish in his own output. It is a richly ornamented affair: Ferrey endowed its interior with much beauty by the use of diapered tiles arranged in a chromatic gradient that shifts from red to green. He looked to a medieval precedent of wall covering at Westminster Abbey, and the decorative effect is extremely satisfying. To the south, a small chapel adjoins the chancel, separated from the aisle by a carved stone screen. Ferrey, tellingly, stops short from continuing the screen across the chancel itself. Another screen conceals the organ on the opposite side of the chancel. Overhead, a painted timber roof supported by angel corbels adds further richness to the composition. All this could only have been designed for a patron of Lance's theological sympathies. Indeed, one almost wishes that Ferrey had been a High Churchman himself, given what he was capable of achieving under (albeit unusually munificent) Anglo-Catholic patronage.

Whatever his opinions, when his patron at Buckland requested statues of the apostles Ferrey consented, and quite remarkably made provision for twelve niches to house them inside the church, high up above the nave arcade [**100**]. The effect is striking: the apostles, carved by Thomas Earp, look down from on high to the pews below, a glorious company likely to provoke the ire of any Low Church Protestant.

98 A window in St Mary, Buckland St Mary, presented by the church's builder, Henry Davis. On the right Solomon holds the temple, and on the left King David holds the plan of St Mary's.

OPPOSITE
99 The chancel of St Mary, Buckland St Mary, faced with red and green diapered tiles. The reredos of the Entombment of Christ, by James Forsyth, commemorates the Rev. John Edwin Lance.

100 Statues of the apostles by Thomas Earp high up in the nave of St Mary, Buckland St Mary.

101, **102** Two sources of inspiration for the statues in niches at Buckland St Mary: those at St Mary Magdalene in Taunton, and those in the Basilica of St Anthony in Padua, sketched by Ferrey in Scott's company in 1851.

For a precedent Ferrey looked both to England and to Italy. The arrangement was no doubt suggested by the medieval niches high up in the nave of St Mary Magdalene in Taunton [**101**], a church on which Ferrey had been working with Scott about the same time as Buckland St Mary. Ferrey's sketchbook from his trip to Italy with Scott in 1851 also seems to have been formative here. Scott and Ferrey had visited Padua on 22 October 1851, where they 'worked tremendously hard at St Antonio & the Arena Chapel [and took] great delight in both'.[86] One of Ferrey's sketches of the Basilica of St Anthony records the arcade of St James's chapel there, where statues stand above the arches in canopied niches [**102**]. The canopies in Buckland St Mary appear to be subtly anglicised copies of those in Padua.

It has been said that Ferrey was the first Englishman to introduce statues into niches since the Reformation, a suggestion that overlooks not only Laudian statues as at Oxford and Beverley but also the handful of nineteenth-century examples that predate Buckland St Mary. Still, those earlier nineteenth-century examples generally came courtesy of Roman Catholic architects, which Ferrey was certainly not. A few years earlier, he had served as a churchwarden of St Giles-in-the-Fields in London. His rector there was James Endell Tyler, who had dedicated much of his

103 James Forsyth's somewhat alarming monument of 1863 to Madelina Lance (d. 1839) in the chancel of St Mary's.

energy to hammering the Tractarians and the Church of Rome in print. One such publication set out his view on statues rather unequivocally in its title alone: *The Image-Worship of the Church of Rome: Proved to Be Contrary to Holy Scripture*. Ferrey probably concurred with Tyler's view, but was a businessman first.

More so than any other church by Ferrey, St Mary's in Buckland houses a collection of sculpture of quite exceptional quality. On the north wall of the chancel Ferrey built a recess to house a strikingly original monument to John Edwin Lance's first wife, Madelina, who had died in childbirth in 1839 [**103**]. The sculptor was James Forsyth,[87] who also created the reredos installed in the church in 1888 in memory of Lance himself – depicting, with apt solemnity, the Entombment of Christ [99]. There is some uncertainty as to the extent of Ferrey's involvement in designing Madelina Lance's monument; he certainly made provision for the niche, and the window above showing the Resurrection of Christ. It is a quite extraordinary piece of work: Madelina is portrayed clasping her child and violently emerging from the tomb, as though in response to the trumpet call of the Last Judgment. The effect is at once startling and poignant. The composition draws from a Swiss monument by Johann August Nahl in the church at Hindelbank in Switzerland. That monument commemorates Maria Magdalena Langhans, like Madelina the wife of a clergyman, who, like Madelina, had died in childbirth. Nahl's work achieved wide renown and circulated in prints and terracotta reproductions, one of which is now in the British Museum. Despite the fame of the Hindelbank monument, the Buckland monument appears to be the only imitation in Britain – a curious and moving relic of the European Romantic imagination in rural Somerset.

By the time the church was consecrated in August 1863, ten years had elapsed since Ferrey had been engaged on the project. Lance's desire to ensure that 'every part of it should be built as solidly as possible and of the best materials' was cited as the reason for the length of time that it took to build the church. He boasted that there was 'nothing but stone, well seasoned oak, marble, and not a bit of plaster work, or an inch of deal in the whole building'.[88] This was not achieved without considerable financial outlay, which brought its own delays. By 1863 Lance had given £16,000 (about £2.65 million today) of his own money towards the reconstruction of the church; the remainder of the total cost of £20,000 (about £3.3 million) was made up by the parish, along with 'some kind friends, and affectionate relations'.[89] It was certainly not the sum that a small rural parish could easily raise in a short space of time.

Still, the expense was evidently thought worthwhile. The Bishop of Bath and Wells remarked after the consecration that 'it had been his pleasure and his privilege at various times … to open a great many restored churches, and to consecrate many new churches, but [this] was the first time that he had ever consecrated a cathedral'.[90]

104 St Mary the Virgin, Hedgerley, Buckinghamshire, 1852.

Other Churches and Later Practice

By the time Ferrey had designed Buckland St Mary, his best churches were behind him. As the 1850s progressed he settled into a steady practice in which on average he would build two or three churches a year. By the 1860s his restoration work had slowly begun to overtake his church-building, so that by around 1862 he was known as one of the foremost restoration architects of the day.

Around the same time that Buckland St Mary was being designed, Ferrey was working on several other churches which might fairly be described as somewhat less extraordinary. St Mary the Virgin at Hedgerley in Buckinghamshire, built in 1852, might stand as a good example of one of Ferrey's more middling village churches [**104**]. It was built at the behest of Hedgerley's reforming incumbent, the Rev. Edward Baylis, who had had his rectory rebuilt in 1846 and then turned his attention to the church around the spring of 1851. Ferrey drew his plans up very quickly, so that in August of the same year they were being displayed at the rectory for parishioners to inspect between the hours of 10 and 5 o'clock. The drawings would have shown the epitome of an English village church – a good-sized crenellated west tower, an aisleless nave with some Decorated windows (possibly based on those at Long Wittenham, which J. H. Parker had recently measured and drawn), and a shorter chancel with lancets and a large east window. It sits very happily in its pleasant secluded churchyard, a straightforward bit of Middle-Pointed, modestly unextraordinary.

Ferrey would design many more village churches along similar lines. He began to experiment with pyramid-roofed towers, as at St Giles, Barlestone, in Leicestershire, in 1855. St Paul, Foston and Scropton in Derbyshire, built in the same year, is a development of the same model [**105**]. The tower is especially prominent there – wide and lofty, with a tall pyramid roof. The effect is one of sharp, pointed excitement, much augmented by the Puginian high-pitched porch which the Ecclesiologists thought too large.

There were also smaller village churches, towerless and compact. It was a form that Ferrey had first used in the 1840s at churches like Vobster in Somerset [**106**]. That church (since converted to a house) was built as a chapel of ease for the village between 1845 and 1848. It is towerless, simply composed of a well-proportioned nave and chancel, sparingly decorated with a modest ballflower cornice and a roof crest. When *The Ecclesiologist* finally came to review it in 1853, they declared: 'We know nothing of Mr Ferrey's which we have liked better than this church.'[91] Given that they had reviewed St Stephen, Rochester Row, three volumes previously, it

105 St Paul, Foston and Scropton, Derbyshire, 1855. Its pyramid-roofed tower is set off by a steep-pitched porch.

106 St Edmund, Vobster, Somerset, 1845–48.

might seem an extraordinary claim, but Ferrey was perhaps at his best when he was designing on a modest scale. His smaller churches were uncomplicated, well-conceived, and 'correct'.

In the decades that followed, Ferrey would continue to use a similar form for his smaller churches. All Saints at Curland in Somerset of 1855 is probably Ferrey's smallest church, and was also paid for by Lance of Buckland St Mary [**107**]. It is

107 All Saints, Curland, Somerset, 1855.

108 Holy Trinity, Deanshanger, West Northamptonshire, designed in 1853.

in a sorry, overgrown state, having been converted to residential use in 1991. Holy Trinity at Deanshanger in West Northamptonshire [**108**], designed two years earlier, in 1853, shows a development of the model that Ferrey had perfected at Vobster. It is another towerless church with a small lean-to north aisle, but with the addition of a tall double-decker bellcote at its west end. It is the variety of bellcote that we have seen at St Helena [90], which Ferrey would return to several times. Deanshanger makes ready and economical use of lancets at both the east and west ends, the latter recessed rather like Pugin's church of 1844 at Barntown in Ireland. The model that Ferrey would use for these smaller churches was one that was familiar to Pugin and other contemporaries who were looking to revive an appropriate form for a small Gothic church: St Michael, Longstanton, a twelfth-century church in Cambridgeshire [**109**]. Pugin referred to it several times during the 1840s: at St Andrew in Cambridge, St Charles Borromeo in Ryde, and St Alphonsus in Barntown. It even made it out to Philadelphia in the United States complete with a double-decker bellcote, thanks to the Cambridge Camden Society, who sent out plans of Longstanton as a model to copy. Deanshanger was another success: the Northampton Architectural Society proudly reported that they 'had never had a more approvable design before them', considering the budget that Ferrey had at his disposal.

Ferrey's practice, like that of so many of the early Revivalists, was based on taking good medieval precedent and adapting it. We have seen several occasions when Ferrey replicated elements of existing buildings in his own work. Only once, however, would he be tasked with exactly replicating a medieval church. In 1848 he received the commission to rebuild St Andrew's at Kingswood in Surrey, a small

109 St Michael, Longstanton, Cambridgeshire, a small medieval church used as a model by many Revivalists, including Ferrey.

unattributed church of 1835 in the Norman style. It had become apparent within ten years that it was too small, so its patron, Thomas Alcock, asked Ferrey to design a church to replace it. Alcock had regularly worshipped at St John the Baptist at Shottesbrooke in Berkshire [84] when he had been a guest of the Vansittart family at Shottesbrooke Park. Shottesbrooke is a delightfully uniform church of 1337 which, much like Ferrey's church at Penn Street, is defined by its elegant spire, rising over a crossing tower. Alcock requested that Ferrey recreate the church for him at Kingswood, which he duly did, completing the work in 1852 at a cost of about £9,000 (about £1.7 million today); its all-important spire would be added two years later. Ferrey's replication is good and precise, although ironically the spire of Penn Street [83] has an elegance and slenderness far closer to Shottesbrooke.

The world of ecclesiastical design changed drastically in the 1850s with the birth of new forms of naturalistic Gothicism, buoyed by the work of Ruskin *et al.* Street and Butterfield had brought in polychromy, the High Gothic was born, and the archaeological Middle-Pointed of the 1840s began to appear outdated. Pugin had died in 1852, yet Ferrey would continue to cling doggedly to his architectural legacy. In 1857 he received a commission to build a new church for Blackheath in south London. The by now familiar tale of urban expansion had left residents without a conveniently placed church, leading in turn to the foundation of a new parish there. Ferrey's church, All Saints' [**110**], is of Kentish rag, its spire placed asymmetrically to the south in an arrangement reminiscent of St Stephen, Rochester Row [86] and St Michael and All Angels at Chetwynd in Shropshire [117]. It has all the monumentality of those two churches, and of Christ Church at Esher in

OPPOSITE
110 All Saints, Blackheath, London, 1857–58.

Surrey, but none of the coarseness. It is small and well formed, intended to be built on a small budget (which was eventually exceeded by double). All Saints is one of Ferrey's best-known churches, almost entirely thanks to its extraordinary situation in the middle of the heath itself. It is isolated, quite away from any nearby buildings, and marooned in the expanse of grass that surrounds it. It almost has the appearance of an architectural model dropped from the sky.

All Saints' was built when another All Saints' continued to rise across the river at Margaret Street, Butterfield's polychromatic masterpiece. Ferrey's church at Blackheath could have been built in the 1840s. It was his old tried and tested model, which he would return to again and again well into the 1860s.

Still, Ferrey would continue to experiment and invent even within the self-imposed limitations of archaeological correctness. In 1857 he would address the RIBA with a paper entitled *Notes on Stamped or Incised Stucco*. In it, Ferrey revealed a new method of decoration which he had himself developed while working on designs for St Mary's at Maulden in Bedfordshire that same year. It was really a revival of an existing method of sgraffito, in which stucco surfaces are stamped or incised while wet to make a recessed pattern or decoration which could then be painted. In his paper Ferrey explained the 'very cheap and simple mode of ornamentation':

111 St Mary, Maulden, Bedfordshire, 1857. 'Incised stucco', the experimental method of decoration that Ferrey developed in the 1850s, was first used here.

> It is well known that the external roughcasting on old timber houses was stamped or wrought in small devices, known by the term 'pargetting'; but it never assumed the importance of extensive wall decorations, as when stone and brick entirely superseded the use of quartered oak framing the system of pargetting also ceased. The plan now proposed is to impress the common stucco with geometrical and other forms, and applied according to taste, either under string-courses, around arches, in spandrels, soffits, or in large masses of diapering; and texts may be imprinted on the plaster instead of being simply painted on the walls. If colour be desired, it can be effected by mixing the desired colour with the coat forming the groundwork, then, by laying the stencilled pattern against it, and filling in the solid portions of the device with the ordinary stucco or plaster.[92]

At Maulden Ferrey covered almost every available surface with this incised decoration, filled in with blue and red [**111**]. Text runs over every arch in the church, with geometric devices placed at regular intervals above. It is an interesting effect, and has preserved the original decorative scheme which would probably over time have flaked away from the wall. As a method of decoration, in a somewhat revised form, it would gain popularity in the decades that followed.

From 1862 Ferrey's church-building practice would begin steadily to wind down, as his restoration and country house practice took up more of his time. The consecration of Buckland St Mary in 1863, which had taken a decade to build, marked his last truly successful church building. If Ferrey's style had been unfashionable in the 1850s, it was even more so in the 1860s, and yet we see him returning to the forms he had developed over twenty years earlier. In 1864 at St Mary, Cefn Meiriadog, in Denbighshire in Wales, he once again returned to the old Longstanton model [109] for a small church with its bellcote and short nave [**112**]. Here, though, Ferrey added a flourish and placed a vaulted polygonal apse at its east end; we might look back to its equivalent at Compton Valence and observe how much more accomplished his earlier work was. St Peter and St Paul in Lufton, Somerset, begun a year later in 1865, is another trotting out of the same model, hardly altered during the course of two decades.

There are occasional flourishes of imagination in the 1860s, but they increasingly represent eccentric reworkings of old motifs. At St Mary and St Peter at Pett in Sussex [**113**] and at the Church of the Blessed Virgin Mary at East Lydford in Somerset [78], both begun in 1864, Ferrey is once again experimenting with octagonal towers. At Pett the tower, surmounted by a squat shingled spire, forms the north porch. It is an unusual and imaginative arrangement, but one that can hardly be described as beautiful. Ferrey had more success at East Lydford, where the tower is crowned with a handsome stone spire and is placed at the north-east corner of the nave with a vestry at its base. Both of these towers

112 St Mary, Cefn Meiriadog, Denbighshire, 1864.

113 St Mary and St Peter, Pett, Sussex, begun in 1864.

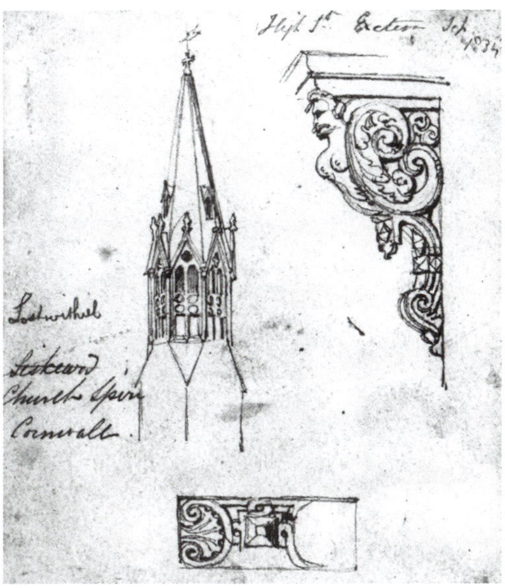

114 An early sketch of 1834 by Ferrey showing the octagonal spire at St Bartholomew, Lostwithiel, Cornwall.

were inspired not only by Welford, as has previously been noted, but also by St Bartholomew at Lostwithiel in Cornwall with its distinctive octagonal spire that Ferrey had noted in his sketchbook [**114**].

St Mary at Lower Slaughter in Gloucestershire is one of the most attractive of Ferrey's churches built in the 1860s [**115**, **116**]. He replaced the medieval church there but retained a thirteenth-century arcade. A well-proportioned spire sits at the east end, and Ferrey's good sense of proportion governs the interior, which is well

115, **116** St Mary, Lower Slaughter, Gloucestershire (1867), from the north-west.

OPPOSITE
117 St Michael and All Angels, Chetwynd, Shropshire (1865–67).

executed and unostentatious. Chetwynd is probably the most ambitious church Ferrey would design during the 1860s in terms of scale [**117**]. As at Lower Slaughter he returned to a more traditional broach spire, again set in the favoured position at the north-east corner of the nave. Chetwynd is well thought-out and has good proportions, especially in its interior, but it can hardly be said to belong to the age in which it was built. Ferrey was, it seems, sticking blissfully to the models with which he had already had success.

The 1870s brought some unusual developments. Ferrey was by this point becoming far less prolific in all areas of his practice. The death of his wife Ann in 1871 and the beginning of a new marriage in 1872, coupled with the fact that he was no longer considered a fashionable church architect, all conspired to slow down his work. The commissions for new churches that he undertook in this decade are marked with some unusual developments. At St James in Birlingham, Worcestershire, he introduced highly uncharacteristic polychromatic banding into the nave arcade [**118**], recalling E. W. Pugin's church of 1865 at Barton-upon-Irwell.[93] In 1870 at Christ Church, Colbury in Hampshire Ferrey experimented with an extremely unusual shingled bell turret punctuated by four rather naïve corner spirelets [**119**]. While shingled belfries are part of the Hampshire vernacular, Colbury's

118 The interior of St James the Great, Birlingham, Worcestershire, 1871–72.

is more reminiscent of Scandinavia than of England. Ferrey had designed similarly experimental belfries before at Sambrook in 1856 and Dorking a year later.

By the middle of the 1870s Ferrey had passed on much of his church building to his son. The lion's share of the work at St Mary Magdalene, Wookey Hole in Somerset was left to Edmund, who produced a remarkably amateurish church built of leftover material from his father's ongoing restoration at Wells Cathedral nearby. St Luke's at Burton in Wiltshire tells a similar story. It is a return to the old model of a smaller towerless church, but is executed rather meanly in brick. Both inside and out it is a very unassuming building, realised on a tight budget – hardly the work of the hand that produced the churches at Morpeth or Rochester Row. Burton, built in 1875, is almost entirely the work of Edmund rather than Benjamin. This handful of churches with which Ferrey had little involvement has not helped his posthumous reputation.

119 The unusual bell turret at Christ Church, Colbury, Hampshire, 1870.

In 1876 Ferrey designed his final church, Holy Trinity at Dorchester in Dorset [**120**]. A medieval church had stood on the site, directly beside the road without a churchyard. It had largely been rebuilt in the 1820s, and a series of modifications had been made inside to gain seating. By the 1870s it became clear that there would have to be a more substantial addition or a total rebuild. Ferrey was consulted at the end of 1874 and produced a design for the total replacement of the old church. It almost appears as a single block when viewed from the south-east, with all the hallmarks of a Puginian composition. The nave and chancel are of the same height. An extremely narrow aisle which provides an entrance from the street is tacked on to the south side of the church, extending only halfway down the nave. The church is largely built of an attractively light Pokeswell stone, with Bath stone for the interior.

So, after forty years of church-building, Ferrey's ecclesiastical career ended somewhat anticlimactically. He had achieved greatness in the 1840s and early 1850s, but could not quite sustain the ingenuity of his younger years. As we have seen, a large part of that was to do with his stylistic stubbornness: by 1870 he

120 Holy Trinity, Dorchester, Dorset (1875–76), Ferrey's last church.

was still building in much the same way as he had in 1840, but crucially without much of the same imaginative energy. Those accomplished churches – Morpeth, Littlebredy, St Stephen, Rochester Row – should not be forgotten or overshadowed by some of those that followed.

CHAPTER 5

A Foreign Interlude

OPPOSITE
121 The earliest surviving portrait of Ferrey, a photograph taken in the early 1850s.

[**121**] Somewhat unusually among his contemporaries, Ferrey was almost universally well-liked by his professional peers. What might today be called a talent for 'networking' proved invaluable for him, winning not only a steady stream of commissions but also many lasting friendships. Chief among these was his friendship with Sir George Gilbert Scott [**122**].

Ferrey found himself co-opted onto many committees throughout his career, just as he had been during the competition to rebuild the Palace of Westminster. One such committee was that of the London Architectural Society founded in 1831, a precursor of the Royal Institute of British Architects. Scott too had joined the Society by the mid-1830s, and it was probably during one of those meetings that the two men had become acquainted. The details of their developing friendship over the next decade and a half remain sparse, but a vivid glimpse into their relationship emerges in Scott's memoirs when he recounts a joint tour of Europe undertaken by the pair in 1851. This account offers the most substantial surviving portrait of Ferrey's character, and goes a long way toward illuminating the personality behind the practice.

122 Sir George Gilbert Scott (1811–1878), one of Ferrey's greatest contemporaries and his greatest friend.

It also happens that one of the most substantial surviving collections of Ferrey's sketches relates to this tour. Later in life Ferrey revisited his sketchbooks, selecting what he regarded as his finest work and cutting those pages out of the books. The chosen sheets were then compiled into a presentation volume which he inscribed to his second wife: 'Emily Ferrey from her loving husband'. In due course, Emily reorganised the drawings into a series of volumes which she gifted in 1910 to her youngest stepdaughter, Annie. Two of these volumes now survive at Tyntesfield in Somerset, that exuberant house built on the profits of guano to designs by John Norton, a student of Ferrey's. How exactly the volumes came to be at Tyntesfield remains unclear. A third volume composed of the sketches made during his Continental tours is preserved in a private collection.

The tour began in October 1851 in Berlin, a city where the upheavals of 1848 were still palpable. Just three years earlier its streets had been barricaded by revolutionaries, and although order had been restored, the political and social climate of the city remained tense. Ferrey and Scott would have sensed this febrile atmosphere, but much of their visit took on a rather Pickwickian tenor. Both men possessed a dry wit, and Scott would later recount with some relish the many amusing episodes that befell them during the tour. The first occurred almost immediately in Berlin, when a hotelkeeper greeted Scott with extravagant enthusiasm. Flattered, Scott assumed this to be a recognition of his work at St Nicholas in Hamburg. The truth, however, was rather different. When the hotelkeeper proceeded to address him as 'the greatest of English poets' Scott soon realised – with no small sense of embarrassment – that he had been mistaken for a certain Sir Walter.[1]

From Berlin the two travellers continued on to Prague. Ferrey, wearied by the monotony of the North German plain, had fallen into a state of gloom. It was only upon observing the mountainous splendour of Saxon Switzerland, with its dramatic pinnacles and wooded crags, that his spirits suddenly shifted. The landscape so thrilled him that Scott became convinced that he might fling himself out of the carriage window in sheer excitement. What occurred in Prague itself is less clear; Scott makes no reference to their time there in his memoirs, and Ferrey's sketchbook does not provide any elucidation. The same silence envelopes their stay in Vienna. The road out of Vienna brought some comic relief. Travelling in a droshky – a low open carriage – through the Semmering Pass, they encountered more of the rugged scenery that so delighted Ferrey. His enthusiasm, though, was punctuated by the repeated detachment of his wideawake hat by the alpine winds; each instance of the hat blowing from his head provoked such convulsions of laughter from both Scott and the coachman that the latter 'fell off the carriage, but cat-like came down on his legs'!

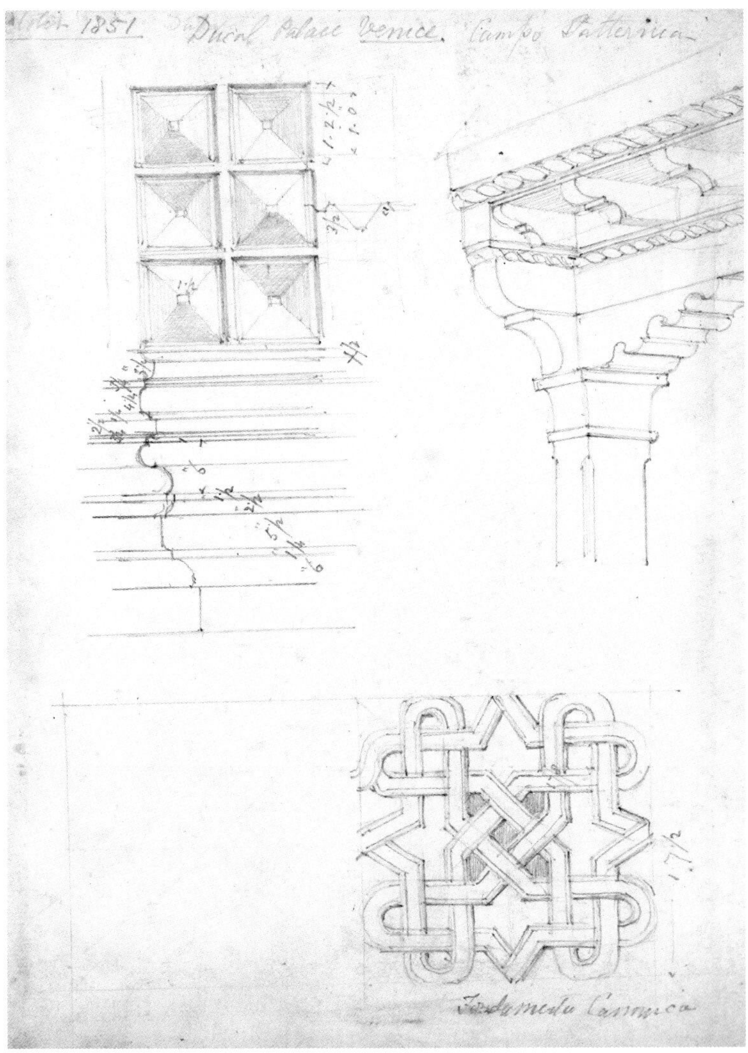

123 Sketch by Ferrey of details of the Doge's Palace in Venice, 1851.

The real goal of their tour lay over the Adriatic: Venice, where for Scott 'all was enchantment'. Ferrey, by contrast, was reportedly 'enraged at it', and would continually mutter the words 'Batty Langley' – that early and most unsophisticated practitioner of the Gothick style. Ferrey was proving a

124, **125** Sketches by Ferrey of details of St Mark's Basilica in Venice, 1851. The 'compartment of the nave' of is one of those on the external north side of the west end.

discriminating and opprobrious architectural critic. His sketches from Venice reflect this antipathy: they are largely confined to details of domestic buildings. Ferrey made several drawings of capitals and mouldings in the Doge's Palace [**123**], a building that he admired, but he produced only three sketches of ecclesiastical architecture, all of them exterior views of St Mark's Basilica [**124**, **125**]. Scott's impressions of St Mark's were, by his own account, 'stronger than [he] could describe', and he regarded its interior as the most impressive he had ever seen.

Just a month before Ferrey and Scott set out from Berlin, Ruskin and his wife Effie had arrived in Venice [**126**]. In that same year, 1851, Ruskin had brought the buildings of Venice to the forefront of public attention with the publication of the first volume of *The Stones of Venice*. Ferrey and Scott arrived shortly after, full of enthusiasm. They not only encountered the subject-matter of that most influential text, but its author, too, enjoying 'a most delightful evening' in his company. Scott was already personally acquainted with Ruskin, and Ferrey probably was too: they shared membership of several societies, including the Oxford Architectural Society, and it is likely that they first crossed paths at meetings of that group.

126 John Ruskin (1819–1900).

The first volume of *The Stones of Venice* opened with a haunting evocation of the city's faded magnificence:1 Venice 'is still left for our beholding in the final period of her decline: a ghost upon the sands of the sea, so weak – so quiet, – so bereft of all but her loveliness, that we might well doubt, as we watched her faint reflection in the mirage of the lagoon, which was the City, and which the Shadow.'[2] As Ruskin suggested, Venice was a city whose future rested precariously between ruination and restoration. In many ways both fates would be realised, one the result of the other. It was during the years in the 1850s that a tourist might have seen Venice as it truly was for the last time. Scott, for example, was enraptured by the Fondaco dei Turchi, a thirteenth-century palace which in the seventeenth century had become a warehouse for Turkish merchants. Ruskin described it as a 'ghastly ruin' and an 'unsightly heap festering to its fall'.[3] Whatever the truth in that assessment was, Ruskin, Scott or Ferrey could not possibly have applauded its insensitive 'restoration' in 1869. Scott sketched the Fondaco repeatedly, and came to use its densely spaced round-headed arches in one of his proposals for the Foreign Office.

All three men were also engaged in an enterprise that would bear fruit the following year. Scott had for some time been considering the need for a public collection pertaining to English Gothic architecture, and it would appear that the meeting between Ruskin, Ferrey and Scott in Venice went beyond a social gathering and touched on the practical matter of endowing and organising such an institution. The aim was not the display of architectural artefacts for passive appreciation, but an explicitly practical one: the Royal Architectural Museum [**127**] was to be a didactic resource for the nation's workmen. Scott and others believed that these workmen had been reduced to replicating a narrow range of bad exemplars, lacking access to a fuller visual archive of medieval work.

In order to discourage any antiquarian market in original artefacts, Scott made it a firm rule that only casts, not genuine medieval fragments, were to be accepted. Ferrey was among the earliest and most active supporters of the cause, and when the museum opened in the attic of a wharf on Canon Row in 1852 it already contained thousands of objects, among which were Ferrey's own casts of

127 The Royal Architectural Museum in 1854.

the medieval statuary from the west front of Wells Cathedral. Ruskin contributed generously too, presenting a huge collection of casts including a complete set of panels from the north doorway of Rouen Cathedral and forty-three casts from the Doge's Palace in Venice.

A letter home from Ruskin offers another account of this meeting, which appears to have been entirely spontaneous. He recounts that Scott arrived just in time to be asked to tea, an occasion which, in Ruskin's words, became 'a great architectural séance'.[4] Although Ferrey is not named, his absence from the letter is not necessarily significant; the note was only a very brief dispatch to Ruskin's father, written primarily to remind him of Scott, 'who you must remember [from] Denmark Hill'.[5]

Moreover, there is a telling shift in the subjects that Ferrey sketched after 21 October, the date of the 'architectural séance'. At the time Ruskin was also engaged in making notes and sketches of the city in preparation for the next volumes of *The Stones of Venice*. While it is tempting to imagine that he and Ferrey sketched side by side in Venice, reasonable conjecture can hardly go that far. What is more plausible is that Ruskin suggested some sites of interest to Ferrey, who we must remember spent much of his time in Venice muttering 'Batty Langley'.

One such suggestion may have been the Sagredo Palace. Detailed sketches of one specific balcony there appear in both Ruskin's and Ferrey's sketchbooks [**128**, **129**]. Ferrey might have been inspired to pay another visit to St Mark's, where Ruskin had been toiling away, listing and analysing the thirty-six carved capitals of the lower arcade on the basilica's west front. Ruskin made a comprehensive catalogue of all the figures carved in these elaborate (and at times somewhat naïve) fourteenth-century capitals. The day after their encounter, Ferrey returned to the basilica. He had already spent some time there sketching part of an elevation of

128, **129** Sketches by Ferrey and Ruskin of the balcony of the Sagredo Palace in Venice, 1851.

130 Ferrey's sketch of a capital of St Mark's in Venice showing the Virtues, a favourite of Ruskin's, 1851.

the west front, but this time he turned his attention to the ninth capital in Ruskin's sequence, a finely carved representation of the Virtues [**130**]. His drawing shows three of them: Justice, Prudence and Hope. Ruskin had thought it one of the better capitals.

That autumn, Venice might have seemed overrun by a huge flock of English artists and connoisseurs. Scott recalled three more notable individuals who he and Ferrey had encountered during their stay there. The first was Thomas Gambier Parry, a gentleman artist and energetic squire of Highnam in Gloucestershire, where just sixth months earlier his great architectural triumph – a church designed by Henry Woodyer and frescoed by Gambier Parry himself – had been consecrated. Gambier Parry was returning from a honeymoon tour of Europe with his second wife and was considering forming what would become a very significant collection of early Italian painting, a genre still largely overlooked in Britain during the 1850s. Scott maintained a friendly relationship with Gambier Parry for some time, though that friendship would later unravel in a fierce row over the painted ceiling at Ely Cathedral.

131 Edward William Cooke (1811–1880), a friend of Ferrey's from Pugin's drawing school, in Venice for its maritime world.

A more familiar companion for Ferrey came in the form of Edward William Cooke [**131**]. The two had been classmates at Pugin's drawing school on Great Russell Street, and Cooke's uncle, William Bernard Cooke, had engraved several of Ferrey's drawings for *The Antiquities of the Priory of Christ-Church*. Like Ferrey, Edward Cooke had enrolled at the drawing school in 1825, though he left within the year, later claiming that Pugin had found him 'to be in need of no instruction'.[6] Whether that claim holds much truth is debatable, but either way Cooke soon returned to his real passion: drawing and painting ships. It was this pursuit that occupied him in Venice twenty-five years later. He had first visited the city in 1850 and was so taken with it that he would return regularly throughout his life to produce pictures of Venice and its maritime traffic, most powerfully at sunset. His diary entry for 19 October 1851 offers a vivid outline of a typical day's activities: 'Called on Ruskin, he out … [Mrs Ruskin] lent me his *Pre Raphaelitism* which I read. At ¼ p 11 I went to call on Mr Cheney (out).[7] Went in gondola and worked on Ducal Palace … at ½ p 8 went to Ruskin's to tea. Met Lady Sorrell and daughter. R showed me his two Turners.'[8]

Another artist who Ferrey and Scott met in Venice was David Roberts. Roberts was perhaps the most distinguished architectural painter of the day in Britain, and had been spending time in Venice executing a series of Canalettian views. It was Ferrey and Scott who persuaded him to stop in Vienna on his return journey – a suggestion that led to the creation of 'two noble pictures' of the interior of St Stephen's Church, one now housed at the Guildhall, the other at the Birmingham Art Gallery. Roberts was also a frequent visitor to Ruskin's apartment, and the two men maintained an unusual friendship – unusual, since Ruskin would repeatedly publish extremely unfriendly assessments of Roberts' work.

Ferrey and Scott left Venice after a few stimulating days. Their next stop was Padua, where they 'worked tremendously hard'[9] sketching the Basilica of St Anthony [**132**] and the Scrovegni Chapel [102, **133**], with Giotto's remarkable frescoes. Ferrey's sketchbook paid no attention to the paintings, and focused solely on the architecture of the chapel and its furnishing. The sketches would become useful during his work at Buckland St Mary.

Padua was the scene of another amusing episode. Scott and Ferrey were in the habit of rising at dawn for breakfast in order to leave much of the day for sketching. Scott was evidently the first to rise on this occasion, and saw out of the hotel window 'a Gothic domestic ruin' in the dim light. His initial delight soon turned to disgust when he realised that he had been fooled by a *trompe l'œil* painting on a yard wall. The opportunity for mischief was not missed, and Scott, summoning Ferrey, played the trick on him. Ferrey returned the favour the next day in Vicenza, catching Scott out with a similar deception.[10]

The pair were both 'charmed beyond measure' by Vicenza,[11] though their time there was brief. This is reflected in Ferrey's sketchbook, which contains only a single rapidly executed drawing from this leg of the journey. From Vicenza they continued to Mantua, where Scott made 'precisely the same sketch of the tower of the cathedral which Street made the next year'[12] (in fact two years later). George Edmund Street would publish notes from his tours in Italy in *Brick and Marble in the Middle Ages* (1855), a highly influential volume which in due course

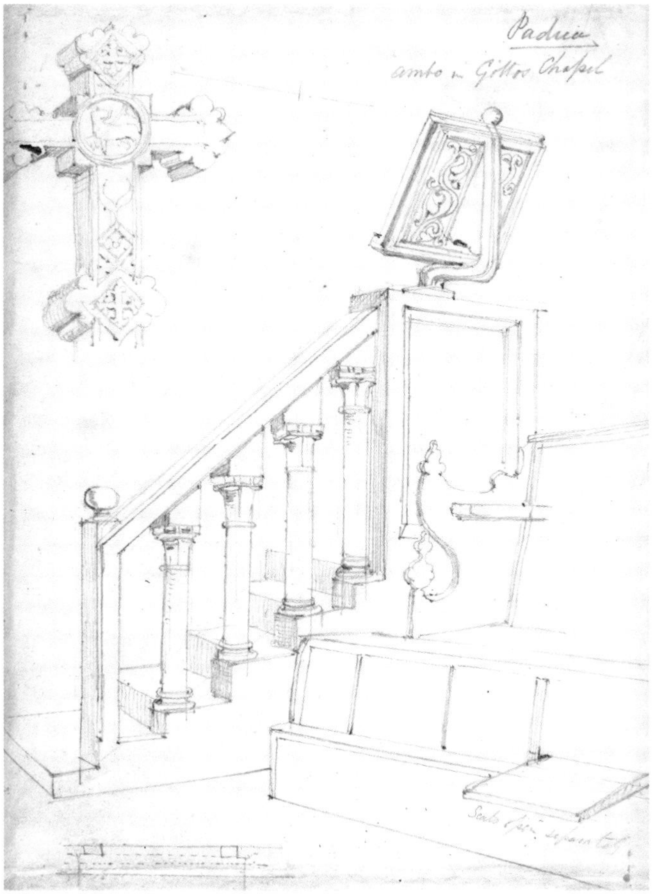

inspired church architects in Britain to reassess architectural colour and take up polychromatic brickwork. Incidentally, the book includes drawings by Street of several specific architectural features that Ferrey had recorded a year earlier.

A humorous interlude in Bologna, reached by way of Modena, occurred when Ferrey attempted ‘a little speculative Italian’. The pair, in search of St Stephen’s Church, encountered a genial-looking elderly man and asked him for directions. Scott recalled the man’s response: ‘He, seeing that we had exhausted our knowledge in the question, made no reply, but, taking one of us by the button … led us silently through two or three streets, and, conducting us into the very middle of the church, shook hands with us both in dumb show, and departed.’[13]

This, and no doubt other such episodes, made clear their need for a translator. Fortunately, they found one in Anthony Salvin, the twenty-four-year-old son of the well-known castle architect of the same name. Both Scott and Ferrey knew the elder Salvin from the RIBA, and Ferrey had worked with him a few years earlier at Wells Cathedral. It is unclear at what point the younger Salvin joined them, but he was evidently touring with his father, who visited Ruskin’s apartment in Venice only a few weeks after Ferrey and Scott had left that city.

Next came Florence. For Scott it ranked second only to Venice, but one suspects that for Ferrey it eclipsed all other Italian cities. In his sketchbook the drawings

ABOVE LEFT
132 Ferrey’s sketch of a dome of the Basilica of St Anthony in Padua, 1851.

ABOVE
133 Ferrey recorded that his sketch in the Scrovegni Chapel of St Anthony in Padua showed the ‘ambo in Gittos Chapel’, but he ignored Giotto’s frescoes.

ABOVE
134 Details of the Palazzo Vecchio, sketched by Ferrey during his stay in Florence, 1851.

ABOVE RIGHT
135 A sketch by Ferrey of 'Giottos Campanile' of Santa Maria del Fiore in Florence.

of Florence are executed with a noticeable attention to detail – many of them measured, a practice otherwise reserved for his Venetian studies [**134**, **135**]. The impression is given that he intended these sketches for some practical use, yet with a few minor exceptions Ferrey never seems to have meaningfully incorporated any of these Continental precedents in his work at home. Often an architect returns from such a journey profoundly altered: Street is a prime example, and Scott's work, too, bears the imprint of these new influences after 1851, but Ferrey seemed largely immune to the appeal of Italy. He remained, as has been noted, 'a Puginian rather than a Ruskinian Goth'.[14]

Even the new enthusiasm for polychromatic brickwork, popularised during the years when Italy swarmed with English artists and architects under the spell of Ruskin, passed Ferrey by. He experimented with it a few times, perhaps most confidently in a rectory for Fleet in 1854 and again in the interior of his church at Birlingham in 1871–72 [118], but rarely. A confidently polychromatic rectory in Thames Ditton (where Ferrey had restored the church) has been rumoured to be his work, but it seems to be rather too bold.

From Florence, where Ferrey lavished particular attention on sketching the cathedral, the pair travelled to Siena. There, Scott recorded that he undertook 'the hardest three hours work in [his] life, and the pleasantest'.[15] Ferrey also put his

ABOVE LEFT
136 Sketches by Ferrey of Siena Cathedral, 1851: a diagonal view under the dome, and a plan of the pulpit.

ABOVE
137 Nicola Pisano's pulpit in Siena Cathedral, sketched by Ferrey.

pencil to good use: his sketches of the cathedral are among the best in his sketchbook [**136**, **137**]. But by now it was nearly November, and Ferrey was becoming anxious about the return journey. According to Scott, he was 'in fits at the idea of crossing the Alps in the snow'.[16] The pace was therefore quickened, and after only a day in Siena they made for Pisa.

At Pisa they encountered a new companion, a 'young English architect … [who] had the happy knack of giving offence to the police authorities'.[17] Austrian soldiers, as Scott noted, were an almost constant presence from Saxony to Tuscany; Europe was still unsettled by the revolutions of 1848 and continued to be wary of further uprisings. The company of so provocative a figure was therefore unwelcome. Scott and Ferrey were both terrified of his conversation being overheard in cafés by Austrian officers. Scott tactfully does not name him, but his remark that this individual 'had been arrested at Verona for sketching the fortifications' allows us to identify him as Harry Robert Newton (1828–1889), an obscure pupil of Sydney Smirke. Newton had reportedly been mistreated while in custody, prompting his father, the miniature painter Sir William John Newton, to have Joseph Hume raise the case in Parliament on 16 November 1852. Lord Stanley, then serving under his father as Parliamentary Under-Secretary of State for Foreign Affairs, promised to investigate, though he remarked that it was evident that the arrest had not been without cause.

Ferrey and Scott also visited Verona, a stop omitted from Scott's *Recollections*. Ferrey made several sketches there, including a view of the imposing Lamberti Tower from precisely the same angle later taken by Street in *Brick and Marble* [**138**, **139**]. As Newton had learned, the political atmosphere in Verona under Austrian rule was especially tense. Since 1849 Verona had been transformed into the Empire's

138, **139** The Lamberti Tower in Verona, sketched by Ferrey in 1851 and illustrated by Street in *Brick and Marble in the Middle Ages* (1855).

most heavily fortified city, and Austrian troops were seemingly everywhere. Ferrey and Scott being more peaceable than Newton attracted no suspicion from the troops – in fact they were greatly struck by 'their fine persons and equipments'.[18] During the return coach ride Ferrey was 'ecstatically' describing the Austrian soldiers to a retired English officer just returned from India. His response predicted the course of the 1859 Second Italian War of Independence: 'aye, but if they ever go to war with the French, you'll see how the French will walk into them'.[19]

Ferrey's haste to avoid the snow proved in vain. By the time they reached Genoa, the Carrara mountains were already covered in snow. Scott wrote: 'I shall never forget looking back upon them as we walked up the hill at Spezzia in the morning and seeing them again radiant in fiery glory in the last rays of the setting sun. I never saw, nor since have seen, anything more magnificently splendid.'[20]

Whether Ferrey was able to share this appreciation is uncertain. By now his anxiety was making him a trying companion. Scott later wished that they had stayed longer in Europe, but their friendship was undiminished, and the final stage of the journey, from Genoa to Milan, was as cheerful as ever. Scott considered the western front of Genoa Cathedral 'the best Gothic architecture' he saw in Italy,[21] though Ferrey's sketchbook records nothing from the city. In Milan, their last day of sketching in Italy, Ferrey concentrated on the unusual octagonal brick tower of San Gottardo [**140**]. This tower also caught Street's eye, who wrote of it: 'it is certainly a rich and picturesque tower, and well deserves inspection'.[22]

140 Ferrey's sketch of the tower of San Gottardo in Milan, 1851.

Bypassing Pavia in their haste, they reached Como only to find that the snow was already six feet deep. Sledges – 'deal boxes nailed on ash poles'[23] – were required to cross the Alps. The conditions were harsh; they were lucky to have some twenty men going ahead to dig a way for them, but 'nothing [was] to be seen but snow and fog'.[24] It was during this passage that one of their horses jumped over a precipice. Ferrey saw it happen, woke Scott, and together they looked over to find the creature suspended in a tree. With ropes it was hauled to safety.

Their return journey was broken with one notable stop-off at Freiburg. Ferrey was back in the more familiar territory of the Gothic North. He took out his sketchbook once more, to record not the cathedral's imposing late Romanesque portal but a more understated entrance on its south side [**141**]. Either way, there was no trace of Batty Langley to be seen there. Scott, meanwhile, visited an old acquaintance, a commissionaire with a curious collection of 'quaint English books and letters'.[25] From Freiburg they returned to England, arriving back in London in mid-November.

This lengthy account of the tour is justified by the rare and vivid picture it offers of Ferrey's character. Posthumous accounts present him as a kindly, agreeable man. Scott's *Recollections* do not contradict this, but they reveal something more: a combination of energy and mischief otherwise absent from accounts of his life. There is a boyish vigour in the tour's episodes – the mutual foolery, the good-humoured irritations, the sarcastic asides in Venice, and the anxious but ultimately vindicated haste to beat the Alpine snow. Moreover, Ferrey's presence in Italy in 1851 placed him at the centre of a remarkable circle of connoisseurs, theorists and architects. As we have seen in the case of Street, such tours would prove decisive in shaping the direction of British architecture in the 1850s and beyond. But Ferrey, almost uniquely, remained unmoved. He had found an architectural language that suited him, and patrons who valued it. He saw no reason to tamper with a secure

141 The 13th-century portal of Freiburg Cathedral, sketched by Ferrey in 1851 on the way back to England.

formula. Scott, writing in 1879, summed up the tour in much the way Ferrey himself might have done:

> In spite of all the violence now indulged in, against every lesson learned south of the Alps, I must say that I gained very much by this journey, and much desire to repeat it. I was convinced, however, that the Italian Gothic, as such, must not be used in England, but I was equally convinced, and am so still, that the study of it is necessary to the perfecting of our revival.[26]

CHAPTER 6

Restorations

It would require at least another book to do justice to the movement that resulted in the restoration of thousands of medieval churches during the nineteenth century. John Betjeman's poem beginning 'The Church's Restoration/In eighteen-eighty-three/ Has left for contemplation/ Not what there used to be' does much to encapsulate the popular modern assessment of Victorian restorers as senseless vandals. The truth is not nearly so straightforward. These debates thundered as passionately during the nineteenth century itself. Indeed, at the end of his career, Ferrey would find himself facing headlong the polemics of the 'Anti-Restoration' movement.

The popular drive to restore churches coincided in many ways with the development of the Cambridge Camden Society. There had of course been earlier restorations, particularly of cathedrals, but a growing understanding of medieval architecture meant a new approach to restoration soon developed. In 1846 Edward Augustus Freeman published a book entitled *Principles of Church Restoration*. Freeman, a friend of Ferrey's from the Oxford Architectural and Historical Society, named three categories of church restoration: 'destructive', 'conservative', and 'eclectic'. The 'destructive' type was a hangover from earlier decades, associated with such alarming names as James Wyatt 'The Destroyer'; some Victorians still persevered in this tradition. 'Conservative' restorations created facsimiles of what had been replaced – Ferrey very occasionally fell into that category. The 'eclectic' form of restoration is what Ferrey most often found himself undertaking. This was a *via media* between the other two approaches: buildings were carefully studied, and new work was executed in accordance with the general character of a church. A mere copy of what had once been there was avoided. In short, eclectic restorations represented a form of 'church improvement' rather than derivative reconstruction.

The earliest of Ferrey's church restorations date from around the period when Freeman was formulating these categorisations. Many, as we shall see, were carried out in relation to his work as the Diocesan Architect for Bath and Wells, a post to which he was appointed in 1841. From 1850, as Ferrey entered the zenith of his career as a church architect he began to take on noticeably less work as a restorer of churches. There were however several restorations in the late 1840s and early 1850s, many of them in Oxfordshire. These commissions include work on the parish churches of Harpsden, Cuddesdon and Swyncombe. Ferrey had moved to Henley-on-Thames in 1846, and as luck would have it, in 1847 Bishop Wilberforce of Oxford decided that he would appoint a Diocesan Architect. Having heard this,

OPPOSITE
Detail of Figure 158.

Ferrey applied for more work in the diocese, perhaps in an attempt to prove his suitability for the job. It may have seemed a done deal for him, especially in light of his work building a chapel for the Bishop's Palace at Cuddesdon. Wilberforce had even written to one of his clergy in 1849 advising him not to advertise a competition to rebuild his church, but to opt for 'the safe way' – 'to take Scott or Ferrey'.[1] Nevertheless, on 12 December 1850 Wilberforce appointed George Edmund Street, the only other applicant, to the post. It seems that the decision simply boiled down to money: Street offered his services free of charge, whereas Ferrey sought £100 (about £17,000 today) a year.

Still, one diocese was enough to keep Ferrey's restoration portfolio full. His work restoring the cathedral and the Bishop's Palace in Wells would occupy him for the best part of three decades and would in turn lead to several other important commissions both within and without the diocese. Around 1860 his workload as a restoration architect overtook his work as an architect of new churches. This was the decade when the great stream of church restorations flowed at its fullest. The vast majority of the restorations referred to in this chapter took place during this decade. The year 1862 marked the commencement of several of Ferrey's most important restorations.

Ferrey was a prolific restorer, and no doubt even more prolific than his own fragmentary list of works suggests. Quite often his restorations amounted to little more than a reworking of a chancel or an aisle, but, as we will see, he was frequently occupied with projects to restore larger, more important buildings. The following provides a representative overview of a large body of work.

Wells Cathedral – Early Restorations

Ferrey had been appointed as Diocesan Architect for Bath and Wells in 1841, a position he held until his death in 1880. As a thirty-one-year-old Ferrey was inexperienced as a church architect, the vast majority of his work up to that point being represented by civic buildings. He had however proved himself at Compton Valence, and the first of his Romanesque churches were beginning to take form. One of his earliest and most useful patrons was William Thomas Parr Brymer, rector of Charlton Mackrell in Somerset and, from 1840, Archdeacon of Bath. A list of works published with Ferrey's obituary in *The Builder* suggests that he had built Brymer a rectory and restored the church at Charlton Mackrell; there is however very little evidence in support of this. The rectory is eighteenth-century; the church was restored around the time when Brymer had a local architect, Charles Edmund Giles, design a village school in 1847, and it is likely that Giles was responsible for the restoration too. Either way, Ferrey knew the church and its incumbent, who would recommend him to be Diocesan Architect.

The interior of Wells Cathedral in the early nineteenth century would be unrecognisable to modern eyes. Canon H. W. Barnard wrote a manuscript account of the restoration work that took place at Wells between 1834 and 1854. He began with a description of the cathedral as it once appeared:

> From time immemorial to the year 1843 the whole interior of our beautiful Cathedral, from East to West, from North to South, & from the floor to the ceiling presented an unbroken mass of whitewash, & yellow ochre; – not a trace of the natural stone could be seen; – the fine sculpture of the capitals, and other ornamental portions were scarcely to be distinguished under the accumulated layers of the odious wash; and even the polished Purbeck marble columns in the Presbytery, & Lady Chapel, had shared the same ruthless fate. – The Choir at this time was fitted with very plain Oak stalls, with canopies running in a line in front of the arches destroying their proportions, and hiding the columns and capitals. Above these were three galleries on each side with tabernacle work in front of blue pannels with gothic tracery in white and gold; they were approached by staircases from the north and south aisles, & were altogether very great disfigurements, & unsightly encumbrances.[2]

Edward Blore had been consulted in 1830 with a view to receiving the commission to restore the cathedral. His report was never followed by any substantial action, although a few alterations were made in 1832, including the cleaning of the interior and the repaving of the north and south aisles. Edmund Goodenough, who became Dean in 1831, envisaged a more considerable restoration. His determination was matched by Brymer's coordination and a financial contribution from the Archdeacon of £1,000 (roughly £140,000 today). By 1842 an extensive scheme of restoration could therefore be considered.

In an 1842 letter of appeal the Dean wrote: 'from the date of the Restoration of Charles the Second, very little indeed has been done … the greatest desire is now entertained for the perfect restoring of the whole in a style & age suitable to the Architecture of the Church'.[3] The first undertaking was to remove hundreds of monuments, mostly dating from the eighteenth century, which had covered almost every surface of the cathedral walls. Barnard recalled how tablets had been allowed to 'partially block up the windows, & otherwise intersect the mouldings, and deface the walls'.[4] This was executed under the auspices of Goodenough, who with some considerable tact and charm was able to avoid any major complaints arising from the families of those whose monuments had been removed to the cloisters.

With the walls of the cathedral cleared, Ferrey was able to begin scraping away at the 'odious wash' in the chapels at the east end of the cathedral, revealing for the first time in centuries the stone and marble with which it had been built. This process continued for some time, and in 1844 the final stage of scraping began at the west end of the cathedral. It was a method of working which would later become controversial.

Strictly speaking, Ferrey's role was one of superintendence. In restoring the Lady Chapel, he left many of the decisions about decoration and design to the stained-glass artist Thomas Willement, with whom he had worked before, including at East Grafton. Willement filled the windows with stained glass and executed stencilled decoration on the vault above. He would later carry this stencilling through to the nave, having found some medieval painted foliage under the whitewash – an attempt at 'conservative' restoration that divided opinion. Ferrey had Minton pave the Lady Chapel, and after the renewal of some damaged carving its restoration was complete. He continued in a similar way, restoring (with Willement's artistic input) the north and south choir aisles in quick succession. Much had been completed by the beginning of 1845, when work was suspended for want of money.

It was at this point that a series of minor setbacks were experienced, not least the death that May of Goodenough who had done so much to instigate and oversee the restorations. Goodenough was soon replaced by a new Dean, Richard Jenkyns, and all that remained of the envisaged scheme was the reordering of the choir, then disfigured by lurid blue galleries. Jenkyns would quickly realise that this final portion of restoration would not be straightforward. The question of finance was solved in due course by another public appeal, but a diversity of opinion within the chapter became apparent over what might replace the galleries. After a hiatus, the chapter met once again to consider the restoration and decreed that Anthony Salvin should also be engaged alongside Ferrey so that the work might be executed 'in the best possible manner'.[5] Rather than representing a snub, it seems likely that Ferrey, sensing difficulties ahead, requested assistance at a time when he was increasingly busy elsewhere.

Although the chapter were unanimous in their desire to remove the unsightly galleries, they were conscious that valuable seating capacity would be lost as a result. One of the challenges for Ferrey and Salvin was therefore to provide as much possible accommodation in the stalls without giving them the appearance of being overcrowded. Debates raged at chapter meetings about these stalls – where they should be placed, how old medieval woodwork might be incorporated, whether or not there should be canopies. The real bone of contention was whether the material used should be stone or wood – it took some three years before the matter was finally settled.

This work was left almost entirely to Salvin. At the beginning of October 1848, after much work on Salvin's stalls had already been undertaken, the chapter decided to suspend work in the choir so they could deliberate once more over whether the canopies should be of stone or oak.

One correspondent in the *Bristol Times and Mirror* reported news of this suspension 'with extreme regret',[6] suggesting that two strong-willed individuals within the chapter had caused the delay through their determined disagreement. Work was suspended on 2 October, and it was not until 17 July in the following year that a decision was reached: the stall canopies should be executed in stone. However, it soon became apparent that there was not enough money to see that through. Had it not been for Jenkyns himself coming forward with a benefaction of £1,000 (about £160,000 today), the saga might well have continued indefinitely. The stalls were eventually executed by James Forsyth [**142**], who worked with Ferrey at Buckland St Mary [99, 103].

This first phase of Ferrey's restoration of Wells Cathedral was sufficiently complete for a meeting of the Archaeological Institute to examine the work in July

142 The stone stalls of Wells Cathedral as completed by James Forsyth.

1851. Freeman read a paper at that meeting 'on the rage for restorations' which quite remarkably tailed off into an attack on Lord Elgin for the 'vandalism of transferring the Elgin marbles from their proper locality to the walls of the British Museum'.[7] Robert Willis then gave a lecture on the history of the cathedral, and Cockerell spoke of the medieval statues on the west front before the restoration work was finally considered. It might say something in favour of Ferrey and Salvin's work that such a discriminating antiquarian audience examined their restorations 'with critical care and occasional approbation'![8]

Christchurch Priory

The First Phase

There was perhaps no restoration that Ferrey was better placed to carry out than that of Christchurch Priory. It had not only formed the view from his childhood home [4], but had been the subject of his archaeological research in *The Antiquities of the Priory of Christ-Church*, which he had published with Brayley in 1834. In many ways that book was itself an appeal for the restoration of the priory church, which had been in a 'dilapidated and unsightly condition' for centuries.[9] The ambition to restore was held by Ferrey and also by the dedicatee of *Antiquities*, the Earl of Malmesbury [**143**]: it was Lord Malmesbury who would invite Ferrey to draw up plans for the restoration of the priory in 1846. In October that same year, a public meeting was held in the town hall where Ferrey's plans were unveiled. It was noted at the same meeting that work had already begun. At this stage the restoration committee envisaged the reinstatement of a vault on the north porch, and the complete restoration of the medieval stone choir screen. One correspondent reported: 'the screen is miserably defaced, yet happily there still exists the faint outlines of its original beauty'.[10] Ferrey himself had noted its sorry condition in 1834. This element of the restoration would eventually attract a great deal of attention.

143 James Howard Harris, 3rd Earl of Malmesbury (1807–1889).

Some restoration work had previously taken place at Christchurch, including the construction of a rather convincing nave vault by William Garbett in 1819. Still, the power of the church's interior remained obscured by cumbersome Georgian galleries and furniture. The late fourteenth-century screen had had much of its carved work hacked away in the eighteenth century in order to accommodate pews which were built against it, and the organ that

144 An engraving based on Ferrey's 1831 watercolour of Christchurch Priory in Dorset, showing the box pews that obscured the medieval screen and the organ on top of it.

had been placed on it in 1788 was judged to be a great eyesore [**144**]. It is an amusing coincidence that the priory's organist happened to be Ferrey's brother, George, who had also been appointed Mayor of Christchurch in 1846. Thomas Talbot Bury, one of Ferrey's old classmates from Great Russell Street, produced two engravings around this time showing Ferrey's proposals for the restoration of the screen [**145**] and of the north porch [**146**]. One view looking east through the church showed 'the effect that would be produced by the removal of the Organ and the restoration of the Ancient Stone Screen', and work towards achieving this effect was soon underway. By October 1847 the organ had been removed, and the pews had been taken out.

It was not long before a critical letter appeared in the press, written from Winchester under the pseudonym 'Archæophilus'. Its author accused Lord Malmesbury of planning to demolish the stone screen, which was rather overambitiously judged to

ABOVE LEFT
145 Ferrey's proposed exposure and restoration of the stone screen of Christchurch Priory, engraved by Thomas Talbot Bury.

ABOVE
146 Ferrey's proposed vaulting of the north porch of Christchurch Priory, 1846, engraved by Thomas Talbot Bury.

be 'one of the finest monuments of the taste and skill of our forefathers that has yet been spared to us'.[11] Archæophilus went on to note that Ferrey himself had opposed the plan and refused to carry out the demolition.

Malmesbury, replying in January 1848, began reassuringly by claiming that he had 'never as yet moved in Committee any alterations excepting the removal of the pews and organ from the top of the screen'.[12] He however went on to say that Ferrey had never been appointed to execute the work so could not have refused his services, but that he had indeed been consulted on the question of demolition. Lord Malmesbury himself seems to have been the originator of the proposal: he noted that far from being a 'very fine monument' the screen was in fact an 'unsightly and mutilated wall'.[13] Its removal would not only save a good deal of money which Lord Malmesbury doubted could ever be raised another way, but it would also give much needed additional room for seating. He intended to forward his plan to the Bishop for his approval. This correspondence only served to confirm Archæophilus's worst fears.

The restoration committee met at the beginning of February 1848 to consider the question of the screen. A lengthy discussion followed, with a majority seemingly fixed on the demolition of the newly exposed screen. Having listened to the arguments, Ferrey rose to speak and put across an impassioned plea to preserve it. Rather than refer only to its historical significance, he pointed to its structural importance: by interfering with it, not only would the spatial effect of the church be ruined, but the remains of the crossing tower could potentially collapse (in pointing to the screen's structural importance, he unwittingly foreshadowed the collapse of Chichester Cathedral's spire in 1861). So strong was Ferrey's conviction that he offered a subscription of £20 (about £2,800 today) towards the restoration of the screen and offered to waive his fees as architect. It was enough to convince the committee to revise their intentions and agree to the screen's preservation and restoration.

Ferrey's proposals were accepted fully, and by the end of the year the screen had been restored according to his scheme. As it appears today, the carved work dates almost entirely from 1848, based on those fragments that remained. Still, having expended a great deal of energy in securing funding, the committee stopped the restoration short of the north porch; that would have to wait for another decade.

The Second Phase

Ten years after Ferrey's restoration of Christchurch Priory was complete, it had become clear that a second phase was necessary. The first restoration of 1846–48 had hardly made it beyond the screen, and the fact remained that the structure of the church was in a potentially perilous condition. Ferrey surveyed the site and produced a report on the condition of the building. In it he noted that the exterior stonework was in such poor condition that any delay in addressing it could prove disastrous. There were cosmetic repairs to be considered in the suggested replacement of pinnacles and other carved stonework, but Ferrey also found that there were three buttresses that needed complete rebuilding. Elsewhere, Norman walls were on the brink of collapse, and the timber roofs of the aisles had almost entirely rotted away. He suggested a course of action for the comprehensive repair of this decaying work, which was approved early in 1859.

By the end of 1860, as well as having tackled urgent structural work Ferrey had been able to clear the north transept of its Georgian galleries, carry out a restoration of the Norman arcade, and fill several windows with stained glass. During work on the north transept, Ferrey discovered an apsidal Norman crypt crammed with over two thousand bones. More discoveries were to follow. On inspecting St Michael's Loft, a curious room above the Lady Chapel, Ferrey noticed a series of holes in the plaster. These holes had traditionally been explained, somewhat absurdly, as having been made for hooks on which Cromwell's soldiers would hang the saddles of their horses. Upon inspecting the holes in good light, Ferrey spotted the outline of a thirteenth-century window drawn between them. This, he realised, was the medieval master mason's design for a window; upon comparing the measurements of this drawing to a filled-in window in the south aisle, Ferrey realised that it was the design for this lost window, and was thus able to recreate it.

Ferrey was also afforded the opportunity to realise his 1846 plans for the north porch [146, **147**]. The vaulting that he placed there is striking. The earlier design was only slightly amended by an uncharacteristic touch of polychromy: instead of leaving the stone vault undecorated, Ferrey faced it with bands of white and green stone. Despite this progress, work once again stopped short of completion owing to a lack of funds. Christchurch was not a wealthy parish.

Just a few years later, 'by the exercise of great energy and proportionate self-denial',[14] its new curate, Zachary Nash, managed to collect a further £3,000 (about

147 The north porch of Christchurch Priory, vaulted by Ferrey.

£500,000 today) towards the restoration. By the beginning of 1864 work was able to recommence on replacing the flat timber roofs of the transepts and crossing lantern. Although still overseeing this restoration, Ferrey was noticeably less involved in this phase. Nash had taken on the running of the priory in the absence of its infirm incumbent, and as such sat as the chairman of the restoration committee. He was efficient and effective in this role, but would unfortunately re-ignite the old controversy surrounding the chancel screen.

In October 1865 Ferrey received an anxious letter from Lord Malmesbury relating the events of a meeting of the restoration committee. The meeting had been called to consider the ongoing work at the priory and to discuss the progress of public subscription towards it. After a brief discussion of those points, Nash and two other members unexpectedly proposed that the choir screen should be demolished. It was, in Malmesbury's estimation, a tactic to catch their opponents off guard; a revival of the old controversy had certainly not been anticipated. Nash argued that the screen ruined the appearance of the interior and that it made the celebration of Holy Communion near impossible. Ferrey replied immediately to

Malmesbury's letter, to express his 'very decided opinions'. He rehearsed the same arguments – namely, that removing the screen would harm the appearance of the church and destroy its archaeological integrity. He also repeated his warning about the screen's structural significance: 'I believe that the screen as now built into the piers of the centre tower does afford strength to the piers and arches, and could not be removed without some risk'.[15] This was an even starker warning now that the removal of a stone screen had caused the collapse of Chichester Cathedral's tower four years earlier. Scott joined his voice to Ferrey's to protest the proposed demolition; he was well placed to do so, having at the time been engaged on reconstructing Chichester's crumpled tower.

It was an ironic turn of events that Lord Malmesbury found himself leading a campaign to preserve the screen, having himself called for its demolition years earlier. After spending a month gathering support, in the national press he published a letter that he had written to Nash. There he outlined Nash's arguments and countered them one by one, assisted by Ferrey's letter. 'In 1847', he wrote, 'this subject was thoroughly discussed … eminent architects were consulted' and the decision was taken on several grounds not to demolish the screen. Subsequently 'the screen was admirably restored by means of a subscription of £600 (over £100,000 today) … seventeen years after this decision and outlay on the part of the subscribers, many of whom are still living, you propose to demolish their work'.[16]

Malmesbury had made himself quite clear in his very public 'protest against playing with our ancient monuments in this capricious manner'.[17] It was a bold act of open warfare designed to encourage public outrage, and in that it was successful. Within days of the publication of Malmesbury's letter, Nash had been inundated with correspondence objecting strongly to his intentions. Groups like the RIBA and the Society of Antiquaries wrote to express their opposition to the plan. Perhaps unsurprisingly, Nash's hopes for the demolition went no further.

In 1866 correspondents from *The Ecclesiologist* visited Christchurch Priory to inspect Ferrey's work. They were seemingly impressed by much of what they saw. The amount of medieval work that Ferrey had retained, like the choir stalls, was pleasing, and they were particularly complimentary about his 'splendid vaulted … porch'.[18] Ferrey's work on the screen, however, was denounced as a 'tame reproduction' and one which, while interesting from an archaeological perspective, was, in the absence of a 'people's altar', thought inconvenient for the celebration of Holy Communion.[19] Nash may have found some satisfaction from this vindication which came from an unexpected quarter. Still, their impression of Ferrey's restoration was overwhelmingly positive.

By the 1870s Ferrey's restoration had been more or less seen through to completion [**148**]. It was for him one of his proudest. To have spent so much of his youth in the shadow of the priory, and then to return to oversee its restoration, was a fitting testament to his close personal attachment to the building. In restoring the church that first awakened his love of Gothic architecture he was able, in some measure, to bring his work as an architect full circle.

OPPOSITE
148 Christchurch Priory.

St Mary Magdalene, Taunton, Somerset

Ferrey had been engaged at St Mary Magdalene since 1842. On his arrival in 1840 the vicar, the Rev. James Cottle, found the building in what he described as a 'most dangerous and dilapidated condition'. He went on to add that 'it was quite evident that unless something should be speedily done, divine service could not be conducted in it with safety to the congregation'.[20] With the backing of his ratepayers, Cottle appointed Ferrey to oversee the much-needed restoration.

Ferrey's task was twofold: to secure the church's structure, and to refashion its interior in accordance with the rising tide of ecclesiological reform. Cottle, evidently proud of the result, produced a handsome volume giving an account of the restoration. His narrative reveals a sense of the strong resistance he faced from many of his parishioners, especially regarding the removal of the box pews. The system of rented pews had long been condemned as being incompatible with the egalitarian principles that had gained traction within both the Church and wider society. The Incorporated Church Building Society had been founded in 1818 with the primary motivation of providing 'free' seating to churches. Ferrey regularly applied to the ICBS for funding, and indeed applied to them for his work at Taunton.

Two contrasting drawings published by Cottle of the church before and after the restoration give a good impression of Ferrey's work at Taunton, and indeed more generally what he was capable of as a restoration architect [**149**, **150**]. The rented

149, **150** St Mary Magdalene, Taunton, Somerset, before and after Ferrey and Scott's restoration of 1857–62.

box pews, which in Cottle's estimation provoked 'unchristian tempers',[21] were replaced by low uniform benches. Some medieval character was thus reintroduced to the church, and new sightlines were opened up, not least between the vicar and his parishioners who had previously been afforded 'every facility for irreverent behaviour … and all kinds of improprieties … behind the curtain of a high pew'.[22] The restoration in 1842 and the years that followed thus represented the triumph of the principles of the Victorian Church over what many saw as the complacent and class-bound parish religion of the previous century.

Ferrey contributed a chapter on Somerset's medieval church towers to Cottle's 1845 volume on the restoration of St Mary Magdalene. In it he observed that 'amongst the many admirable towers of the county … none was more justly admired than the splendid tower of St Mary's Church, Taunton'.[23] Indeed the tower, untouched during Ferrey's restoration in the 1840s, was a consummate example of a Perpendicular Somerset tower. Built between 1488 and 1514 and rising to a height of 136 feet crowned with finely pierced tracery parapets, it was long held to be among the finest parish towers in the country.

Despite Ferrey's earlier work at Taunton, it soon became apparent that the tower, too, was in an advanced state of structural decay. Rather than employ Ferrey once again, the parish initially turned to a local architect, Charles Edward Giles, who proposed strengthening the tower with buttresses. Beginning at the north-west corner, Giles set to work before quickly discovering that the sandstone of the tower was too weak to support the work. Sensing that he was running into potentially catastrophic trouble, Giles appealed to George Gilbert Scott, who was widely regarded as 'the most eminent authority in the kingdom on such matters'.[24] Scott, in turn, enlisted the help of Ferrey.

Their joint report was published in *The Builder* early in 1857. In it Scott and Ferrey presented two alternatives: the first was to stabilise the existing tower by reinforcing its base with cement and stone; the second, more radical, option was to proceed with a complete demolition and attempt a 'perfect reconstruction'.[25] In the end, the latter course prevailed. Demolition was completed within just three months, and the foundation stone for the new tower was laid in 1858 amidst a grand Masonic procession and ceremony.

Four years later, Scott and Ferrey's work at Taunton was brought to completion [**151**]. The construction itself had been carried out by Henry Davis, who was simultaneously engaged on Ferrey's church at Buckland St Mary. Public reception was enthusiastic, and a grand day of celebration marked the completion, concluding with a display of fireworks launched from the tower. It would however be remiss not to note a regrettable epilogue to the story of the work at Taunton. Just four years after completion, Ferrey was called back to address signs of subsidence, this time in the newly rebuilt tower. It was only through a concerted effort, and no small degree of persuasion, that he and Scott managed to dissuade a vestry meeting from embarking upon yet another demolition. One might sympathise, not without reason, with Taunton's more indignant parishioners on this occasion.

151 The tower of St Mary Magdalene, Taunton, completely rebuilt by Ferrey and Scott in 1857–61.

Wells Cathedral – the West Front

Ferrey would remain in post as the Diocesan Architect for Bath and Wells until his death. In practice, most of the work executed as part of this role involved the construction or restoration of parish churches in the Diocese. However, as we have seen, Ferrey had already carried out substantial restoration work during the 1840s on the interior of Wells Cathedral itself, and had extended the Bishop's Palace there from 1846. His work was however not yet over.

In 1868 attention was drawn to the famous west front of the building [**152**]. A canopy had fallen. The Dean, fearing for his cathedral, immediately had a scaffold constructed and summoned Ferrey to examine the stability of the buttresses. Ferrey duly produced a report in which he noted 'much decay … in almost every portion of the splendid façade'.[26] It was a façade that Ferrey called 'the finest in England'; he continued, 'it is the glory of this city; of Somerset, and of the west'.[27] Its restoration was therefore imperative.

In August 1869 a committee chaired by the Earl of Cork met to consider restoration. Ferrey's report was read, and a worrying account of the west front's condition was given therein. The report noted defective masonry and crumbling statues which could at any time fall to the ground. Regarding the latter, Ferrey suggested the immediate removal of those that were in danger of disintegrating, and replacing only those that were of particular interest or of which the features could be easily discerned. He estimated that the full restoration of the west front would cost £5,000 (about £770,000 today). For another £1,000 (about £155,000)

152 Wells Cathedral's west front before restoration, engraved after a somewhat idealised drawing by Charles Robert Cockerell.

attention could be given to the chapter house, which he suggested needed interior work, reroofing, and new windows.

When the committee next met, the resolution was passed that they would seek a second opinion from Scott. A sum of £5,800 (about £900,000) had already been raised, but before Ferrey's proposals were to be accepted the committee sought to double-check the accuracy of his report. It might not seem an unusual course of action, but Scott's response was somewhat defensive. He wrote in reply that having spoken frequently with Ferrey about the west front, he found that he disagreed with him on no point of the proposed restoration; moreover, 'having already engaged as your architect a man of eminence and experience I should not like to appear in any prominent position in reference to a work known to be in his hands excepting as a friendly referee or a second opinion'.[28] The committee found this response disappointing, not least since it seems they would have liked to have Scott appointed to the job. They wrote back to Scott, alerting him to the fact that although Ferrey had been consulted in his capacity as Diocesan Architect, it was ultimately for the committee to decide who was appointed to oversee the works. Scott, having conferred with Ferrey personally, arranged to visit the cathedral with him on 16 November to consider the restoration of the west front and the chapter house. In his report Scott went into a great amount of detail and was at pains to point out how his opinions corresponded with what Ferrey had already suggested. In reality their approach was slightly different. Whereas Ferrey had suggested the replacement of a handful of statues, Scott insisted that they all should be retained, repaired, or, only if absolutely necessary, faithfully replaced. Scott also suggested that the chapter house needed only the slightest amount of work. It was a principle of 'reparation, protection, and preservation' that Scott insisted on, 'rather than entire restoration'.[29]

Scott's detailed report reveals his astonishing ability in the field: it reads as the reflections of a clear, experienced, and astute restoration architect. It also reveals the strength of his friendship with Ferrey. Sensing that the committee might be seeking to promote him over his friend, Scott filled his report with more praise of the 'excellent architect Mr Ferrey'.[30] He did not intend to usurp Ferrey, especially not on his home turf.

Scott's and Ferrey's reports were both accepted by the committee, and Ferrey was tasked with finding a suitable clerk of works for the west front. Almost a year had passed since the committee had first met, and Ferrey had finally been given permission to begin work on the central portion of the west front. A scaffold was erected, and a clerk of works was found who had just finished work at Salisbury Cathedral under Scott. Defective stonework was to be replaced like-for-like, using the original Blue Lias rather than the Doulting stone that had been used experimentally during minor restoration work in 1842.[31] Work was underway, and yet the committee remained determined to consult Scott at almost every juncture. He responded rather sternly in June 1870 to another request from the committee that he inspect Ferrey's work, writing that 'the time for such consultations … has now passed'. Ferrey, he noted, was 'the proper and the most competent judge of how to carry out the principles on which he and I were so closely in agreement and which he was definitely appointed to carry into effect'; his continued involvement would, Scott thought, be 'an undue interference with the duties and responsibilities of your official architect'.[32]

Ferrey may well have been embarrassed by this constant undermining of his authority, but in reality he appears to have actively wanted Scott's input on the restoration. Having already sent his rebuttal to the committee, Scott revised this refusal at Ferrey's own request. His visit in September 1870 must have been somewhat uncomfortable. Scott was repeatedly asked questions as to whether Ferrey's work was up to scratch, to which he gave one-word answers: 'Yes'. Ferrey revealed in a letter, published after Scott's death, that the committee had been desperate to engage Scott's services as they believed that his name, associated with several major restorations, would attract wide attention and therefore financial contributions. It was however galling for Ferrey to see the restoration of Wells Cathedral in Scott's list of works in one obituary in 1878, and he felt it 'due both to [Scott's] memory and my own position' to set the record straight in a letter of correction.[33]

Either way, the nerves of the committee had evidently been settled by Scott's unequivocal endorsement of Ferrey: following Scott's visit, Ferrey was permitted to continue with his work uninterrupted. By the summer of 1871 much of the central portion of the west front had been conserved. Purbeck marble columns had been replaced, buttresses strengthened, and decayed carvings carefully replicated. The question of preserving the statues was now under consideration. Ferrey brought a series of photographs to a meeting at Lord Cork's London residence in May 1871. These photographs are extremely evocative: not only do they show the statues up close for the first time ever, but they afford glimpses of the somewhat alarming wooden scaffold [**153**, **154**]. The photographs were released commercially and received widespread critical acclaim; Ruskin bought several sets for himself and for donation to 'schools of art'.

Ferrey suggested that only the statues that were in perilous condition should be replaced, at a cost of about £500 (about £80,000 today). Otherwise, his stonemasons were to exercise the utmost caution in renewing decayed sections of otherwise intact statues. Several benefactions were duly made for the repair or replacement of those statues, including £100 (about £16,000) from Lord Cork for the repair of the figure of Christ at the top of the west front.

Ferrey's work progressed happily, and at a public meeting in October 1872 he was able to present a report of the ongoing restoration. Work continued steadily, and by the summer of 1873 the majority of the statues had been preserved. Attention was finally then given to the lowering of the ground level at the north corner of the west front. At the beginning of 1874 Ferrey reported that the restoration was nearing completion. The committee did not meet again.

This was to be the final stage of Ferrey's revival of Wells Cathedral, and his last major restoration. He was by now slowing down in his work as an architect. The much-anticipated proposals for the chapter house went unrealised, but Ferrey

153, 154 Two of an acclaimed series of photographs taken during the restoration work on the west front, showing the statue of Bishop Duduc of Wells surrounded by scaffolding, and Robert of Normandy and Fulk of Anjou.

had nevertheless achieved a great deal during this second phase at Wells. For the first time in centuries, the west front seemed 'complete'. Where weathering had undone the effect of the thirteenth-century carvings Ferrey had carefully recreated their effect. It might have been tempting to replace eroded statues, but they were retained, preserving some appearance of the façade's antiquity. It was the most ambitious demonstration of Ferrey's later approach to restoration, honed over almost four decades of practice: archaeological conservatism.

Parish Church Restorations

Ferrey began restoring medieval parish churches during the 1840s. In many ways he had been thrown in at the deep end at Wells: when he was given superintendence of the proposed restorations there in 1842, he had never restored another church of any description, certainly not a cathedral. It should be said that a very faint question mark remains over this claim. The list of projects published with Ferrey's obituary in *The Builder* provides a series of problems, not least in its several omissions. Among the churches listed are several restorations that seemingly never took place, at least not under Ferrey's supervision: Charlton Mackrell may be one example (see p. 134), and Ackworth in Yorkshire is another. Meanwhile other difficulties arose in the form of insecurely dated restorations. St Mary at Tyneham in Dorset is possibly the most problematic, in respect of a local assertion that the south transept was built by Ferrey in 1832. This seems impossibly early. A more sensible suggestion is made by Pevsner, who dates the restoration to some time before 1852. Still, the proximity of Tyneham to Christchurch and the relatively naïve execution of the new transept means that an earlier date cannot be entirely discounted, perhaps one that predates his work at Wells. Surely, though, it is not as early as 1832.

Putting the question of Tyneham to one side, Ferrey's earliest parish church restorations date from the mid-1840s. Ferrey had inspected the Chapel of St Catherine in Abbotsbury around 1841 and had produced some notes on its architectural history. It seems though that he stopped short of actually restoring it, again despite its appearance in the aforementioned troublesome list of works. Ferrey was actively engaging with the archaeological study of medieval church architecture which in turn informed his own architectural practice (at East Grafton in the case of Abbotsbury). In 1845 Ferrey began work on several restorations. His restoration of the parish church of Chilton Foliat in Wiltshire is a good example of the sort of work that he was carrying out [**155**]. There, he put in a new east window and added a spacious south aisle with angels carved into its stone cornice. The nave

155 The restored interior of St Mary, Chilton Foliat, Wiltshire (1845).

was reordered, with its box pews removed in favour of open benches. A wooden pulpit was put up to Ferrey's design, accessed directly from the vestry. It was an extensive restoration, and one which has given the interior all the appearance of a Victorian church.

Ferrey's restorations often followed a similar pattern. The main motivation of the incumbents who commissioned them was generally to increase seating capacity. This was primarily achieved by replacing rented box pews with 'free' seating and tacking aisles onto existing naves. Chancels too were often the focus of restorations, since in those days incumbents were traditionally responsible for the upkeep of that part of the church. Ferrey's restoration of the chancel at Holy Trinity, Nuffield, in Oxfordshire around 1845 is one typical early example of his approach. The fabric of the walls was substantially retained along with some medieval tiles, but the windows were rebuilt, the walls were recovered, and the roof replaced so that it appears almost as new.

Another example in Oxfordshire is St Botolph's in Swyncombe – one of Ferrey's most sensitive and pleasing restorations. St Botolph's is a remote church with a substantial amount of early Norman work preserved. It had already been restored in 1831 when the chancel arch (now obscured by Walter Tapper's rood screen) was widened. Much however remained to be done, and Ferrey, having been commissioned in 1850 to continue restoration work, gave back to the building some of the character that it had lost over time. The cumbersome south porch was replaced by a more modest structure, and the tracery of some of the nave windows was replaced. However, it was in restoring the apsidal east end that Ferrey excelled. Its integrity had been much harmed by the insertion of square-headed windows in the place of small round-headed Norman originals. Using one original window which survived in the north wall of the chancel, Ferrey inserted two others to match it, restoring the chancel to how it would have looked when it was first built. During the process, Ferrey also uncovered traces of wall paintings – these were duly reinstated with a scheme taken directly from what had been revealed of the original. The painted chancel, with its starry canopy, is entirely convincing – a pleasingly 'conservative' restoration [**156**].

This restoration practice continued rather sporadically through the 1840s and 50s. When he had gained experience in cathedral restoration, several large and important churches came his way, including Ottery St Mary in Devon, a church which has been described as Exeter Cathedral in miniature. There, Ferrey worked under the close supervision of the Bristol Architectural Society. He cleared away the west gallery, removed partitions that separated the transepts from the chancel, and rebuilt the roof in English oak. This restoration was complete in 1848. Further ambitious work was undertaken in his role as Diocesan Architect soon after. From 1851 Ferrey was employed at Castle Cary in Somerset, where he lengthened the nave by a bay, built a new transept, reordered the chancel, and rebuilt the tower. This restoration, which took four years to complete, also saw the interior substantially remodelled, with the addition of new pews, Minton tiles, and carved stonework on

OPPOSITE
156 The apse of St Botolph, Swyncombe, Oxfordshire, with its original fenestration restored and its wall paintings renewed in 1850.

the east wall which Ferrey would call a reredos. Despite all these interventions, he was judged to have 'studiously preserved the characteristics of the old church'.[34]

Not all of Ferrey's work fell into this rather conventional category. His restoration of St Mary at Funtington in Sussex in 1858 almost amounts to a rebuild [**157**]. However, just enough of the medieval fabric was retained to consider it a restoration; the tower, north arcade, and south chapels were preserved. It was in building a new chancel that Ferrey expended most of his creative energy [**158**], and did so in an uncharacteristically eccentric way. A peculiar arcade with clustered marble shafts runs the whole length of it, opening the north and south chapels. On its east wall, the chancel is decorated with the same form of 'reredos' of stone arches that he employed at Castle Cary and elsewhere. Above it sits the east window of three lancets, accentuated with yet more marble shafts. All these arches of different proportions, thrown together in such a small space, create a sense of overwhelming dizziness. Outside, Ferrey set the east window into a cavernous arched recess, a curious and seemingly inexplicable arrangement. It is so unlike the archaeologically-concerned work that one meets with elsewhere, and yet it is not

157 St Mary, Funtington, restored by Ferrey in 1858 in a somewhat eccentric way.

158 The chancel of St Mary, Funtington, Sussex, 1858.

entirely without its charm. At Funtington Ferrey's hand appears to be developing in a 'roguish' direction, a style in which other architects would build with great panache and energy. The restoration is so convincingly eccentric that Ian Nairn somewhat overzealously attributed it to Samuel Sanders Teulon. Yet it was not a wholesale departure from what Ferrey had built elsewhere, merely a development in an unknown direction. It is interesting to consider what might have been had Ferrey pursued this development further. Might he have considered joining the ranks of those practitioners of a freer form of Gothic, amongst whom were fellow Low Churchmen with Huguenot ancestry like Teulon and Robert Lewis Roumieu, and indeed his own cousin-in-law, Joseph Peacock (see pp. 193–4)?

Ten years earlier, around the time when Ferrey's restoration practice was gathering steam, George Gilbert Scott was working on a paper which he would deliver before the Buckinghamshire Architectural and Archaeological Society. This was in time expanded and published in 1850 as *A Plea for the Faithful Restoration of our Ancient Churches*. Having sensed some public support for destructive restorations in which caprice had triumphed over conservation, Scott called for a sensitive approach, urging respect for the individual character of churches. This went beyond the popular ambition to restore churches to how they might have looked before the Reformation, towards an approach that preserved good post-Reformation work. It was an ambition that would be expressed more radically in later decades by the anti-restoration movement. Scott was of course a great friend of Ferrey, and the two of them had travelled through Italy together in 1851. In 1853, having been employed to rebuild Doncaster Parish Church, a church Ferrey had previously furnished, Scott fought unsuccessfully to have Ferrey appointed as joint architect. In turn Ferrey suggested Scott's name to the committee which appointed him to restore Lichfield Cathedral in 1855. The two friends would come to work together on a number of restorations, including at Taunton in 1857 [151]. They also worked together at Martock in 1860 [**159**] and Warmington in 1876 [163]. Unsurprisingly, these all represent suitably 'conservative' restorations.

In 1862 Ferrey received a typical commission for the restoration of a village church. The church in question was St Denis at Stoke-sub-Hamdon in Somerset, which has since been re-dedicated to St Mary the Virgin. This restoration is worth noting since its enterprising incumbent published some of Ferrey's initial correspondence in *The Ecclesiologist*. Ferrey begins with a flattering assessment of the building, writing that he had 'seldom met with a more interesting parish church' or one with a more satisfying diversity of medieval styles. What follows is a revealing explanation of his intentions in restoring the church:

159 All Saints, Martock, Somerset, jointly restored by Ferrey and Scott in 1860.

> Such a building is deserving of the greatest care, and on removing the various modern obstructions, I should observe the greatest possible caution in renewing any of the ornamental features which have been ruthlessly hacked away. Happily there is nothing of a conjectural kind needing to be replaced, as there is ample evidence of the form of every feature which has been destroyed.[35]

The restoration at Stoke-sub-Hamdon did indeed turn out to be conservative.

By the mid-1860s the amount of work Ferrey undertook as a restoration architect was beginning to match the amount he undertook as the architect of new churches. The restorations followed a pattern that had by now been tested many times. Often he was mainly brought in to build new aisles for growing congregations, as at the Surrey churches of St Nicholas at Thames Ditton in 1864 and St Mary the Virgin

160 St Mary, Wingham, Kent, after restoration.

at Merton in 1866. New and fertile territory for restoration was opened in Wales through the patronage of Sir Watkin Williams-Wynn, for whom Ferrey had been working on Wynnstay from 1859 (see pp. 180–1). These Welsh restorations largely took place in the early 1870s and were often less satisfying than their English equivalents. At St Cedwyn in Llangedwyn Ferrey practically rebuilt the medieval church, which had already been subjected to a Romanesque restoration by Thomas Penson in the 1840s. The effect of Ferrey's somewhat pedestrian restoration there was in turn greatly altered by the addition of dormer windows during the first decade of the twentieth century.

By the 1870s Ferrey's son Edmund had become heavily involved in many of his father's restorations. During these years several chancels were rebuilt rather straightforwardly, including those of two churches in Somerset: St Luke at Brislington in 1874 and Holy Cross at Babcary a year later. These may well have been executed alost entirely by Edmund. Another restoration of 1874, at St Mary, Wingham, in Kent [**160**] displays some of the same eccentric flair that was experimented with at Funtington. Ferrey replaced a circular Georgian east window with a large Decorated window with rather peculiar tracery; the chancel arch was rebuilt, its seventeenth-century screen removed, and all of the Georgian furniture of the nave discarded. Images of the interior before the restoration show quite how drastic Ferrey reorderings could be [**161**].

161 St Mary, Wingham, before restoration, with a circular window and tall Georgian Tables of the Law at the east.

Although the vast majority of Ferrey's work concerned the restoration of medieval churches, there were a handful of occasions when he was called on to alter more modern buildings. At Highcliffe in Dorset, near his native Christchurch, Ferrey enlarged St Mark's Church which had been built in 1842 perhaps with some of his own input. In 1873 at St Mary the Virgin at Bransgore in Hampshire Ferrey added a chancel to an especially basic brick Commissioners' church. Of more interest is his restoration in 1871 of St George's, Hanover Square, in London, a church built in 1721–24 [**162**]. Ferrey, who lest we forget worshipped at a Classical church, wisely did not think to impose Gothic details on St George's. Rather he took aim at the furnishings, cutting down the height of the box pews and removing their doors. He also took away the pulpit canopy and reduced the

162 St George, Hanover Square, London. In 1871 Ferrey lowered the box pews and removed the canopy of the pulpit of John James's church of the 1720s.

double-decker reading desk by half. It was hardly a restoration – rather, a Victorian rationalisation of eighteenth-century church furnishings.

By the end of the 1870s the restoration of ancient churches had become a subject of intense public controversy. An anti-restoration movement had begun to form around William Morris, whose campaign was rapidly taken up by the likes of Ruskin, Edward Burne-Jones, William Holman Hunt and Thomas Carlyle. Their campaign would result in the foundation of the Society for the Protection of Ancient Buildings, or the 'anti-scrape' movement, as Morris himself referred to it. Scott, having been such a vocal supporter of the movement to restore medieval churches, received a significant amount of criticism from this newly-formed group. Ferrey, who had 'scraped' a significant number of ancient churches, would also be embroiled in the polemics that issued from Morris's campaigners. At a meeting of the RIBA in 1877, the Scottish architect J. J. Stevenson launched an attack on Scott, suggesting that an 1865 paper entitled *Conservation of Ancient Monument and Remains – General Advice to the Promoters of the Restoration of Ancient Buildings* had both justified and led directly to the destruction of many post-Reformation church interiors. Ferrey was present at that meeting and publicly supported Scott, not least since Stevenson's tirade also by implication denounced his own restorations. He rose to insist that Scott should be given a right of reply, which he duly was.

163 St Mary, Warmington, restored by Ferrey and Scott in 1876 – Ferrey's last restoration.

Ferrey and Scott were taken aback by such a direct attack on the principles of restoration which they had both developed during their long careers. The two men however had lived long enough to see their architectural philosophies become the target of outrage and attack. Whether it was the result of old age or changing tides in popular thought, Ferrey would not carry out any substantial restorations after the attacks of the anti-restoration movement were launched. His final major restoration was of St Mary the Blessed Virgin at Warmington in Northamptonshire, work in which he was joined by Scott [**163**]. With Warmington restored, the old order finally changed.

CHAPTER 7

Other Buildings

OPPOSITE
Detail of Figure 191.

Ferrey was first and foremost an ecclesiastical architect. Churches consumed almost all his energy and attention, and after his death he was remembered almost solely as a church architect. This is neither a surprising reflection of his career nor is it an inaccurate one. Nevertheless, Ferrey cut his teeth designing a series of public buildings, and he would cultivate a lucrative country house practice in later life. That aspect of Ferrey's career will be considered in this chapter, alongside the other secular buildings he worked on, many of which might struggle to be placed in a category of their own.

Ferrey's earliest surviving sketchbook is packed with drawings of domestic rather than ecclesiastical architecture. These were sketches made in the early 1830s when he was finding his feet as an architect in London. The most significant design he was working on during that period was his Tudor proposal for the new Palace of Westminster, but in the absence of that lost scheme we can only speculate how the buildings he recorded in his sketchbooks might have inspired him that competition entry. Still, Ferrey would be afforded several opportunities to build in Tudor style in the years that immediately followed.

164 Ferrey's Tudor gatehouse at Baynards Park in Surrey.

One of his first commissions after Bournemouth came from the Rev. Thomas Thurlow, son of the Bishop of Durham and nephew of the Lord Chancellor. In 1832 Thurlow bought Baynards Park in Surrey and immediately set about modernising the late Tudor brick house there. For this, the services of Thomas Rickman and Ferrey were called upon, probably at some point in the early 1830s. It is difficult to discern precisely what the division of labour might have been between the two architects, but it seems that Rickman was naturally given the bulk of the work and Ferrey took on whatever was left, including the gatehouse nearest the house [**164**]. Rickman may well have had a small input in its design, but Ferrey by all accounts had free reign here. It is a perfectly convincing attempt at a Tudor gatehouse. Built of brick and enriched with diapering and stone dressings, it consciously avoids a symmetrical arrangement, with an off-centre carriageway and oriel window above; the Tudor royal arms are rather whimsically incorporated in the oriel – a nod to a visit from Henry VIII. Elsewhere, tiny quatrefoil windows admit light to a projecting staircase turret. The variety and execution of the fenestration is delightful. The whole building is playful and rewarding.

It is possible that Ferrey had been preparing for this commission as early as 1833, when his sketchbook records several visits to Athelhampton. One sketch shows the gatehouse there, which had been built in the 1550s (it was to be demolished in 1862), and it is clear that Ferrey's gatehouse at Baynards represents a close reworking of that model. The use of brick rather than stone and the generous lower-storey window at Baynards give the design an additional elegance, but details like the battlemented oriel and the unusual projecting staircase are lifted directly from Athelhampton. Ferrey's careful drawings of 1833 might suggest a much earlier date for the gatehouse at Baynards than has been supposed.[1]

Tudor was to become Ferrey's style of choice during the earliest years of his practice. In 1838 he had designed a rather pedestrian Tudor stable block for Robert Williams at Bridehead [**165**], the interest of which lies not in its own quality but in the other buildings that would follow it. As we have seen, Williams [42] had been pleased with Ferrey's work there and would engage him again several times; after Williams's death his son [92] would do the same. Williams had served as MP for Dorchester from 1812, and having handed his parliamentary seat to his son in 1835, he was able to concentrate his efforts on regenerating the town. In 1839 he gave land in Back West Street for the foundation of a Dorset County Hospital, and advertisements were duly put out inviting suitable designs. One Mr Malpas of Frome was initially awarded the commission, but Ferrey, having heard of Williams's

165 Ferrey's 1838 stable block on the Bridehead estate at Littlebredy in Dorset.

166 Ferrey's proposal for the Dorset County Hospital, 1839.

project, submitted his own plans which were recognised as being far preferable and more economical than those of poor Malpas. Ferrey had proposed a symmetrical building of Portland stone on an E-plan [**166**]. It bore all the outward appearance of an Elizabethan house, with a Middle-Pointed chapel forming its south wing. By March 1841 the first phase of work was complete; it would continue in two more phases, one from 1844 and another in 1859, so that by the end of that year the whole hospital was complete. Its *Buildings of England* entry suggests that Ferrey's Elizabethan hospital was really running 'away from the design problem. It was not the solution Pugin was at that moment formulating.'[2]

Whereas Pugin's ideal 'Catholic town' was entirely Gothic, Ferrey approached the design of public buildings less dogmatically: a hospital could be Tudor, but its chapel would still quite naturally be Gothic. Newman and Pevsner point to the hospital's visual similarity to Loseley Park. It was Sir George More of Loseley who built the old brick house at Baynards, and it is no doubt more than a mere coincidence that Ferrey should have looked to Loseley when designing the hospital.

In 1862 a young Thomas Hardy set off to London with a letter of introduction in his pocket. Before pursuing literary work, Hardy had been articled to John Hicks, who had become Dorchester's town architect. It was Hicks who wrote the letter of introduction and addressed it to Ferrey. The exact course of events is not clear, but the letter did not have the intended effect. Ferrey's son Edmund had joined the practice that year, and it is likely that Ferrey had no space to accommodate another pupil. John Norton, a former pupil of Ferrey's, would instead give Hardy a desk in his office, perhaps at his former master's suggestion. Within very little time Hardy had found work as a draughtsman for Arthur Blomfield, the architect son of Bishop Blomfield.

Ferrey's work in Dorchester would come to form the backdrop of Hardy's Casterbridge. He rebuilt All Saints Church from 1843 in partnership with Arthur

167 The Dorchester Corn Exchange, built by Ferrey in 1847, with a clock tower added in 1864.

Acland [200], who was serving as the first chairman of the hospital committee. Hardy would later criticise Ferrey's remodelling of the town. In 1910, on receiving the freedom of Dorchester, Hardy condemned Ferrey for demolishing the old All Saints, and in no uncertain terms: 'a milder-mannered man never scuttled a sacred edifice',[3] he said. Either way, Ferrey's Corn Exchange [**167**], still in a rather free Tudor in 1847, would become the Corn Exchange in *Far from the Madding Crowd* and *The Mayor of Casterbridge*. Its eccentric corner clock tower, which boldly juts outwards and upwards, was added later in 1864. Ten years after that, Ferrey would leave his final mark on the town when Holy Trinity Church was completed in 1875–76 [120].

So much of what Ferrey and his contemporaries would work on was essentially moralising architecture. For some, like Pugin, this was expressed outwardly through the use of correct Gothic forms. Ferrey was less concerned with expressing morality through style in his secular architecture, but a significant proportion of his work was inherently concerned with social improvement. Projects like St Stephen, Rochester Row, provide the best evidence for this concern, but another example can be observed in the continued endowment and construction of almshouses. Ferrey received his first commission for almshouses in 1842, from Susan, 10th Baroness North.[4] Her

168 The almshouses at Kirtling, Cambridgeshire, built by Ferrey for Susan, 10th Baroness North, in memory of her sister, the Marchioness of Bute, 1842.

169 The Market Cross at Glastonbury in Somerset, designed by Ferrey in 1846.

sister had been the first wife of Lord Bute, for whom Ferrey had been working at East Hyde. The Marchioness of Bute died in 1841 as work progressed on Ferrey's church at East Hyde, and her sister sought to commemorate her by endowing six houses for the poor of the village of Kirtling in Cambridgeshire. Lord Bute recommended Ferrey to his sister-in-law, and by the end of the year the almshouses had been built – a small, low brick building with a gabled central doorway [**168**]. It was an arrangement suggested by seventeenth-century examples, especially the Pemberton Almshouses in St Albans and the Tregonwell Almshouses in Milton Abbas.

It has been suggested that Ferrey also had a hand in the almshouses built in Dorking in 1847–48. These also bear a strong resemblance to seventeenth-century brick examples, but they are on a much larger scale. At Scott's suggestion, Ferrey was also invited to judge the competition to build a set of almshouses in Faversham in 1860. Ferrey selected four entrants, out of which he favoured the proposal of two little-known Kent architects, Robert Wheeler and John Marshall Hooker; they would build a relatively Ruskinian brick affair with a monumental stone chapel tacked on to it – not quite what Ferrey himself might have built. It was in 1868 that he made his final foray into the genre, at Shepton Mallet in Somerset, with a tall heavily gabled building in dark coursed rubble.

Other than almshouses, Ferrey received commissions for a number of other 'miscellaneous' projects as his career progressed. In 1846 he designed a market cross at Glastonbury [**169**]. There had been a medieval cross on the site, a covered octagonal structure with clustered pillars arranged around a central column, but it had fallen into disrepair and was eventually demolished in 1808. Thomas Porch of Edgarley Park, who owned Glastonbury Abbey, commissioned Ferrey to replace it almost forty years later. Ferrey instinctively looked to the Eleanor Crosses built by Edward I between 1291 and 1295, a prototype for scores of Victorian imitations: three years earlier, Scott had erected one of the most prodigious tributes in his Martyrs' Memorial at Oxford, inspired by the Eleanor Cross at Waltham Cross. But Ferrey's Glastonbury cross was informed much more heavily by the early sixteenth-century Fountain of the Croix-de-Pierre in Rouen, which he had seen during his 1825 tour with A. C. Pugin. Drawing on this precedent (with a degree of restraint and indeed imagination), Ferrey designed a satisfying and elegant market cross, the only such structure within his body of work.

In 1850 another atypical commission came Ferrey's way. In July that year Prince Adolphus, Duke of Cambridge, died at the age of seventy-six. Apart from his sister, Princess Mary, Adolphus was the last surviving child of George III, who had spent much of his reign at Kew Palace. In 1806 the King had given Adolphus a house on the west side of Kew Green, which later became known as Cambridge Cottage. The Duke expressed a wish to be buried in St Anne's Church, an early eighteenth-century building very near the house, and shortly after his death in 1850 Ferrey received the commission to build a mausoleum for him there. It was his first royal commission. Quite how he came to be appointed is not entirely clear. By 1850 he had developed a reputation as a capable architect with an easy manner. It is perhaps worth noting that Angela Burdett-Coutts was a close friend and correspondent of Prince George, the Duke of Cambridge's eldest son. Was Ferrey's ongoing work at Rochester Row part of the reason why he received the commission at Kew? We might also remember the interest that the Duke of Cambridge's sister-in-law, the Queen Dowager, took in Ferrey's work both for Angela Burdett-Coutts and at for the Curzons at Penn Street.

Whatever the explanation, Ferrey set about designing a mausoleum to be built onto the east end of the church [**170**]. It is conspicuous among Ferrey's work as an unapologetically Classical building. Built in a style matching the eighteenth-century brick church (but now attached to the chancel rebuilt in 1884), the mausoleum is a small semi-circular building with Italianate stone niches running round its exterior wall. It is covered by a half dome, its lead roof decorated with ornamental bands, in turn surmounted by a cross; in its basic outline it is vaguely reminiscent of Bramante's Tempietto in Rome. Ferrey was present at the small ceremony which saw the Duke of Cambridge's remains transferred from their temporary position in the church into the mausoleum. As a fully-fledged Classical building it stands alone in Ferrey's œuvre, and yet it is not wholly unexpected. Ferrey's training under Wilkins had grounded him in the Classical style; he worshipped in a Classical church, and lived in a Classical house. His obituarist would later observe:

> Mr. Ferrey, though originally brought up in a Gothic school, and known as one of the early workers in the Gothic Revival, was never bigoted as regards the Classic

170 The Cambridge Mausoleum, added onto the east end of St Anne, Kew, in 1850, Ferrey's only work in a consciously Classical style.

> styles, with which his pencil was always quite familiar. He never took the strong line that Sir Gilbert Scott did in that respect, though he undoubtedly preferred Medieval architecture, with which he was more at home.[5]

Ferrey would also be asked to work on a mausoleum in 1859 at Maulden in Bedfordshire, but the Cambridge mausoleum remains the most interesting of his smaller buildings.

Another building concerned with memorialisation was being erected from 1848 by Frederick, Lord Dufferin [**171**] – a tall lookout tower situated on a hill in his Irish estate, Clandeboye. The architect employed there was the Scottish Baronial Revivalist William Burn. Unusually, the recipient of this architectural tribute was very much alive when it was built – Dufferin's mother, Helen. Helen was the granddaughter of the playwright Richard Brinsley Sheridan, and she and her two sisters had been hailed as the 'Three Graces' of London society. She was beautiful, cultured, and charming. Her son, by now starting out on a diplomatic career which would eventually lead to the viceregal throne of India, was utterly devoted to her. Their relationship went far beyond the usual bonds of attachment between a mother and her child. Such was Dufferin's all-consuming filial love for Helen that he built 'Helen's Tower' as a monument to her during her lifetime. Ferrey had already decorated

171 Frederick Hamilton-Temple-Blackwood, 1st Marquess of Dufferin and Ava (1826–1902).

172 The interior of Helen's Tower at Clandeboye in Northern Ireland, 1848.

a back room of Dufferin's London house on Grosvenor Square in the 'style of Edward IV',[6] and the interiors of Helen's Tower with rich panelling and wooden vaulting are almost certainly his work too [**172**].

It is unclear when Ferrey and Dufferin first met, but both men were certainly present at a tea party hosted by Ruskin in Venice in 1851. Much of Ferrey's work for Dufferin is dated, somewhat insecurely, to the period about ten years after that meeting, but the decoration of Helen's Tower is probably somewhat earlier than the rest. Ferrey had made proposals in the 1850s to remodel Clandeboye in the style of a French chateau, but Dufferin's vision for the house constantly changed, and nothing came of Ferrey's plans. Still, he was eventually engaged at Clandeboye to build a railway station and a bridge at the edge of the estate towards the end of the decade. The whole complex was executed in Dufferin's favoured style, Scots Baronial, and was finished by 1862. The station with its crow-stepped gables must be one of the most remarkable in Ireland [**173**]. The railway bridge, a solid construction framed by turrets, marks the private entrance to Clandeboye [**174**]. A path runs through an arch adorned with Dufferin's arms, and down a three-mile avenue towards the house. This was to be Ferrey's sole attempt at railway architecture.

Only two of Dufferin's commissions were seen through to completion. One was the station and bridge; the other, conceived around the same time, was the

173 Helen's Bay Railway Station at Clandeboye, opened in 1865.

construction of a gatehouse and walls for Killyleagh Castle [**175**]. The ownership of the gatehouse had been the subject of an ancient quarrel with Dufferin's cousins, the Hamiltons, which, much to his own delight, Dufferin had resolved by requesting an annual homage from them: the family would on alternate years give him a golden rose and a spur. As Dufferin's biographer Andrew Gailey points out, it was 'pure [Walter] Scott'.[7] Dufferin's romantic imagination was expressed once again by Ferrey in the Scottish Baronial style. The gatehouse with its battlements and soaring turret boldly proclaims its own strength, and the enclosing walls with corner towers copied from the castle lend the whole arrangement an air of fantastical romance. One of Dufferin's Hamilton cousins wrote to him on first seeing Ferrey's work and described it as 'out of a page of romance'.[8]

174 The bridge at Helen's Bay, its arch signalling the private entrance to Clandeboye, 1862. One of the crowstepped gables of the station is just visible at the far right.

175 The gatehouse and walls at Killyleagh Castle in Northern Ireland.

Schools and Rectories

An architect building a new church was often expected to build a rectory and a school to accompany it. In some instances only the rectory was required, in others only the school, and often only the church would rise, for lack of funds. Ferrey followed this church, school, rectory pattern on several occasions, most notably at St Stephen, Rochester Row, but his work in this regard was often piecemeal. He would regularly be asked to design a rectory or school without being responsible for the church.

Ferrey's schools have suffered more than any other type of his work. He designed more than twenty-five, mostly in the Tudor style, but they are generally unlisted, many more are unattributed, and a majority have been demolished. St John's, Angell Town, in south London, offers a representative example of a larger building of this kind [**176**]. Erected in 1853, it followed an L-shaped plan with broad stone-mullioned windows; its ornament was confined, rather effectively, to stone quoins. Much smaller schools adopted a plainer approach. St Mark's in Battersea Rise, built in 1866 also in South London, is typical of these: modest in scale, well-proportioned, and unassuming.

There were also schools less easily classified, where Ferrey employed loosely conceived Gothic motifs with

176 The schoolhouse of St John, Angell Town, in London, 1853 (now apartments).

177 Oakhill Church School, Somerset.

a degree of freedom unusual in his other work. The school at Buckland St Mary, although never formally attributed to him, is almost certainly his work; its design unites a Tudor outline with stray Gothic details, here the unconventional elliptical window at the east end. Oakhill Church School in Somerset, of uncertain date, represents one of the most successful examples of this hybrid type [**177**]. It comprises two principal wings: one in a Tudor manner, with quoined windows, and the school hall attached to it with an unusual projecting gable filled with a large arched window, most of which is taken up by plate tracery. At the top is a circular window below which sit three shouldered-arch windows.

Ferrey worked in this unusual style once again in 1858 at the National Schools at Esher in Surrey [**178**], where he was also responsible for the adjacent church. The patron was Prince Leopold, later King of the Belgians, with his niece Queen Victoria taking an active interest in the project. It is perhaps Ferrey's most engaging

178 The National Schools at Esher, Surrey, 1858.

and certainly his most idiosyncratic educational building. It is built on a large scale, with provision for infants, boys, and girls, and Ferrey reprised the use of a striking variety of windows – lancets, trefoils and circles. The roof is enlivened with bands of red and brown tiles laid in fishscale patterns. What makes the Esher Schools of particular interest are the many gables of varying heights and proportions. The porch of the infants' school rises so steeply that it terminates scarcely seven feet from the ground. The adjoining schoolhouse, a modest, cottage-like building, employs the same vocabulary of mixed window forms and prominent gabling. Ferrey seems to have drawn repeatedly on this group of motifs in designing school buildings. In 1868 at Chetwynd, a building closer in scale to a modest rectory, he used the familiar banded tiles and varied windows once more, though with greater restraint than at Esher. Even within the limited scope of parochial school design Ferrey managed to introduce variety and a sense of character to his buildings. This makes the loss of so many of his schools all the more regrettable.

Ferrey's designs for rectories tell a similar story. By the late 1840s he had settled into a comfortable standard pattern: compact Tudor houses, gabled and modest, often arranged on an L-plan. The rectory at Tarrant Hinton in Dorset however is a good example of his earlier style. Built of brick, it comprises a single block in the Tudor idiom, its chief visual interest being derived from two slender gabled dormers that recall the proportions of those of his stable block at Bridehead [165]. There has been uncertainty as to the date of this rectory, with some suggestions being as late as 1850. Surely though it must date from the earliest years of his practice, probably around 1836. It belongs to the same family of brick rectories as that at Hedgerley [**179**], where Ferrey would design the church in 1852. The rectory

179 The Old Rectory at Hedgerley in Buckinghamshire, 1846. Its authorship is uncertain, but it bears many of Ferrey's hallmarks. (The splendid Gothick conservatory was added in 1994 by Eric Throssell for the owner of the house and author of this book's Foreword, Lucinda Lambton.)

180 The rectory at Maiden Newton in Dorset, designed in 1842.

there, dated 1846, cannot be assigned to him with certainty, but it bears several hallmarks of his manner – the brick diapering, the firm and grounded proportions, and the overall sense of solidity.

There are, of course, outliers. Perhaps the most significant of these is one of Ferrey's earliest rectories, Maiden Newton in Dorset [**180**]. This he designed in 1842 and it is one of his first substantial attempts at the form. Otherwise unattributed and little known, it is an ambitious building: an impressively large rectory, remarkably convincing in its appearance – a grand sixteenth-century stone building. A drawing in Ferrey's sketchbook of what he called the 'ancient rectory' before his intervention suggests that much of the earlier building may survive with Ferrey's work [**181**]; if not, his replacement was an incredibly close replica. The south range of the original building, that Ferrey sketched, had a wing added to it, forming an L shape. From the north the whole building perches happily at the top of a lawn, and bears all the appearance of a small Oxford college.

181 Ferrey's sketch of the 'ancient rectory' at Maiden Newton.

By the 1850s Ferrey's rectories had begun to exhibit more nuanced footprints, moving away from blockier forms. The one at Penn Street in Buckinghamshire, completed in 1850 at a cost of £7,000 (about £1.2 million today), was a smaller vicarage and an incredibly charming example at that [**182**]. The chief interest of this building – now demolished – lay in a gabled wing that projected very subtly to the right of the front elevation.

182 The vicarage at Penn Street in Buckinghamshire, completed in 1850 (now demolished).

Here, the Gothic fenestration was purer and included a rather unusual septfoil light at attic level. It was a vicarage modelled on a more Puginian plan, but alas still with a certain degree of Georgian formality in the placement of its windows.

183 The clergy house at Romsey, Hampshire, 1855 – one of Ferrey's finest houses.

Pugin's influence appears more directly in Ferrey's vicarage for Mentmore in Buckinghamshire, built in 1851, the year before Paxton's Mentmore Towers would rise. This three-storey vicarage, constructed of dark brown ironstone, returns to the use of large square-headed mullioned windows. It evokes, if only vaguely, Pugin's house at Ramsgate, which Ferrey had visited and sketched from beyond a wall [82]. Yet Mentmore still lacks the all-important Puginian quality of having been designed from the interior outward. That principle becomes more evident in 1855, in Ferrey's clergy house at Romsey in Hampshire [**183**], where the function of the house's interior is expressed in its exterior. The asymmetrical entrance front, set away from the main road, is a delight. It is a sophisticated composition, with Gothic fenestration varying from trefoiled lancets, including a charming gradated set of three high in the gable, to a long traceried staircase window beside the recessed entrance porch. Here the exterior speaks unmistakably of the interior's arrangement and purpose. In the garden Ferrey fashioned a rather playful folly in the form of a ruin of a church; what would the anti-restorationists have made of such frippery? Romsey must be the finest vicarage designed by Ferrey.

The Country House Practice

While Ferrey may have by and large stuck to tried and tested Puginian models when designing rectories, in his country houses he experimented with styles that were otherwise left untouched.

His introduction to building country houses came at the very beginning of the 1840s. His first identifiable large house is Clyffe House, which he built in the village of Tincleton in Dorset for Charles Porter in 1842 [**184**]. Porter's biography is somewhat obscure; either way, it seems that it was his work on the nearby Dorset County Hospital that brought Ferrey to Tincleton. Porter engaged him from 1840 to build a schoolhouse, a church, and a country house. The school was the first to be built, then the church in 1849. When Ferrey came to build Porter's house, he was still looking to Elizabethan houses for inspiration: as Loseley had been a significant model for the Dorset County Hospital, so it was also for Clyffe. Porter's house is built to resemble an Elizabethan manor house, of which Ferrey had studied several in Dorset; Kingston Maurward was one particular model, many-gabled and based on an H-plan. Clyffe House is built in brick, with some occasional diapering that here looks incongruous. In the entrance front Ferrey deviated slightly from the plan and attempted to create some rhythmic interest. The two-storey porch is flanked by two projecting gabled wings which are joined to the main building by angled bays. The whole façade is thus given an interesting sense of 'folding in'.

If Tincleton was Ferrey's first attempt at building a country house, his earliest work in the field had come slightly earlier, courtesy of Robert Williams of Bridehead at Littlebredy in Dorset. Williams's father, a London banker, had bought the estate in 1797 but his primary seat was in Hertfordshire, so Bridehead received little attention during his lifetime. It was his son, Ferrey's patron, who would begin substantially altering the estate when he inherited in 1814. Eventually in 1830 he engaged Peter Frederick Robinson to remodel both the house and the estate village. Robinson had been strongly inspired by Uvedale Price's theories, which sought to analyse the sources of beauty within a landscape. In outlining his ideal landscape, Price gave an apt description of Robinson's ambition for Bridehead. It was a landscape of 'green meadows with fat cattle; canals or navigable rivers; well fenced, well

184 Clyffe House in Tincleton, Dorset, 1842, Ferrey's first large house.

cultivated fields; neat, clean, scattered cottages; a humble antique church, with churchyard elms, and crossing hedge-rows, all seen under bright skies'.[9]

Robinson rebuilt the old house between 1831 and 1833 in a picturesque Tudor style, 'of excruciating awkwardness' according to Pevsner.[10] A survey of Bridehead and Littlebredy made by Acland in 1836 showed the extent of Robinson's work: the crenellated house sat happily in a large pleasure garden with waterfalls and ornamental cottages beyond. Having designed a stable block for Bridehead in 1838 [165], Ferrey was engaged to extend the house westward, which he did in collaboration with Acland, perhaps slightly earlier than the '*c.* 1850' date previously suggested. Outside, the substantial extension is, at Williams's behest, indistinguishable from Robinson's work. Ferrey may have wished to build more boldly, but his instructions were clear.

It was in designing the interior that Ferrey expended most of his creative energy. The library and a large corridor which runs the width of the house are the two finest elements of Ferrey's interior [**185**, **186**]. The corridor is panelled in a beautifully coloured oak, with Puginian bookcases that continue on into the library, centred on a grand Perpendicular fireplace formed of an ogee arch; even its grate, supported by flying buttresses and pierced with quatrefoils, is delightfully stylised. The library bookcases are decorated with foliage pateras which are found elsewhere, in those instances executed in papier maché: Ferrey modelled these pateras directly from A. C. Pugin's *Gothic Ornaments*, published in 1831 alongside Ferrey and Pugin's *Ornamental Gables* [**187**, **188**].

185, **186** The library and a corridor running the width of the house at Bridehead, introduced by Ferrey.

187, **188** A papier maché patera from Bridehead and the source from which it was copied – A. C. Pugin's *Gothic Ornaments*.

Ferrey continued to receive a steady stream of commissions for the remodelling of existing houses. He had apparently prepared a scheme for some minor work on Lord Bute's house at Luton Hoo in 1840, and he had also worked on the Bishop's Palace at Wells in 1846. However, he would build relatively few new houses until the end of the 1850s. His first major commission did not come until 1858, when he was brought in by Sir Watkin Williams-Wynn, 6th Baronet [**189**], to rebuild his seat at Wynnstay. Like Robert Williams, Sir Watkin was a Tory MP, holding the seat of Denbighshire from 1841 until his death in 1885.

The story runs that at some point in the 1850s Sir Watkin was travelling by rail when he fell into conversation with a gentleman in his carriage. Sir Watkin's large Classical house had been reworked several times by his father, and he had been considering extensions to it; this was evidently the topic of conversation in that train carriage. At some point, Sir Watkin's companion revealed himself to be an architect: Benjamin Ferrey, no less. By the end of their conversation, Ferrey and Sir Watkin had agreed to correspond further, and Ferrey was duly employed at Wynnstay around 1855 to make alterations to the house and create a new picture gallery. Ferrey would subsequently encourage his pupils always to travel first class!

189 Sir Watkin Williams-Wynn, 6th Baronet (1820–1885).

A disaster was soon to occur. In the early hours of 5 March 1858, a fire tore through Wynnstay, destroying most of its contents, and that same day Ferrey received a frantic telegram requesting his immediate presence. He duly set off to North Wales. On arrival he found the old house reduced to a shell; it had to be rebuilt from scratch. Before he had been given a chance to make any suggestions, Ferrey was told by Sir Watkin that he wanted his new house to be built in the French style – unknown territory for Ferrey.

Work began almost immediately, and went on until 1861; the interior was still being decorated in 1865. Ferrey had embarked for France almost immediately after the fire and his sketchbook shows that he visited several chateaus, no doubt to gain inspiration for the work he was about to undertake for Sir Watkin. His sketchbook records visits to Villandry [**190**], Chenonceau, and Amboise. What Ferrey eventually designed was a large house 'in the Henri III style, with the influence of Ancy-le-Franc much in evidence' [**191**].[11] It is dominated by a huge tower with a two-storey bow window, under which is a porte cochère. This opens immediately to the great hall, which Mark Girouard described as 'enormous, barren, [and] coarsely decorated',[12] with a coffered ceiling, organ gallery, and an incredibly flamboyant chimneypiece – surely not a product of Ferrey's imagination. Scale was the primary motivation here and throughout. The low wings are punctuated by pavilion towers, much shorter than the central tower,

LEFT
190 Ferrey's sketch of the château of Villandry, made in preparation for his work at Wynnstay during a tour of France in 1858.

BELOW
191 Wynnstay, in North Wales, 1858–61.

one at a corner and another sandwiched into a wing. This seems to be an idea suggested (and then much developed) from Villandry. The visual effect of Wynnstay is much to do with the severity of mansard roofs of those towers, quite in contrast to the low roofs of the rest of the house. At the time the French domestic style in England – a style which would take off during the 1870s – was often much more formal and devoid of the asymmetry that Ferrey introduced at Wynnstay.

There is a slight possibility that Ferrey designed a French Renaissance conservatory at Orwell Park in Suffolk in 1854, which is unattributed but appears in his sketchbook [**192**]. There was also an unrealised plan to build a 'French chateau' at Clandeboye, but Wynnstay stands rather conspicuously as Ferrey's only executed attempt at the style.

While he was building Wynnstay, Ferrey received a commission from the 12th Duke of Somerset to rebuild his country house, Bulstrode, near Gerrards Cross in Buckinghamshire. This commission seemingly came through Lord Dufferin, for whom Ferrey had been working at Clandeboye. His mother, Helen, was the older sister of Somerset's wife, Jane Sheridan, one of the 'three beautiful Sheridan girls'.[13]

The original house at Bulstrode had been built in 1686 for the infamous Judge Jeffreys and in due course was sold to the Dukes of Portland. They commissioned alterations from Stiff Leadbetter in the 1740s, and from James Wyatt in the first decade of the nineteenth century. The estate was then sold in 1811 to the 11th Duke of Somerset. In 1860, five years after inheriting the dukedom, Edward Adolphus

192 Orwell Park with its French Renaissance conservatory, a drawing in Ferrey's sketchbook, 1854.

193 Ferrey's sketch of Bulstrode before his own interventions, showing Wyatt's ruined gatehouse at the centre.

Seymour, the 12th Duke, demolished the house, retaining only Wyatt's monumental gatehouse, of which Ferrey imagined a full reconstruction in his sketchbook [**193**]. The commission was given to Ferrey in 1861 as his work at Wynnstay was drawing to a close, and he set to work immediately.

The Duke of Somerset was an easier patron than Sir Watkin Williams-Wynn had been: his request was simply for a house that spoke to the estate's history. In 1861 Ferrey published a rather far-fetched romantic history of Bulstrode in *The Builder*, full of Saxons, Normans, Roundheads, and Cavaliers. The resulting building, which Ferrey described as being 'designed in the old English manorial character',[14] is perhaps the most imaginative of his country houses. At its core is a gabled red brick Tudor-style house, the sort of rather pedestrian house he was building in the early 1840s, but at Bulstrode the elevations are enlivened with varied and gripping architectural punctuation [**194**].

194 Bulstrode Park, Buckinghamshire, 1860–62, from the south.

195 The entrance front of Bulstrode Park.

The entrance front, facing a sweeping courtyard, has a large tower jutting forward with a pyramid roof; with its two-storey oriel, it has a hint of Wynnstay about it [**195**]. The west elevation [194] looks out toward Wyatt's fragmentary gatehouse. At the south-west corner Ferrey placed a slender polygonal turret which thrusts upward, capped with a sharply pointed roof. It is this turret that gives Bulstrode its distinctive outline. The central portion of the south garden elevation is set back behind an integral veranda which is supported by adventurous barleytwist columns in pairs [**196**] – almost a parody of the cloister of St John Lateran in Rome. This

196 The veranda of Bulstrode Park.

197 The staircase hall of Bulstrode Park with its barleytwist columns.

idea is carried through to the interior, where the columns run along the landing in groups of four, holding up an unusual half-vaulted, half-domed ceiling [**197**]. The effect is bizarre.

Bulstrode has suffered an unfortunate fate. Even by the end of the nineteenth century most of Ferrey's interiors had been replaced by F. C. Eden's Classical interiors. The estate was inherited by a daughter of the 12th Duke; her son in turn sold the estate in 1932 but kept the house. On his death in 1958 Bulstrode was sold to a religious sect, and it has since been in the hands of several commercial owners. At the time of writing Bulstrode is once more on the market, with no buyer seemingly forthcoming, continuing to decay.

Churchmead House at Datchet in Buckinghamshire is a smaller country house which is worthy of briefly being mentioned, not least since it has remained misattributed for over a century. Precisely when it was built is uncertain, but it must have been at some point between 1865, when the land was bought, and 1876, when the house appears on an Ordnance Survey map. Ferrey's client was William Good, a London barrister, who bought the site in order to have a country house within easy reach of the railway and thus London. William Good's father was Joseph Henry Good, a little-known London architect who had trained under Soane. Coincidentally, Joseph Good grew up in Sambrook in Shropshire where his father was rector of a church which Ferrey would rebuild in 1856.

Given the fact that William's brother was also reportedly an architect, it had been presumed that Churchmead must have been designed by a member of the family. However, it appears in a list of Ferrey's work, and on further inspection, close stylistic resemblances to other houses by Ferrey begin to appear. Churchmead was demolished in the 1950s, having become derelict after the War, but photographs

show it to have been a typical Tudor brick affair, with diapering, prominent gables, and mullioned windows. In scale it resembles a large rectory rather than a country house, but on the entrance front we see Ferrey's trademark tower porch with a pyramid roof and first-floor oriel window [**198**]. We might note, too, the patterned banding below the roofline achieved through depressed brickwork; Ferrey experimented with an identical pattern when building the rectory for St Paul's in Dorking [**199**]. Churchmead was, in essence, a country house in miniature.

Ferrey would work on a handful of larger country houses in the later 1860s–70s, including, from 1868, Huntsham Court in Devon. It was the house of Arthur Acland, a constant patron and indeed collaborator, from the very beginning of Ferrey's career [**200**]. Acland, who had married the daughter of Robert Williams of Bridehead and with whom Ferrey had worked at Dorchester, Bridehead, and Littlebredy, had inherited Huntsham in 1852 on the death of a distant relative, the Rev. Dr Edward Troyte. Troyte had spent much of his time hunting and cock fighting and had not given his estate much attention, so when Acland inherited Huntsham he found acres of overgrown land with a decaying Tudor house for good measure. The

198 Churchmead House at Datchet, Buckinghamshire, demolished in the 1950s.

199 Ferrey's rectory for St Paul, Dorking, Surrey, 1857, with brickwork matching that of Churchmead House.

only condition attached to his inheritance of the estate was the addition of 'Troyte' to his name. Acland had become a regular correspondent and friend of Ferrey's, so it was natural that when he was finally able to consider rebuilding the house he would turn to his old friend.

200 Arthur Acland, latterly Dyke-Troyte (1811–1857) – capable amateur architect and stonemason, and a steady patron and collaborator of Ferrey's.

This could only happen some sixteen years after Acland had inherited Huntsham. He had spent that time reordering the estate, tending diligently to his tenants, and rebuilding the parish church, a task which fell to Ferrey in 1854 with much input from Acland Troyte. The house that Ferrey designed for him was a Tudor creation which, although extremely competent, might well have been built several decades earlier [**201**]. It is a large house on an irregular plan with two projecting wings; on the entrance front Ferrey inserted a turret to ease a corner and add some intrigue – a well-tested formula that he used from Clyffe House through to Bulstrode. The impression remains of a conservative and somewhat forbidding house.

Huntsham's main point of interest may well be its kitchen: an octagonal structure set in a service court, this was based on the medieval Abbot's Kitchen at Glastonbury. It is a delightful bit of whimsy in an otherwise serious composition, but as a Victorian recreation of the Glastonbury kitchen it does not stand alone. Eight years earlier, in 1860, the Oxford Museum of Natural History had opened, housed in a fine Ruskinian brick building by Deane and Woodward. Ruskin had been heavily involved in its construction, and so too had Acland Troyte's brother, Henry Acland. Henry Acland was a fellow of Christ Church and a close friend of Ruskin,

201 Huntsham Court, Devon, 1868–70, as viewed from the tower of All Saints, Huntsham, a church rebuilt by Ferrey and Acland.

202 Bagshot Park, Surrey, 1877.

and it was he who had instigated and overseen the Oxford building project. Part of that project was to build a chemistry laboratory, which Acland insisted should be kept separate so that 'all noxious operations are removed from the principal pile'; the solution was to build a free-standing laboratory based on the Abbot's Kitchen. It cannot be a coincidence that Ferrey built a version of this distinctive model at Huntsham a few years later for Acland's brother.

Ferrey's most famous house, Bagshot Park in Surrey, was built in the final years of his life – indeed, it was the last building that he would work on [**202**]. The commission came from twenty-eight-year-old Prince Arthur, Duke of Connaught and Strathearn, the favourite child of Queen Victoria [**203**]. A marriage had recently been contracted for him to Louise Margaret, the daughter of Prince Friedrich Karl of Prussia, so Connaught was in need of a private residence. Ferrey by this point was well known to the royal family, having received the royal commission at Kew, and also possessing an attractive set of establishment credentials: the vice-presidentship of the RIBA and a recipient of its Gold Medal. However, it was his work at Bulstrode, just twenty miles from Bagshot, that would gain Prince Arthur's attention. He requested from Ferrey a grander version of what he had achieved at Bulstrode.

203 Prince Arthur, Duke of Connaught and Strathearn (1850–1942).

Having received the commission, Ferrey set to work drawing up plans in his tried and tested Tudor style. The house was to be built of brick on an irregular plan, with a central block flanked on the east by an extensive service wing. The first task was to demolish the old house, which had been built by Inigo Jones for Charles I but latterly much altered by James Paine and Soane. An article in an 1877 edition of *The Builder* suggested that the 'Lombardo Gothic' style had been considered, which might have made for an eccentric final flourish to Ferrey's career.[15]

Having supervised the demolition and selected a site for the new house, Ferrey suffered a stroke in October 1877 (the story of his declining health, culminating in his death in 1880, is told in full in the next chapter). As a result, he delegated much of the work at Bagshot to his son, Edmund, and spent the next few months resting in London. By the end of 1878 he was able to visit the site regularly, staying a few weeks at a time to oversee the works and to benefit from the bracing country air.

We might turn at this point to Ian Nairn's assessment of Bagshot, which has become the prevailing view of Ferrey's work there. In the *Buildings of England* guide for Surrey, Nairn wrote of Bagshot's 'Bad, purposeless ugliness'; it is a building, he continued, that is of a 'scarifyingly ugly brick-and-stone Tudor like a Bournemouth hotel. Either mid-Victorian heartiness had a shattering effect on the sensitive designer of buildings like St Stephen Rochester Row, or – to be more charitable – he left most of the designing to his son in old age.'[16]

Characteristically, Nairn shoots dead the elephant in the room. Bagshot is not a successful building. Ferrey had shown himself capable of an entertaining and spatially interesting form of 'mid-Victorian heartiness', but here it is all jumbled. The suggestion that Edmund might have been responsible for much of the design is rather plausible. The elements of a typical Ferrey entrance elevation are all there: the pyramid-topped tower with a two-storey oriel, the asymmetry, the mullioned windows with their quoins, but the effect is lost [**204**]. The asymmetry is jarring; the fenestration, especially in the westernmost gable, is clumsy; and the thrusting effect of the tower is negated by a veranda and porte cochère that disguise its verticality. It is telling that the latter, and a separate building to the west connected by a corridor, do not appear in Ferrey's original designs. There is however clumsiness elsewhere which is more difficult to account for. On the west front, which originally

204 The entrance front of Bagshot Park.

ABOVE
205 The Prince's Room in Bagshot Park.

ABOVE RIGHT
206 The saloon of Bagshot Park.

overlooked a tennis court, a large ecclesiastical-looking staircase window bears no relation to any other window and sits uncomfortably halfway up the wall.

The interior is formed on a rather basic plan, but with some enjoyable moments: the Prince's Room has an interesting fireplace set at an angle between two walls [**205**], and the hall, or saloon as it is named on plans, rises the whole height of the house and is lit from above but retains a sense of homeliness [**206**]. In these previously unpublished photographs, one can see the Duke of Connaught's furniture and collection sitting very comfortably in the house. They provide a real insight into the taste of Bagshot's owner, with glimpses of Zulu shields, busts of Prince Albert, and several old masters hanging on the walls.

The real issue with Bagshot is the way that it sprawls aimlessly and endlessly. The placement of the service wings, which have a larger footprint than the house itself, is regrettable. They give Bagshot the outward appearance of a provincial boarding school, or indeed 'a Bournemouth hotel'. These wings compete for attention with the house and block the view of its proportions at every angle. Without them, Bagshot would make much more sense as a well-formed country house. A youthful Ferrey would no doubt have avoided this problem.

207 Bagshot Park seen from the west.

Happily, though, Bagshot is the only one of Ferrey's major houses still to serve its original purpose [**207**]. Built for the son of Queen Victoria, it remains the family home of their Royal Highnesses the Duke and Duchess of Edinburgh.

AGED LXIX YEARS

CHAPTER 8

Personal Life

208 A chalk portrait of Benjamin Ferrey, made about 1860.

[**208**] In the absence of personal letters, files or journals we are left to study Ferrey's life largely through the buildings he designed. From the Italianate villas of the 1830s through the Romanesque experiments of the 1840s to the Ecclesiological churches of the 1850s and finally to the stylistically various country houses of the 1860s and 70s, an insight is gained into Ferrey's developing mind and his place in the history of nineteenth-century architecture. From the age of fifteen to the day of his death in 1880 he was immersed in the world of architecture.

It is however possible to reconstruct some aspects of his life from what few private papers do survive.

As we have seen, Ferrey's childhood was a happy one. He enjoyed a good education at Wimborne, and until the death of his mother in 1824 he was encouraged by two supportive parents. On entering Pugin's drawing school in London, Ferrey's fate was practically sealed: he was to become an architect. After his education, both with Pugin and under Wilkins, his career begun to gather steam. He published a book to critical acclaim, and threw himself headlong into the competition of rebuilding Parliament. Unlike his siblings, there was no question of his remaining in provincial Christchurch. He would keep at least one foot in London for the rest of his life.

The closest Ferrey came to returning to native territory is when he began work for Sir George Tapps-Gervis at Bournemouth in 1836. He took a house nearby to supervise the works, no further than five miles from his family home in Christchurch, and his father appears to have taken an active role in selling the villas on the Westover estate. It was by virtue of this work and the improved professional prospects which it heralded that Ferrey was able to take a wife that same year. On 30 April 1836 he married Ann Lucas at St Mary's, Islington, the church in which he had attended A. C. Pugin's funeral four years earlier.

Ann, the daughter of William and Sarah Lucas, was born in 1812 into a prosperous Quaker family at Stapleton Hall. Stapleton was a modest country house and remained the only house in rural Hornsey, north of London, as late as 1861, when the nearby suburb of Islington finally encroached on it. It had been bought by Ann's bachelor uncle Joseph, a successful merchant in the South Seas whaling industry and a keen investor in property and land. On Joseph's death the house passed to Ann's father, William, who in turn died in 1832. Ann's mother would die

OPPOSITE
Detail of Figure 210

shortly after in 1836, the same year that her daughter married Ferrey. It must have seemed a period of great personal change.

No portrait survives of Ann. The impression one gains is of an intelligent and affectionate wife who showed a great interest in her husband's work. She is known to have prepared the heraldic drawings for St Stephen, Rochester Row. Her only surviving letter offers a clear sense of her character. It was written during her courtship with Benjamin in 1835, less than a year before their marriage. Ann had been staying in Ramsgate with members of the Judkins family, who had contracted marriages with the Lucases over the course of two generations. She writes a long and amusing letter to her 'dearest Ben', who is planning to join her later in the week in order to visit Canterbury and Dover. Several sketches from that trip survive in Ferrey's sketchbook. In her letter Ann records how she had travelled to several towns on the Kent coast, including Margate ('a concentration of vulgarity') and Broadstairs. She liked the latter town very much, but went on to write: 'what annoys me most is that [Broadstairs] has a church with no "heaven pointing spire."' For 1835 this is a remarkable statement, and one which is worthy of more attention. 'Heaven-pointing spire' was a phrase used by Pugin in his 1841 *True Principles of Pointed or Christian Architecture*.[1] It became a common parlance thereafter, but it does not appear to have been published before then. The fact that Ann had placed that phrase in quotation marks suggests that she had heard it before. Was it some sort of mantra that Ferrey had picked up from Pugin? Whatever the true origin of that famous phrase, Ann's comments reveal an early interest in Gothic ecclesiastical architecture, an interest which is equally apparent in her account of a saga that saw her locked inside St Laurence's Church in Ramsgate. Ann had, according to her letter, wished to sketch the medieval church while her relatives visited Dover. She wrote:

> I set off for St Lawrence alone and went boldly to the sexton and asked for the key of the church and he told me he never let anybody have it. I remonstrated and he offered to accompany me and show me the church. I told him I wished to be there all morning and as there was a vestry meeting he would be there and let me out when I wished. After this was over he asked me how much longer I wished to stay. I told him till one o'clock. He locked me in and to my great annoyance did not come at the time appointed.

After frantically searching for a means of escape, she eventually found a door with a rusty lock which she managed to open. Having done so she discovered that she was once again trapped, this time in a locked churchyard surrounded by a high wall. More chaos ensued, including a vain attempt to seek help from local urchins. Mercifully Ann eventually caught sight of her 'jailer advancing' who she thought must have forgotten all about her!

The 1835 letter provides a tantalisingly brief portrait of its author. Ann was evidently a keen artist in her own right, and shared her husband's genuine interest in ecclesiastical architecture. Their marriage would form a familial connection between Ferrey and a much-underappreciated architect, Joseph Peacock. Elizabeth Lucas, Ann's paternal aunt, married John Peacock in 1815, and in 1822 she gave birth to Joseph, a cousin for Ann. He would in turn become a gifted Rogue Goth, most famous for the church of St Simon Zelotes in Chelsea.[2] It is curious that there should exist no further evidence of a friendship, but certain vague similarities might be observed between the work of the two men.

Ferrey's first child, a daughter, Alicia, was born in June 1838. Evidently it had come as a great joy after two years of marriage. Ferrey received a letter of congratulation from his brother-in-law, the surgeon Rudd Lucas, who said: 'great and manifold were the joyful palpitations of my heart when I learned from your infinitely welcome letter that the wife has been happily and comfortably blessed into mother'. The Lucases evidently had a predisposition for florid prose!

In 1840 and 1842 Ann gave birth to two more daughters, Ellen and Eleanor. Both were sickly babies: Ellen died shortly after her first birthday, and Eleanor shortly before her third. These were significant blows to the Ferreys, especially since both daughters had survived past the usual few days. Eleanor's death in January 1845 may have been part of Ferrey's motivation to move his family to Oxfordshire later that year. Buoyed by his appointment as Diocesan Architect for Bath and Wells and the extra work that brought in, Ferrey bought a large stuccoed house a mile from the centre of Henley-on-Thames. They moved there with their son Benjamin Edmund (who always went by his middle name), who had been born in June that year. His birth was a source of great joy for Ferrey: he had longed for a son to inherit his practice, which is eventually what Edmund did.

The seven years that the family spent in Henley were extremely happy. Ferrey, a keen fly fisherman, was finally able to enjoy his country pursuits, and Ann could raise her family in a spacious and unpolluted setting. During this happy period Ann gave birth to their final child, another daughter, Annie, in 1847. A year later, in 1848, Ferrey designed a new church in Henley: Holy Trinity, built of local flint for the new parish of Rotherfield Greys [**209**]. It is difficult to get an impression of Ferrey's church now, since it was encased by two long aisles, built rather carelessly in 1891. Only the nave and chancel are his. The profile of Ferrey's west end, with its two-tiered bellcote, is remarkably similar to St Paul's on the Island of St Helena [90], which he was designing around the same time. His cousin-in-law Joseph Peacock's church of St Simon Zelotes, which would be built in Chelsea a few years later, bears perhaps more than a passing resemblance to Holy Trinity's west end and quatrefoil clerestory. Ferrey's eldest daughter, Alicia, would marry Peacock's brother John in 1870.

Two months after the birth of Annie in 1847, Ferrey's father, Benjamin, died in Christchurch at the age of sixty-seven. While managing the draper's shop, Benjamin Sr had been becoming more and more involved in local affairs, having been appointed Mayor of Christchurch in 1840. It was the honour of his life, and he lived long enough to see his son George, the organist of Christchurch Priory, appointed to the same mayoral office in 1846. Ferrey had been carrying out his

209 Holy Trinity, Henley-on-Thames, designed in 1848, with two large aisles added in 1891.

restoration of the priory at the time of his father's death, so had been spending more time in his company. Eventually, in 1851, Ferrey was able to pay tribute to his father when he installed a window in the south aisle of the church in memory of him [**210**]; it shows scenes of the Entombment of Christ and the visit of the two Marys to the sepulchre on Easter morning.

Ferrey would move back to London in 1853. His practice had reached its zenith a few years earlier and commissions were still continuing to come in. Still, his financial situation was always more precarious than that of many of his contemporaries like Scott. Having his family home at a distance from London had affected his ability to oversee several projects, testified by the difficulties encountered in the final stages of St Stephen, Rochester Row. The Ferreys would eventually occupy 55 Inverness Terrace in Bayswater, a short distance from where Paddington Station opened in 1854.

Just before Ferrey's move back to London, his childhood friend Pugin had died at the age of forty in 1852. The relationship between the two men has been explored already throughout this book. Their friendship was formed as teenagers.

210 Benjamin Ferrey Sr's memorial window at Christchurch Priory.

Ferrey usually couldn't travel home to Christchurch for weekends, so he ended up spending much more time with Pugin than his other classmates. The friendship was genuine, but drifted after Pugin's conversion to Roman Catholicism. Ferrey's work for the committee which sought to reverse the result of the competition to rebuild Parliament probably led to a more permanent cooling of their friendship. Ferrey and Pugin seem to have met privately only once more, during a chance encounter at a railway station in 1844. Ferrey recalled that Pugin seemed agitated during that meeting, and only later learned that he had been rushing home to be with his dying wife. When Scott and Ferrey had attempted to set up their Architectural Museum and requested support from Pugin, just months away from death, the response revealed just how difficult and doctrinaire Pugin could sometimes be. He responded: 'In the present state of society and the total absence of anything like the faith and religious feeling that actuated men in past ages, I believe it is impossible to do much good.'[3]

Not having published a book since 1834, Ferrey suddenly decided to produce a biography of Pugin. Ironically, it would become Ferrey's best-known work. Its genesis is murky, so our main insight into Ferrey's motivations in writing the biography must be discerned from the text itself. In the preface Ferrey wrote of his decision to become Pugin's biographer, claiming that his own 'intimacy with [Pugin] commencing from boyhood' and the 'peculiar opportunities' he had of 'watching Pugin's whole career' made him uniquely well placed to make a record of his friend's life. He continued (writing about himself in the third person):

> The step now taken has been deferred from time to time under the impression that a more competent person might undertake the task; but at the desire of many friends he no longer hesitates, and the moment seems well-timed when a Public Memorial in honour of Pugin is under consideration. Anxious also that this Memoir should be faithful, as well as acceptable to the members of Pugin's family, and feeling that he could not describe Pugin's character from a Roman Catholic point of view, the Author has, at the request of Pugin's widow, admitted an Appendix written by a friend of the family.[4]

This revealed Ferrey's personal difficulty in his role as Pugin's biographer: he could not get to grips with his Roman Catholicism, which was so central to the life itself. Ferrey kept the subject at arm's length and commissioned Edward Sheridan Purcell to write an appendix dealing with Pugin's religion.

Ferrey's *Recollections of A. N. Welby Pugin, and his Father, Augustus Pugin* [**211**] was published in 1861 by Edward Stanford, whose publishing house was next door to Ferrey's offices in Trinity Place near Charing Cross. Cynically one might suggest that a large part of Ferrey's motivation in publishing the biography was financial: he saw a gap in the market and sought to fill it. While there is no doubt some element of truth in this, Ferrey also appears to have been driven by a genuine admiration for his subject. Gothic architecture might have had different connotations and purposes for the two men, but Ferrey was inherently a follower of Pugin. He wrote in total sincerity and 'without exaggeration [that] it may be fairly said that Pugin ranked among the most eminent Architects of the present or former days'.[5]

Ferrey's biography was on the whole well received at the time. As we have seen, some of his former classmates objected to the portrayal of Pugin's mother as a stern and overbearing disciplinarian, but it was nevertheless in the recollections of A. C. Pugin's drawing school that the book was at its most engaging. The rest of the biography was often in danger of meandering, and Ferrey was not ideally placed to write about Pugin's later life and work. There are also a number of errors,

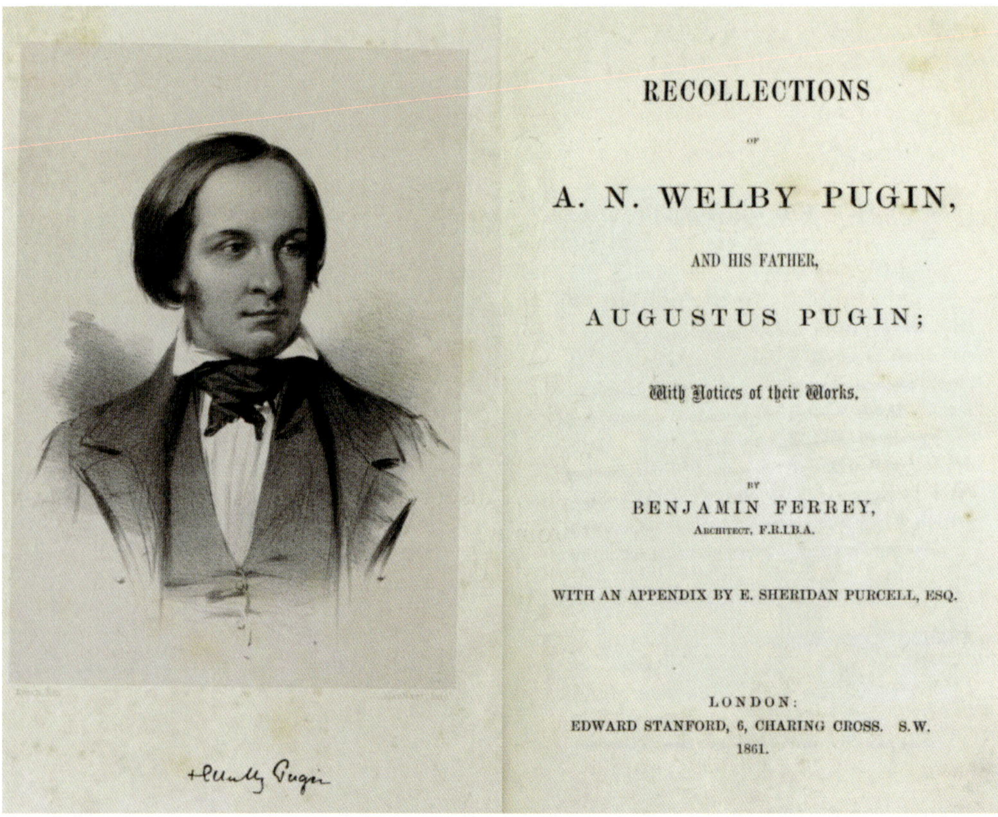
RECOLLECTIONS

OF

A. N. WELBY PUGIN,

AND HIS FATHER,

AUGUSTUS PUGIN;

With Notices of their Works.

BY

BENJAMIN FERREY,

ARCHITECT, F.R.I.B.A.

WITH AN APPENDIX BY E. SHERIDAN PURCELL, ESQ.

LONDON:

EDWARD STANFORD, 6, CHARING CROSS. S.W.

1861.

211 The title page of Ferrey's *Recollections of A .N. Welby Pugin, and his Father, Augustus Pugin* (1861).

the most conspicuous of which is the incorrect rendering of Pugin's forenames in the title: 'A. N. Welby' rather than 'A. Welby N.' Ferrey himself can probably be absolved for this error which was almost certainly introduced by an editor, since the incorrect appellation is not repeated elsewhere in the text. For all its flaws Ferrey's biography retains a genuine value in its first-hand recollections of Pugin's early years and in being the first sustained attempt to gather anecdotes, reflections and personal papers relating to him. If nothing else, it secured for Ferrey a lasting place in architectural history.

Ferrey would commit much time to his membership of several institutions, committees, and societies. In 1839 he had become one of the first fellows of the Royal Institute of British Architects, which had been founded two years earlier. It was probably through Phillip Hardwick, one of the RIBA's founder members, that he had become involved. Ferrey would go on to serve two terms as the Institute's vice-president, and was active in its meetings and debates. He regularly contributed papers, of which the following present a comprehensive list: 'Observations on Gothic Vaulting' (1840), 'A Letter, Relative to a Process Described by J. Sylvester, to Render Bricks and Stone Impervious to Moisture' (1843), 'Account of a Curious Double Staircase in the Church of St Editha Tamworth' (1843), 'Notes on the Life of C. Miles' (1849), 'Notes on Stamped or Incised Stucco' (1857), 'Remarks upon Works of Early Mediæval Architects: Gundolph Flambard, William of Sens &c.' (1864), and 'Observations on the West Front of Wells Cathedral' (1870). They show Ferrey's interests to be part antiquarian, part scientific – a rare combination.

In the same year that he was elected to a fellowship of the RIBA, Ferrey was involved in the foundation of the Oxford Architectural Society. This was the first society of its kind, specialising in the promotion of a 'correct' form of Gothic architecture, especially among clergymen. Ferrey was one of thirteen initial honorary members, among whom were a diverse range of antiquaries, dons, and artists, including the architects Anthony Salvin and Edward Blore and the stained-glass artist Thomas Willement, who would design glass for several of Ferrey's churches. Other active members included Robert Williams [92], whose father would give Ferrey some of his earliest commissions, and Thomas Mozley, who would become a key figure in the story of the collapse of the roof at East Grafton. Ferrey would make regular contributions at meetings.

We have also noted Ferrey's involvement, along with Scott, in the foundation in the 1850s of the Royal Architectural Museum. A member of the committee, he contributed several casts of statues from the west front of Wells Cathedral.

In 1870 Ferrey received the highest honour that could be afforded to him as an architect: the Royal Gold Medal. This was awarded annually by the RIBA on behalf of the Queen in recognition of an individual's contribution to architecture. Scott, Smirke, and Salvin had already been awarded it. When Ferrey was told that he had won, his response was oddly sombre: 'I am flattered by the commitment you have made to me in proposing the desire of the council that I should be the recipient of the gold medal this year', but he continued: 'it has however come to my knowledge that opposition may be raised by some members at the final meeting.' Ferrey was not eager to refuse the medal, but he ended his letter with a plea that another recipient might be found who would gain unanimous approval. He revealed something of his selflessness when he wrote: 'I value greatly the honour which the Council has conferred upon me, but I value still more all that can tend to the prosperity and peaceful working of the Institute.'[6] Quite what that opposition might have been is unclear. Ferrey admittedly was still clinging on unfashionably to the Gothic forms of his youth; perhaps he feared a reaction from the new modern school of Gothicists. Still, he was duly and happily awarded the Gold Medal seemingly without the opposition which he so feared.

Benjamin Edmund, Ferrey's only son, was by this point well embarked on his own architectural career. He had been articled to his father between 1862 and 1867, during which time he assisted with the steady stream of restorations coming through the practice. Ferrey would later ask Scott to take Edmund on for a year, and he eventually entered Scott's office in 1869. Edmund's own career was notably less successful than his father's – he would occasionally take on work of his own, but in the 1870s he was mostly engaged in working on behalf of his father, whose health began to fail. It is often difficult to discern quite what was designed by who in the later buildings. Edmund's son, Cuthbert, recalled how his father had once told him that 'it was taken for granted that he should follow in the footsteps of his father, Benjamin, and that he was given no choice'; he suggested that his father was 'a struggling architect without much talent and no influence'.[7] That may seem a cruel assessment, but it probably reflects something of Edmund's indifference to his own career. Upon his father's death in 1880, he applied to succeed him as Diocesan Architect for Bath and Wells. This application was unsuccessful, but he continued to carry out occasional restorations in the diocese. One such restoration, which Cuthbert suggested had been won by Ferrey shortly before his death, was for St Nicholas, Kittisford. During a visit to the remote Somerset village Edmund fell for the rector's eldest daughter, Georgiana Browne, and he married her there in September 1881. We have already noted Alicia's marriage to John Peacock, with whom she moved to County Clare in Ireland. Ferrey's youngest daughter, Annie, lived beyond her eightieth birthday but never married.

On 1 November 1871 Ferrey's wife, Ann, died at the age of fifty-nine. Theirs had been a happy marriage and their two families had formed a close connection; Ferrey's grandson Cuthbert would fondly remember visits from the Lucases during his childhood. But hardly a year after Ann's death Ferrey married his second wife, Emily Hopkinson, on 3 December 1872 at Weymouth, a town with which seemingly neither Ferrey or Emily had a connection; the couple may have gone there to enjoy a quiet ceremony away from family and friends.

To mark their marriage, the couple sat individually for photographic portraits. It was to be the final image that we have of Ferrey [**212**]. In it he wears the chinstrap beard that he always had, and his manner of dressing had hardly changed since he was drawn *c.* 1860 [208], but his face is noticeably fuller. His bride, Emily, was

212, 213 Ferrey and his second wife, Emily Hopkinson, photographed shortly after their wedding in 1872.

nineteen years his junior; her portrait suggests a composed and confident woman with a remarkably alert, steady gaze [**213**]. The Hopkinsons were a large Islington family. Emily's grandfather had been a coach maker in Highbury Park, and her father, John, had been one of eleven children. His elder brother had been knighted for service in India, and several others went on to make 'favourable' marriages. We do not know when Ferrey met Emily, but it is almost certain that the introduction must have been made through Dr Robert Druitt, who was married to Emily's sister Isabella. Druitt, four years younger than Ferrey, had briefly been a classmate at Wimborne Grammar School. The Druitts were perhaps the pre-eminent family in Christchurch, and were close friends of the Ferreys. What's more, Druitt was a 'medical officer of health' at St George, Hanover Square, which Ferrey restored in 1871. Had he perhaps, upon seeing his old friend Ferrey widowed, suggested an alliance between him and his spinster sister-in-law? Either way, the marriage proved unpopular with Ferrey's children. It was perhaps difficult for them to accept a new, younger stepmother, especially so soon after Ann's death. Emily would almost, but not quite, outlive all her husband's children, dying at Inverness Terrace at the age of ninety-two in 1922.

Soon after his second marriage, Ferrey's health began to deteriorate. He had begun to take on less work, and Edmund was soon playing a greater part in running the practice: much of the work carried out in the 1870s could just as easily be attributed to him as to his father. Eventually in October 1877 Ferrey suffered a stroke. He had received his commission for Bagshot Park earlier that year, and regular travel to and from the site may have overexerted him. A few months later, on 20 March 1878, he found himself writing to Charles Eastlake to resign the vice-presidency of the RIBA. 'The state of my health', Ferrey wrote, 'though considerably improved, is such as to preclude me from any hope of taking active part in the business of the Institute for some time to come.'[8] A week after writing the letter, Ferrey received the news that his friend Sir George Gilbert Scott had died

214 The funeral of Sir George Gilbert Scott in Westminster Abbey, 6 April 1878. Poor health prevented Ferrey from attending; his son Edmund represented him.

of heart failure. It came as an immense blow, even more so at a time when he was considering his own mortality. He found himself writing to Eastlake once more the day after Scott's death. This time the handwriting is uneven and the letter notably short. It read: 'If any deputation from the Institute attends Mr Scott's funeral, I should wish to be on it. I travelled with him in Italy 30 years ago'.[9]

The RIBA held a meeting on 1 April to consider 'what steps should be taken to do honour to Sir Gilbert's memory'. Edmund found himself writing to make apologies for his father's absence. 'My father's health is not yet sufficiently re-established for him to be able to go out at night, much less to attend a meeting on such a sad subject.' Ferrey was evidently in a delicate state. Edmund went on to write: 'I should be very sorry for my father to be much agitated, as from the nature of his complaint, the result might be very serious.'[10] Edmund would attend Scott's funeral later that month on his father's behalf [**214**].

Ferrey managed to make a partial recovery from the stroke of 1877, and by the end of 1878 he was able regularly to spend three or four weeks near Bagshot superintending the work there. It was hoped that the country air would be of use in recovering his health. However, by the spring of 1880 it became apparent that his condition was worsening and that his heart was growing weaker. Edmund dutifully took over the running of the practice, as well as making sure that his father was well looked after in London. By August, Ferrey was confined to his bed.

Finally, on Sunday 22 August 1880 at half past two o'clock Ferrey died peacefully, unconscious, at 55 Inverness Terrace.

Postscript

When Ferrey was laid to rest on Friday 27 August 1880 a mourner might have noticed that many of his closest contemporaries were missing. The pupils of Pugin's drawing school had all but evanesced. Pugin had died young in 1852; Thomas Larkins Walker, Ferrey's old partner, had died in Hong Kong in 1860; and Thomas Talbot Bury had only made it to 1877. The architect contemporaries with whom Ferrey had once worked were also beginning to disappear. Scott had died two years previously, Blore a year after that in 1878, and T. H. Wyatt expired just seventeen days before Ferrey. That earliest generation of Victorian architects was fading fast. Butterfield however would outlive them all and reach the new century.

Ferrey had lived to see seventy, a respectable age for the nineteenth century. During his life he had watched the world change beyond recognition: parliamentary reform, the Oxford Movement, burgeoning cities at home and a growing Empire abroad; the new age of the railway, of photography, and mass printing. Hardly anything remained as it had been when he was born above the draper's shop in Christchurch.

His career, lest we forget, had begun with Italianate villas in Bournemouth (which by 1880 had a population of 17,000) and Picturesque estate cottages in Dorset. By the time of his death, he had designed almost sixty churches in bold new styles, restored many ancient churches and one cathedral, and built houses and mausoleums for royalty. More importantly, he had been at the very forefront of the debates that led to the ascendency of the Gothic Revival with its 'heaven pointing spires' – that movement which would forever change a nation's architectural landscape.

It is a biographer's lot to be eternally overshadowed by their subject. Ferrey has suffered for too long under the epithet of 'Pugin's biographer'. As even the briefest inspection of his work at Compton Valence or Morpeth or Rochester Row shows, the old story of Ferrey the mediocre church-builder is soon contradicted, and he emerges as a proficient and imaginative architect capable of groundbreaking invention.

This biographer will give the final word to the great historian of the Gothic Revival, Charles Eastlake, who wrote of Ferrey:

> He was one of the earliest, ablest, and most zealous pioneers of the modern Gothic school. His architectural taste was for years in steady advance of his

generation, and as an authority on church planning and general proportions he had scarcely a rival. His work possessed the rare charm of simplicity, without lacking interest. By the use of carefully studied mouldings and a spare but judicious introduction of carved ornament, he managed to secure for his buildings a grace that was deficient in many contemporary designs, which had been executed with far more elaborate decoration and at greater cost.[1]

Notes

Chapter 1

1 James Gairdner (ed.), *Letters and Papers of the Reign of Henry VIII*, vol. 13, pt 1, p. 1117.
2 From the French for 'iron-plated': an armed man.
3 Sarah Howard, 'Making, Measuring and Selling in Hampshire: The Provincial Tailor's Accounts of George and Benjamin Ferrey', in *Material Literacy in Eighteenth-Century Britain: A Nation of Makers*, ed. Serena Dyer and Chloe Wigston Smith (London, 2020), p. 138.
4 Ibid., p. 147.
5 Ibid.
6 *The Builder*, vol. 39, 1880, p. 281.

Chapter 2

1 *The Builder*, vol. 13, 1855, p. 5.
2 Benjamin Ferrey, *Recollections of A. N. Welby Pugin, and his Father, Augustus Pugin* (London, 1861), pp. 1–2.
3 Rosemary Hill, 'A. C. Pugin', *The Burlington Magazine*, vol. 138, no. 1114, 1996, p. 12.
4 Ferrey, *Recollections* (cit. at n. 2), p. 3.
5 Hill, 'A. C. Pugin' (cit. at n. 3), p. 14.
6 Charles Dickens, *Martin Chuzzlewit* (London, 1859), p. 11.
7 Charles James Mathews, *The Life of Charles James Mathews*, ed. Charles Dickens (London, 1879), pp. 37–40.
8 Ferrey, *Recollections* (cit. at n. 2), p. 28.
9 Ibid., pp. 9–10.
10 Ferrey, *Recollections* (cit. at n. 2), pp. 18–19.
11 Ibid., p. 18.
12 Ibid., pp. 20–21.
13 Ibid., p. 22.
14 Ibid., p. 5.
15 Rosemary Hill, *God's Architect: Pugin and the Building of Romantic Britain* (London, 2007), p. 23.
16 Ferrey, *Recollections* (cit. at n. 2), p. 6.
17 Ibid.
18 Ibid., p. 27.
19 Ibid.
20 Ibid., pp. 43–44.
21 Ibid., p. 44.
22 Ibid., p. 33.
23 Ibid., p. 34.
24 Ibid.
25 Ibid., p. 35.
26 Ibid., p. 37.
27 The engraving misattributes the watercolour to 'R Ferry'.
28 A. C. Pugin, *Gothic Ornaments* (London, 1831), title page.
29 A. C. Pugin, *Examples of Gothic Architecture* (London, 1831), p. vi.
30 Ferrey, *Recollections* (cit. at n. 2), p. 70.
31 Ibid., p. 71.

Chapter 3

1 See Caroline Shenton, *Mr Barry's War: Rebuilding the Houses of Parliament after the Great Fire of 1834* (Oxford, 2016).
2 Ibid., p. 33.
3 Ibid., p. 39.
4 A. W. N. Pugin, *A Letter to A. W. Hakewill, Architect* (London, 1835), p. 13.
5 Ibid., pp. 13–14.
6 Benjamin Ferrey, *Answer to 'Thoughts on Rebuilding the Houses of Parliament'* (London, 1835), p. 9.
7 *Catalogue of the Designs Offered for the New Houses of Parliament* (London, 1836), p. 17.
8 Ibid., p. 18.
9 Ibid., p. 19.
10 Ibid., p. 18.
11 Ibid.
12 Ibid., 'Resolutions &c.' (in appendix), p. 1.
13 Ibid., p. 3.
14 Ibid., p. 2.
15 Quoted in Shenton, *Mr Barry's War* (cit. at n. 1), p. 57.
16 *Catalogue of the Designs* (cit. at n. 7), 'Resolutions &c.' (cit. at n. 12), p. 5.
17 Ibid., 'Petition of the Undersigned Architects' (in appendix), p. 1.
18 *Salisbury and Winchester Journal*, 12 September 1831, p. 1.
19 Ibid.
20 Bayly's speculative investments in Bournemouth, including his ownership of the Belle Vue boarding house, put considerable strain on his finances. He was eventually declared bankrupt, and his possessions were auctioned off at the King's Arms Hotel in Christchurch (next door to the Ferrey family shop) on 9 June 1857.
21 Augustus Bozzi Granville, *The Spas of England and Principal Sea-Bathing Places* (London, 1841), p. 527.
22 Ibid.

Chapter 4

1 Demolished in 1951.
2 Michael Hill, John Newman and Nikolaus Pevsner, *The Buildings of England: Dorset* (New Haven and London, 2018), p. 217.
3 Acland's own work as an early pioneer of Gothic church architecture is overlooked. The role he played in designing the church at Compton Valence is at least as significant as Ferrey's own.
4 Basil Clarke, *Church Builders of the Nineteenth Century* (London, 1938), pp. 112–13.
5 *The Ecclesiologist*, vol. 1, 1843, p. 81.
6 Quoted in John Steegman, *Victorian Taste* (London, 1950), p. 79.
7 Ibid.
8 A. W. N. Pugin, *Contrasts: or, A Parallel Between the Noble Edifices of the Fourteenth and Fifteenth Centuries, and similar Buildings of the Present Day; showing the Present Decay of Taste: Accompanied by appropriate Text* (Salisbury, 1836).
9 *The Civil Engineer and Architect's Journal*, vol. 1, October 1837, p. 314.
10 Quoted in Clarke, *Church Builders* (cit. at n. 4), p. 26.
11 *The Civil Engineer and Architect's Journal*, vol. 1, October 1837, p. 314.
12 Ibid.

13 Timothy Mowl, *The Norman Revival in British Architecture 1790–1870*, PhD Thesis, University of Oxford, 1981, p. 372.
14 Nikolaus Pevsner, *The Buildings of England: Bedfordshire, Huntingdonshire and Peterborough* (Harmondsworth, 1968), p. 81.
15 *The Civil Engineer and Architect's Journal*, vol. 1, October 1837, p. 314.
16 I am grateful to Edmund Harris for this information.
17 John Mason Neale, *A Few Words to Church Builders* (Cambridge, 1841), p. 9.
18 Pevsner, *Bedfordshire* (cit. at n. 14), p. 81.
19 Mowl, *The Norman Revival* (cit. at n. 13), p. 373.
20 John Ward, *Manuscript journal of the process of the works at East Grafton Church* (1841–44), p. 1. Wiltshire and Swindon Archives.
21 John Sell Cotman, *Architectural Antiquities of Normandy* (London, 1822), p. 15.
22 *The Ecclesiologist*, vol. 1, 1841, p. 31.
23 Ibid.
24 *A Report of the Oxford Society for Promoting the Study of Gothic Architecture* (1841), p. 24.
25 Ibid.
26 Thomas Mozley, *Reminiscences Chiefly of Oriel College and the Oxford Movement* (London, 1882), vol. 2, p. 183.
27 Ibid., p. 186.
28 Nikolaus Pevsner, *The Buildings of England: Cambridgeshire* (2nd edn, Harmondsworth, 1970), p. 499.
29 Mozley, *Reminiscences* (cit. at n. 26), p. 187.
30 Ibid.
31 Ibid., p. 184.
32 John Lloyd, *Manuscript Memorandum of certain works in building a new church at East Grafton* (1841–44), p. 2. Wiltshire and Swindon Archives.
33 John Ward, *Manuscript journal* (cit. at n. 20), p. 10.
34 Mozley, *Reminiscences* (cit. at n. 26), p. 188.
35 Ibid.
36 *Salisbury and Winchester Journal*, 10 December 1842, p. 4.
37 *Salisbury and Wiltshire Herald*, 2 December 1842, p. 1.
38 Ibid.
39 *London Evening Standard*, 7 December 1842, p. 2.
40 This and all the following quotations come from the account of the inquest in the *Salisbury and Winchester Journal*, 10 December 1842, p. 4.
41 Mozley, *Reminiscences* (cit. at n. 26), p. 188.
42 Often misattributed to Ferrey. It was in fact built decades later as a memorial to Grey.
43 Mowl, *The Norman Revival* (cit. at n. 13) , pp. 373–74.
44 Nikolaus Pevsner, *The Buildings of England: Berkshire* (Harmondsworth, 1966), p. 266.
45 *The Ecclesiologist*, new series, vol. 1 (1845), p. 286.
46 *The Ecclesiologist*, vol. 8 (1846), p. 40.
47 *Sherborne Mercury*, 22 August 1846, p. 4.
48 Charles Dickens, *Household Words* (London, 1850), vol. 1, p. 297.
49 Letter from Blomfield to Burdett-Coutts, 12 January 1846, City of Westminster Archives (CWA hereafter), Loose K Papers.
50 Ibid.
51 CWA, E5 2.
52 CWA, E5 1.
53 The school and the rectory have both been demolished. The latter in particular is a great loss. A 'severely gabled' affair with an unusual attic window, it was the image of a well-formed small Victorian rectory. George Gilbert Scott later emulated it when working on the rectory at Fillingham in 1853.
54 *Buckinghamshire Herald*, 5 May 1848.
55 Nikolaus Pevsner, *The Buildings of England: Buckinghamshire* (Harmondsworth, 1960), p. 597.
56 CWA, G4 14.
57 *The Illustrated London News*, 24 July 1847, p. 8.
58 Ibid.
59 CWA, G4 10.
60 Ibid.
61 CWA, J1 17.
62 CWA, G4 22.
63 Ibid.
64 Ibid.
65 CWA, J1 12.
66 CWA, J1 3.
67 *The Ecclesiologist*, vol. 9, 1849, p. 331.
68 *The Illustrated London News*, 29 June 1850, p. 12.
69 *The Ecclesiologist*, vol. 11, 1850, p. 115.
70 *The Illustrated London News*, 29 June 1850, p. 12.
71 *The Ecclesiologist*, vol. 11, 1850, p. 116.
72 Ibid.
73 Ibid.
74 Ibid.
75 Quoted in Edward Cannan, *A History of the Diocese of St Helena and its Precursors 1502–1984* (St Helena, 1985), p. 37.
76 Ibid., p. 38.
77 Ibid., p. 40.
78 The building firm to which Westminster Cathedral's architect, J. F. Bentley, would later be apprenticed.
79 *St Helena Gazette*, 4 May 1850.
80 *The Ecclesiologist*, vol. 12, 1851, p. 43.
81 Quoted in Jim Cheshire, *Stained Glass and the Victorian Gothic Revival* (Manchester, 2004), p. 1.
82 *Dorset County Chronicle*, 29 April 1830, p. 4.
83 Ibid.
84 *Taunton Courier*, 2 September 1863, p. 6.
85 Ibid.
86 George Gilbert Scott, *Personal and Professional Recollections* (London, 1879), p. 159.
87 Forsyth would later work with Ferrey's son Edmund, who produced designs for a number of sculptures.
88 *Taunton Courier*, 2 September 1863, p. 6.
89 Ibid.
90 Ibid.
91 *The Ecclesiologist*, vol. 14, 1853, p. 367.
92 Benjamin Ferrey, *Notes on Stamped or Incised Stucco* (London, 1857), p. 1.
93 In a somewhat eccentric flourish, at Birlingham Ferrey repurposed the Norman chancel arch as a gateway to the churchyard.

Chapter 5

1 This and the following quotes come from George Gilbert Scott, *Personal and Professional Recollections* (London, 1879), pp. 158–59.
2 John Ruskin, *The Stones of Venice*, vol. 1 (London, 1851), p. 1.
3 Ibid., vol. 2 (London, 1853), pp. 119–20.
4 John Lewis Bradley, ed., *Ruskin's Letters from Venice 1851–1852* (Westport, 1978), p. 44.
5 Ibid.
6 John Munday, *Edward William Cooke: A Man of his Time* (Woodbridge, 1996), p. 34.
7 Edward Cheney (1803–1884), a collector of Venetian paintings.
8 Quoted in Munday, *Edward William Cooke* (cit. at n. 6), p. 297.

9 Scott, *Recollections* (cit. at n. 1), p. 159.
10 Ibid.
11 Ibid.
12 Ibid., p. 160.
13 Ibid.
14 Joseph Mordaunt Crook, *William Burges and the High Victorian Dream* (London, 2013), p.91.
15 Scott, *Recollections* (cit. at n. 1), p. 160.
16 Ibid.
17 Ibid., p. 161.
18 Ibid.
19 Ibid.
20 Ibid., pp. 161–62.
21 Ibid., p. 162.
22 George Edmund Street, *Brick and Marble in the Middle Ages* (London, 1855), p. 328.
23 Scott, *Recollections* (cit. at n. 1), p. 162.
24 Ibid.
25 Ibid., p. 163.
26 Ibid.

Chapter 6

1 Ronald Keith Pugh, ed., *The Letter-Books of Samuel Wilberforce* (Oxford, 1970), p. 162.
2 Quoted in L. S. Colchester, 'The Victorian Restoration of Wells Cathedral Church', in *Transactions of the Ancient Monuments Society*, vol. 4, 1956, p. 79.
3 Ibid., p. 81.
4 Ibid., p. 79.
5 Ibid., p. 85.
6 *Bristol Times and Mirror*, 12 May 1849, p. 5.
7 *The Illustrated London News*, 9 August 1851, p. 6.
8 Ibid.
9 Ferrey, *Antiquities of the Priory of Christ-Church* (London, 1834), p. 32.
10 *Hampshire Advertiser*, 3 October 1846, p. 5.
11 Ibid., 11 December 1847, p. 5.
12 Ibid., 22 January 1848, p. 5.
13 Ibid.
14 *Hampshire Independent*, 18 November 1863.
15 *Morning Herald*, 25 November 1865, p. 4.
16 *Morning Herald*, 25 November 1865, p. 4.
17 Ibid.
18 *The Ecclesiologist*, vol. 27, 1866, p. 311.
19 Ibid.
20 James Cottle, *Some Account of the Church of St Mary Magdalene, Taunton and the Restoration Thereof* (London, 1845), p. 1.
21 Ibid., p. 7.
22 Ibid., p. 25.
23 Benjamin Ferrey, 'The Gothic Towers of Somerset', in Cottle, *Some Account* (cit. at n. 19), p. 79.
24 *Sherborne Mercury*, 10 August 1858, p. 9.
25 *The Builder*, 31 January 1857, p. 6.
26 DC/FAB/1/2/9, MS account of the restoration of the west front (Wells Cathedral Archives), p. 3.
27 Ibid., p. 5.
28 Ibid., p. 9.
29 Ibid.
30 Ibid., p. 11.
31 This work had not been overseen by Ferrey and was criticised by Scott in his report.
32 DC/FAB/1/2/9 (cit. at n. 25), p. 22.
33 *Bath Chronicle and Weekly Gazette*, 18 April 1878, p. 6.
34 *Wells Journal*, 18 August 1855, p. 10.
35 *The Ecclesiologist*, vol. 23, 1862, p. 312.

Chapter 7

1 Its listing places it around 1840.
2 John Newman and Nikolaus Pevsner, *The Buildings of England: Dorset* (Harmondsworth, 1972), p. 183.
3 Quoted in Kester Rattenbury, *Thomas Hardy, Architect: The Wessex Project* (London, 2018), p. 108.
4 Susan North, granddaughter of the Prime Minister, Lord North, inherited her father's barony in 1841 after a thirty-nine year abeyance. It was created by writ and could thus descend through both male and female lines.
5 *The Builder*, vol. 39, 1880, p. 282.
6 Quoted in Andrew Gailey, *The Lost Imperialist: Lord Dufferin, Memory and Mythmaking in the Age of Celebrity* (London, 2015), p. 44.
7 Ibid.
8 A. Rowan Hamilton to Lord Dufferin. Ibid.
9 Uvedale Price, *Sir Uvedale Price on the Picturesque: with an Essay on the Origin of Taste* (London, 1842), p. 9.
10 Newman and Pevsner, *Dorset* (cit. at n. 2), p. 254.
11 Mark Girouard, *The Victorian Country House* (London, 1979), p. 418.
12 Ibid.
13 *Devon and Exeter Gazette*, 27 December 1884, p. 3.
14 *The Builder*, vol. 19, 1861, p. 863.
15 *The Builder*, 1 December 1877, p. 1198.
16 Ian Nairn and Nikolaus Pevsner, *The Buildings of England: Surrey* (Harmondsworth, 1962), pp. 101–2.

Chapter 8

1 A. W. N. Pugin, *The True Principles of Pointed or Christian Architecture* (London, 1841), p. 49.
2 For more on Peacock and the Rogue Goths see Edmund Harris, *The Rogue Goths: R. L. Roumieu, Joseph Peacock and Bassett Keeling* (Swindon, 2024)
3 Quoted in Edward Bottoms, 'The Royal Architectural Museum in the light of new documentary evidence', in *Journal of the History of Collections*, vol. 19, no. 1, 2007, p. 117.
4 Benjamin Ferrey, *Recollections of A. N. Welby Pugin, and his Father, Augustus Pugin* (London, 1861), p. vi.
5 Ibid.
6 Letter from Ferrey to John Pollard Seddon, 31 January 1870. RIBA Archives, LC/7/4/25.
7 'Some notes on the Ferrey Family, Compiled by C.E.C.F.' (1976), unpublished. Private collection.
8 Letter from Ferrey to Charles Eastlake, 20 March 1878. RIBA Archives, LC/16/6/27.
9 Ibid., 28 March 1878. RIBA Archives, LC/16/6/44.
10 Letter from Benjamin Edmund Ferrey to William White, 31 March 1878. RIBA Archives, LC/16/6/53.

Postscript

1 Charles Eastlake, *A History of the Gothic Revival* (London, 1872), p. 220.

Bibliography

Barry, C. (1860). *The Houses of Parliament: A Description of the New Palace at Westminster*. London: John Murray.

Belcher, M. (ed.) (2001). *Collected Letters of A. W. N. Pugin*, vol. 1. Oxford: Oxford University Press.

Bottoms, E. (2007). 'The Royal Architectural Museum in the light of new documentary evidence', *Journal of the History of Collections*, 19 (1), pp. 107–121.

Bradley, J. L. (ed.) (1978). *Ruskin's Letters from Venice 1851–1852*. Westport, CT: Greenwood Press.

Brandwood, G. (2024). *George Edmund Street*. Liverpool: Liverpool University Press.

Britton, J. (1827). *The Architectural Antiquities of Normandy*. London: Longman, Hurst, Rees, Orme & Brown.

Cannan, E. (1985). *A History of the Diocese of St Helena and its Precursors 1502–1984*. St Helena.

Cheshire, J. (2004). *Stained Glass and the Victorian Gothic Revival*. Manchester: Manchester University Press.

Clarke, B. (1938). *Church Builders of the Nineteenth Century*. London; revised edn 1969.

Colchester, L. S. (1956). 'The Victorian restoration of Wells Cathedral Church', *Transactions of the Ancient Monuments Society*, 4, pp. 79–94.

Cotman, J. S. (1822). *Architectural Antiquities of Normandy*. London: Henry G. Bohn.

Cottle, J. (1845). *Some Account of the Church of St Mary Magdalene, Taunton and the Restoration Thereof*. London.

Dickens, C. (1844). *Martin Chuzzlewit*. London: Chapman & Hall.

Dickens, C. (1850). *Household Words*, vol. 1. London: Bradbury & Evans.

Eastlake, C. (1872). *A History of the Gothic Revival*. London: Longmans, Green.

Ferrey, B. (1835). *Answer to "Thoughts on Rebuilding the Houses of Parliament"*. London.

Ferrey, B. (1861). *Recollections of A. N. Welby Pugin, and His Father, Augustus Pugin*. London: Edward Stanford.

Ferrey, B. (1845). 'The Gothic Towers of Somerset', in Cottle, J., *Some Account of the Church of St Mary Magdalene, Taunton*. London.

Ferrey, B. (1857). *Notes on Stamped or Incised Stucco*. London.

Frith, W. P. (1887). *My Autobiography and Reminiscences*, vol. 1. London: Richard Bentley.

Gailey, A. (2015). *The Lost Imperialist: Lord Dufferin, Memory and Mythmaking in the Age of Celebrity*. London.

Girouard, M. (1979). *The Victorian Country House*. London: Yale University Press.

Granville, A. B. (1841). *The Spas of England and Principal Sea-Bathing Places*. London: Henry Colburn.

Harris, E. (2024). *The Rogue Goths: R. L. Roumieu, Joseph Peacock and Bassett Keeling*. Swindon: Historic England.

Hill, R. (1996). 'A. C. Pugin', *The Burlington Magazine*, 138(1114), pp. 11–19.

Hill, R. (2007). *God's Architect: Pugin and the Building of Romantic Britain*. London: Allen Lane.

Howard, S. (2020). 'Making, measuring and selling in Hampshire: the provincial tailor's accounts of George and Benjamin Ferrey', in Dyer, S. and Wigston Smith, C. (eds), *Material Literacy in Eighteenth-Century Britain: A Nation of Makers*. London: Bloomsbury, pp. 138–147.

Langley, B. (1742). *Gothic Architecture Improved by Rules and Proportions*. London: S. Harding.
Lewis, D.F. (2021). *A.W.N. Pugin*. Liverpool: Liverpool University Press.
Mathews, C. J. (1879). *The Life of Charles James Mathews*. Edited by C. Dickens. London.
Mozley, T. (1882). *Reminiscences Chiefly of Oriel College and the Oxford Movement*, vol. 2. London.
Mowl, T. (1981). *The Norman Revival in British Architecture 1790–1870*. PhD thesis, University of Oxford.
Munday, J. (1996). *Edward William Cooke: A Man of his Time*. Woodbridge: Boydell Press.
Neale, J. M. (1841). *A Few Words to Church Builders*. Cambridge.
Newman, J. and Pevsner, N. (1972). *The Buildings of England: Dorset*. Harmondsworth: Penguin.
Newman, J. and Pevsner, N. (1968). *The Buildings of England: Bedfordshire, Huntingdonshire and Peterborough*. Harmondsworth: Penguin.
Newman, J. and Pevsner, N. (1966). *The Buildings of England: Berkshire*. Harmondsworth: Penguin.
Newman, J. and Pevsner, N. (1970). *The Buildings of England: Cambridgeshire*. 2nd edn. Harmondsworth: Penguin.
Newman, J. and Pevsner, N. (1960). *The Buildings of England: Buckinghamshire*. Harmondsworth: Penguin.
Price, U. (1842). *Sir Uvedale Price on the Picturesque*. London.
Pugin, A. C. (1831). *Gothic Ornaments*. London.
Pugin, A. C. (1831). *Examples of Gothic Architecture*. London.
Pugin, A. W. N. (1835). *A Letter to A. W. Hakewill, Architect*. London.
Pugin, A. W. N. (1836). *Contrasts*. Salisbury.
Pugin, A. W. N. (1841). *True Principles of Pointed or Christian Architecture*. London.
Pugh, R. K. (ed.) (1970). *The Letter-Books of Samuel Wilberforce*. Oxford: Oxford University Press.
Rattenbury, K. (2018). *Thomas Hardy, Architect: The Wessex Project*. London.
Ruskin, J. (1851). *The Stones of Venice*, vol. 1. London: Smith, Elder & Co.
Ruskin, J. (1853). *The Stones of Venice*, vol. 2. London: Smith, Elder & Co.
Scott, G. G. (1879). *Personal and Professional Recollections*. London: Sampson Low, Marston, Searle & Rivington.
Shenton, C. (2016). *Mr Barry's War: Rebuilding the Houses of Parliament after the Great Fire of 1834*. Oxford: Oxford University Press.
Street, G. E. (1855). *Brick and Marble in the Middle Ages*. London: John Murray.

Periodicals, Newspapers, and Journals:
Bath Chronicle and Weekly Gazette
Bristol Times and Mirror
Buckinghamshire Herald
The Builder
The Civil Engineer and Architect's Journal
Dorset County Chronicle
The Ecclesiologist
Hampshire Advertiser
Hampshire Independent
Illustrated London News
London Evening Standard
Morning Herald
Salisbury and Wiltshire Herald
Salisbury and Winchester Journal
Sherborne Mercury
St Helena Gazette
Taunton Courier
Wells Journal

Acknowledgements

This biography has been made possible by the support and assistance of innumerable friends and colleagues who have collectively lightened the burden of researching, writing, and editing this volume. I am especially grateful to David Lewis, Emily Lane, and Simon Ferrey whose guidance and proofreading have been invaluable.

The appearance of this volume is much enhanced by the photographic contributions of Ed Gaut, with whom I have travelled the country in pursuit of Ferrey and good light. Ed's dedication to the art of photography has been remarkable, and the results speak for themselves.

A host of friends, colleagues, and kind strangers have provided brilliant pointers, advice, and support throughout the whole process. I am much in their debt. Alphabetically – and by no means comprehensively – I might especially thank: John Bucknall, Janet Burn, the late James Stevens Curl, Lucy Duckworth, Stephen Gadd, Edmund Harris, Rosemary Hill, Lois Heslop Samuel Hughes, Mark Humphrys, Julian Holder, Peter Howell, John Lloyd, Diarmaid MacCulloch, Timothy Mowl, Julian Orbach, Ian Palmer, Peter Thompson, and the late Andrew Saint.

I am equally grateful to Fr George Westhaver and the Chapter of Pusey House for providing me with an ideal setting in which to write the majority of this book. Above all, I am eternally indebted to my parents and grandparents without whose sacrifices I would never have been able to consider writing this or indeed any book.

In drawing these acknowledgements to a close, I must thank the individual to whom, more than anybody else, this book owes its existence: Matthew Ferrey. It was through Matthew's desire to reinvigorate Ferrey's reputation and honour his legacy that I embarked on writing this biography several years ago. Throughout the process, Matthew has been the kindest, most understanding, and generous patron. Matthew and his cousin Simon have proved themselves to be the most devoted descendants that Benjamin could ever have hoped for.

Picture Credits

Author photos: figs. 11, 72, 74, 75, 76, 103, 104, 117, 179

Photography by Ed Gaut: frontispiece, figs. 1, 24, 44, 47, 49, 55, 56, 59 ,63, 64, 66, 69, 70, 71, 77, 83, 87, 87, 88, 91, 93, 94, 95, 96, 98, 99, 100, 101, 110, 111, 115, 116, 119, 147, 151, 156, 165, 209, 210

Other credits: fig. 4 Item No. D10310 Joseph Mallord William Turner 1775–1851, photo: Tate; fig. 6 Ethan Doyle White CC BY-SA 4.0; fig. 10 Angelo Hornak, Alamy; fig. 15 Wikipedia, public domain; fig. 19 National Portrait Gallery, Wikipedia, public domain; figs. 20, 21, 22 © Royal Collection Enterprises Limited 2024 | Royal Collection Trust; fig. 30 National Portrait Gallery, Wikipedia, public domain; fig. 36 Russell-Cotes Art Gallery and Museum, public domain; fig. 40 Mr Eugene Birchall, www.geograph.org.uk, Creative Commons licence; fig. 53 Colin Smith CC BY-SA 2.0; fig. 61 Credit: Mark Humphrys at humphrysfamilytree.com; fig. 78 Mike Searle | *The Old Church at East Lydford* | CC BY-SA 2.0; fig. 85 Rob Stallard, CC BY-SA 3.0; fig. 90 Peter Neaum and Andrew Neaum, CC BY 3.0; fig. 105 Alan Murray-Rust, CC BY-SA 2.0; fig. 106 ChurchCrawler, CC BY-SA 2.0; fig. 107 Derek Harper, CC BY-SA 2.0; fig. 109 Hugh Venables, CC BY-SA 2.0; fig. 112 Llywelyn2000, CC BY-SA 3.0; fig. 113 achurchnearyou.com, photographer unknown; fig. 118 Tudor Barlow, flickr; fig. 120 Manfred Gottschalk / Alamy; figs. 128 & 129 © Victoria and Albert Museum, London; fig. 131 Wikimedia commons Creative license, public domain; fig. 142 Dreamstime.com; fig. 148 Jack Pease Photography, CC BY-SA 20; fig. 155 Nicholas Temple-Fry / Alamy; fig. 157 Bashereyre, CC BY-SA 3.0; fig. 158 Derek Voller, CC BY-SA 2.0; fig. 159 David Bown, CC BY-SA 3.0; fig. 160 Josh Tilley, Wikimedia Commons CC BY-SA 4.0; fig. 162 Angelo Hornak, Alamy; fig. 163 Ken Ince / picturesofengland.com; fig. 164 Martyn Davies, Wikimedia Commons, CC BY-SA 2.0; fig. 167 Dreamstime.com; fig. 168 Robert Edwards, CC-BY-SA 2.0; fig. 170 John Salmon, CC By-SA-2.0; fig. 174 Notafly, CC-BY-SA 4.0; fig. 175 P Flannagan / CC BY-SA 2.0; fig. 176 Lambeth Council, care of Boroughphotos.org; fig. 178 Don Cload, CC BY-SA 2.0; fig. 180 Mr Derek Beauchamp / Historic England Archive; fig. 183 Peter Trimming, CC BY-SA 2.0; fig. 184 Chris Downer, CC BY-SA 2.0; fig. 191 Llywelyn2000, CC BY-SA-4.0; figs. 194, 195, 196 Graham Rimell; fig. 199 Ademac, CC BY-SA 4.0; fig. 201 Boddah, CC BY-SA 4.0; figs. 204, 205, 206 By kind permission of HRH The Duke of Edinburgh

Index

ACP refers to Augustus Charles Pugin (father of Augustus Welby Northmore Pugin; AWP to Augustus Welby Northmore Pugin; BF to Benjamin Ferrey; *ill* to an illustration; port to a portrait